Jimmy Buffett
and Philosophy

Popular Culture and Philosophy®
Series Editor: George A. Reisch

Popular Culture and Philosophy®

Jimmy Buffett and Philosophy

The Porpoise Driven Life

Edited by

ERIN McKENNA

and

SCOTT L. PRATT

OPEN COURT
Chicago and La Salle, Illinois

Volume 39 in the series, Popular Culture and Philosophy®, edited by George A. Reisch

To order books from Open Court, call toll-free 1-800-815-2280, or visit our website at www.opencourtbooks.com.

Open Court Publishing Company is a division of Carus Publishing Company.

Printed and bound in the United States of America.

Library of Congress Cataloging-in-Publication Data

Jimmy Buffett and philosophy: the porpoise driven life / edited by Erin McKenna and Scott L. Pratt
  p. cm.—(Popular culture and philosophy ; v. 39)
  Includes bibliographical references and index.
  ISBN 978-0-8126-9659-2 (trade paper : alk. paper)
  1. Buffett, Jimmy—Criticism and interpretation 2. Music and philosophy.
 I. McKenna, Erin, 1965- II. Pratt, Scott L.,
  ML420.B874J56 2009
  782.42164092—dc22

                   2009006270

Contents

Margarita Metaphysics   169

Jimmy Buffett, Cultural Infidel

ERIN McKENNA and SCOTT L. PRATT

> Philosophy is not for me, laughing is my game.
> —JIMMY BUFFETT, "Cultural Infidel"

Jimmy Buffett and his music have affected millions of people around the world. His work spans generations—he has been performing for over forty years—and genres. Is Buffett's music just a good time, or is more going on?

Jimmy Buffett and Philosophy explores the work of a self-proclaimed non-philosopher and shows that Buffett's work is indeed philosophical. Through an examination of his songs, books, concerts, and his fans, the writers also use Buffett's work to exemplify and clarify important philosophical issues such as the meaning of community, personal identity, the nature of being, and the ideas of beauty, pleasure, and responsibility.

Unlike many of the musicians discussed in Open Court's *Popular Culture and Philosophy* series (and elsewhere), Buffett not only writes and performs his own music, he also reflects on his music and its meaning in his autobiography, *A Pirate Looks at Fifty*, and in the context of his short stories and novels. If anything is clear from his published stories, it's that the music—whether it is taken as simple or simply fun—emerges from his experience and helps him to make sense of good times and bad. For better or worse, his ability to engage his own life connects broadly with others and provides a starting point for new and meaningful experience.

Buffett's fans, called Parrotheads, attend concerts, buy his books and albums, and participate in local Parrothead Clubs. There are more than two hundred clubs around the world, most of which participate actively in charitable work. During the last six years, local Parrothead Clubs raised over thirteen million dollars and provided nearly two million volunteer-hours. These clubs represent another dimension of how the character of Buffett's work provides a framework for more than just parties. In addition to members of Parrothead clubs (probably including fifteen to twenty thousand), his annual concert tours sell well over two hundred thousand tickets. This group of fans and concertgoers crosses boundaries of generation, class, race, and gender. Their commitment speaks to the meaning many find in Buffett's work.

Jimmy Buffett and Philosophy is aimed at providing an accessible approach to thinking about Buffett's music philosophically and for thinking about philosophy from the perspective of Jimmy Buffett's music. Some people dismiss Buffett's work as simple entertainment, but on close examination, it marks a critical engagement with different conceptions of a life well lived. Sometimes the engagement acknowledges the loss of meaning and the limits of human life. At other times, Buffett celebrates pluralism and possibility and makes a case for the idea that engaging in the experience of music is itself a transformative experience. As American philosopher Josiah Royce said, "You philosophize when you reflect critically upon what you are actually doing in the world. What you are doing of course is, in the first place, living. And life involves passions, faiths, doubts, and courage. The critical inquiry into what all these things mean and imply is philosophy" (*The Spirit of Modern Philosophy*, 1892, pp. 1–2). As an author—and as a songwriter and singer—Buffett inquires into the troubles and joys of daily life and, for thousands, returns new meaning.

"A first rate test of the value of any philosophy," John Dewey said, is to ask "Does it end in conclusions which when they are referred back to ordinary life-experiences and their predicaments, render them more significant, more luminous to us, and make our dealing with them more fruitful?" If John Dewey is right about what it means for a philosophy to be successful, then Buffett's work merits attention. Parrotheads agree that if Buffett's music and books are anything, they are fruitful—or rather *"fruitiful."*

Mean Old Backed-Up Farts

Why would we try to put together a book about Jimmy Buffett in the first place? After all, he denies being a philosopher and tells his fans to watch out for "mean old backed-up farts." When we first proposed the topic to George Reisch and David Ramsay Steele at Open Court, their response was that, while Buffett has many followers, most of them wouldn't be very interested in a philosophical investigation of Buffett's ideas. But Parrothead Randy Auxier persuaded George and David to think twice, and eventually they were convinced that their first reaction had been mistaken. We have heard similar instant negative responses from some of our friends and one of us even tried to give up on the project early on because of this discouragement.

But we're philosophers and, as people who take the business of philosophy seriously, we had to keep in mind that philosophy is not the exclusive territory of old farts or brooding smokers in coffee houses. One does not need to be a professor or a student or a hermit to worry about where meaning comes from. One does not need to read volumes of tortured translations from the German to take up the question of what it is to live the good life or how to understand a changing and dangerous world. In *A Pirate Looks at Fifty*, Buffett says "There was a strange stigma I associated with Serious Writers, seeing them as tortured, lonely individuals whose somber fatalistic existences were accentuated by drunkenness, isolation, and depression" (p. 11). "I knew," he concludes, "that I would never be a Serious Writer."

If we're serious philosophers, we need to think again about what it means to do the work of philosophy in a way that combines the two ideas that we mentioned earlier from Royce and Dewey. Philosophy is first of all thinking about living and meaning; but it is not enough to think about life without returning that thought to the living itself. We think that Buffett is a philosopher, despite his denial, in exactly these two senses.

In the midst of the confusion of the everyday, the need to work and make ends meet, we try to find a minute to set aside pressing concerns and kick back. If we are lucky, artists and thinkers like Jimmy Buffett show up to meet us. They give us what appears at first to be a moment away from the grind. But it turns out to be more. It turns into a chance to think again about why we do all this, what makes it worth while, and allows us to return refreshed to our families and friends and the work it takes to keep body and soul together.

"Homemade Music"

Buffett achieves a kind of philosophical practice by setting up a musical performance into which the audience can enter and that has within it the resources for an experience that is laden with meaning. On this view philosophy is not only a process of analytic reflection, but is also an experience that calls meaning into question and opens the possibility of new meaning. A Buffett performance is not a philosophical act in itself; it is rather an occasion for philosophical practice. When one is handed a copy of Plato's *Republic*, it is not itself a philosophical practice. It is an occasion for engaging in a certain kind of reflection constrained both by the text and the reader.

You might challenge this and say that there is a big difference between the text written by Plato and a performance of "Margaritaville" and, of course, you would be right. The philosophical resources offered by Plato and passed through 2,300 years of reading, translation and response provide a vastly different starting point for philosophy. Plato's resources establish and try to respond to a range of questions that were significant in his day and are significant today. But not everyone can get into Plato and the problems he sets out do not speak to every situation in which a reader might find herself.

What's significant about a philosophical text, however, is that it provides the reader with the resources for reflection in a way that intersects with her lived experience and challenge her presumptions about what that experience means. "Margaritaville" is not the *Republic*. It is nevertheless an occasion for the audience to engage in an experience that first takes them in and then calls for a moment to think anew about what matters.

The desire by some Buffett fans, as you will see later in the volume, to escape from a dreary job or worse is, in part, a reconstruction of the meaning of a person's life. It marks the search for new values, not simply a weekend binge. It means seeking a way of life that fulfills in ways that a person's present job or circumstances does not. This does not guarantee that the change will succeed or that the new life will not spiral into something that also must be escaped. There are no guarantees that philosophical practice will always save. It is the case, however, that philosophical practice, the reflection on and ordered transformation of meaning, will lead to change.

There are those who will read this, our professional colleagues for example, and respond that this is to cheapen the noble business of philosophy. To compare Plato and the likes of Jimmy Buffett is a kind of sacrilege that should lead to excommunication. We would respond by saying that the comparison doesn't cheapen Plato or philosophy. Instead, we're claiming two things: first, with Dewey, if philosophy is a viable human practice and not simply a profession for some group of elites, then to recognize that Plato and Buffett and an array of work in between can serve as occasions for philosophical practice is to emphasize the democratic character of meaning-making and criticism. Different outcomes will emerge from the *Republic* and "Margaritaville," but we shouldn't make the mistake of concluding that these mark a difference in kind.

By paying attention to the character of philosophical practice in the context of the performances of Jimmy Buffett, we offer a chance to become better at the practice. Philosophy is a practice, a way of doing and thinking, that, like every other way of doing and thinking, can benefit from reflection. This is not to say that Parrotheads have, until now, missed the import of the concerts they attend and the books they read. Meaning-making goes on whether guided by critical reflection or not. If philosophy is a practice of this sort, then even those who know every song in Buffett's discography and every book and story can still benefit from re-engaging these works in the same way that philosophers who have engaged and re-engaged Plato over the centuries have helped lead us to new meaning.

Buffett gives support to this approach to his work in two ways. First, as he often declares, he sees himself as a performer and not a musician. While there are different ways to understand the distinction, it seems that Buffett understands a musician as one whose performance is given in a way that is characterized by virtuosity relative to an ideal standard of the piece performed. In this case, the audience plays a small role at best and the musician, in her focus on her instrument and her work, aims to produce something that will transcend the present moment.

A performer, however, is one whose performance is in the present in a way that involves the audience and the band. The goal is not virtuosity, though skillful playing or singing will make a particular contribution to the performance, but rather to create for the performer and the audience an experience—a kind of totalizing experience in which, for a moment, things outside are lost to view. An experience that leaves the participants changed.

"More often than not," he says, "the writer's original ideas or inspirations are replaced by those of the listener, and the song takes on a whole new meaning. I have accumulated a huge collection of songs, but I don't think of them as my possessions" (p. 83). Buffett is both a writer and performer of songs. This double function provides him with greater opportunity to set the stage for the experience. His approach, that blends his own experiences with narratives that are performed and adopted by the audience, provides a distinctive way of calling for philosophical practice.

Of course, any performance that can engage its audience in a way that leads to meaning-making could be an occasion for philosophical practice. What's interesting about Buffett's work is that he appears to set out to foster a kind of philosophical practice in the context of his performances, musical and literary. He seems to confirm this when he sings "Homemade music is part of my philosophy."

Living My Life Like a Song

In an early song, "The Wino and I Know," Buffett declared that life ought to be lived like a song. Looking back on his life from fifty, he tells the story of his nearly failed second marriage and the realization one day, presented by his therapist, that "life is not a performance. Performance is part of life" (p. 57). The insight is key to recognizing the relation between Buffett's life lived and his philosophical practice in the context of writing and musical performance. In the end, meaning is not found in performance alone, but only when performance—the experiences of life—are brought into perspective outside the performance itself.

Buffett was born on Christmas day, 1946, in Mississippi, grew up in Mobile, Alabama, and eventually finished a bachelor's degree in history at the University of Southern Mississippi. Along the way he learned to play guitar and began to write and perform songs. It's common for the experiences of our lives to pass as trudging, interrupted now and again by joy or disaster. Buffett, however, used his music to recover and reconsider the passing moments. His work as a songwriter and performer became occasions to transform elements of his life from mere moments of relative sadness or success into the objects of reflection that transcend his own life and become opportunities for others to see themselves; first in the midst of a song, and later as a consequence of the experience.

Offering a Q&A to himself in *A Pirate Looks at Fifty*, he responds to the question, What are you going to do with your life? And answers: "Live an interesting one" (p. 10). Later he tells us what an interesting life is: running out of air while scuba diving at ninety feet. Crashing his seaplane. These near misses provide a kind of extreme in the course of experience that help to give Buffett focus and a willingness to use his time richly. "One of the inescapable encumbrances of leading an interesting life is that there have to be moments when you almost lose it" (p. 33). It would be a mistake, however, to think that all of life is simply a constant quest for new death-defying moments. It's important to note Buffett's commitment to discipline as well, his "middle-class work ethic," as he calls it. He writes, he flies, he learned celestial navigation, and runs a vastly successful business. This kind of disciplined activity is also necessary to living an interesting life. From this angle, life shifts back and forth from moments of experience that are fully engaging to moments of thoughtful and careful reflection. The moments of fully engaged experience (like the plane crash) force us to lose track of the future and past, to be right there. But it is discipline, reflection, and work that make these other experiences both possible and meaningful.

Buffett lives this way and lets us all in on this rhythm of experience when he writes about "Changes in Latitudes, Changes in Attitudes." Both the song and the album of that name act as our guide. On the album, Buffett assembled ten songs that lead us to ask questions, find ourselves, and affirm both the pain and joy of living. We encounter the realization that the years are getting shorter as life gets deeper and we struggle to catch our dreams. We also realize that many of us are living a "second hand American dream" and lying to ourselves. We learn to cherish memories as they are being made when we are told to "drink it all up." The memory of the wind in her hair, swimming naked, or playing by the ocean as a child—these are the moments that make up a life and we'd better pay attention. Similarly, life on the road pales by comparison to the women he loves—relationships matter. The girl who asks "What is it all about?" and answers "I just don't know, but I can't go back home" also understands the importance of relationships by their dysfunction and loss. She has learned that she must live life by going forward not backward as has Buffett himself in "Sail Away." While he's "trying to make a little sense of it all" he notes that "if I had it to do over again I'd just get drunk and jump right back in."

In the song "Changes in Latitudes, Changes in Attitudes" (which sets the stage for the whole album) we learn that it is important to take time to get away from people and work and think about how one's life is going. However, this should be a limited activity. Reflection is part of the activity of living an interesting life, but only a part. So the song begins by taking time to contemplate the past year—he gives himself a weekend to think about "all of the faces and all of the places" and wonder where they all went.

The contemplation doesn't occupy him for long. What he really needs is the company of others to make sense of the past. Spurred by a basic need—he gets hungry—he goes out for a bite and finds a companion to talk with (showing the importance of conversation to reflection) and they go off drinking (another aid to reflection, if not done to excess). Buffett continually points to the importance of fellow travelers (friends). His books especially stress how important it is to be part of a community. Being able to drink with friends and let go is also important, but not an end in itself. His autobiography is full of stories of eating, drinking, sailing, flying, and fishing with good friends. If the good times ended tomorrow, he "could somehow adjust to the fall."

He has also learned to be flexible. Change is part of life and learning to go with it is important. Volcanoes blow, careers end, friends die. How he responds to such contingency, and the contingency of his own mortal life, make him who he is by helping him to move on. "Well it seems I've run out of reasons to be here," he sings, but all is not lost: "If your attitude's appalling, there's a latitude that's calling" ("Party at the End of the World"). Looking back is important, but "there's too much to see waiting in front of me." The point of reflection is to not just to look back, but to live forward.

Buffett frequently says that he does not want to end up as some has-been singer working in a Holiday Inn lounge and there seems no danger of that happening. His ability to laugh and to be crazy does indeed keep him from going insane. It also has helped him build an amazing career and to live an interesting life. He has met interesting people (including some real sons of bitches), been to interesting places (Paris, the Amazon, Antigua, Key West), and done interesting things (flying in a navy jet off of an aircraft carrier, fly fishing for tarpon, spending an afternoon on Bob Dylan's sailboat, taking a 4,700 mile Caribbean vacation in a seaplane). His memories of Paris make him want to go there. Dreaming of the ocean makes him wish he was out sailing. His life has been full and he notes that he "just can't go wrong" if he continues to follow the "changes in latitudes, changes in attitudes."

In the end, the laughter that keeps him sane helps to make sense out of his declaration in "Cultural Infidel" that philosophy is not for him. Philosophy, viewed as the staid business of old farts, is no help. Laughter, as a reflective pause brought on by the contemplation of experience, finally makes for an interesting life—makes life worth living.

The Porpoise Driven Life

Rick Warren begins his book, *The Purpose Driven Life*, by declaring "It's not about you" and argues that the purpose of an individual life is "greater than your own personal fulfillment, your peace of mind, or even your happiness . . . far greater than your family, your career, or even your wildest dreams and ambitions" (Zondervan, 2002, p. 17). The purpose of life, Warren concludes, is a matter of one's relationship to God. To understand this, Warren says, is not the result of philosophy—"when it comes to determining the purpose of life, even the wisest philosophers are just guessing" (p. 19)—but revelation. If you want to know the purpose of your life, Warren says, "ask the creator" and you will be told.

The Porpoise Driven Life, in contrast, *is* about you, fulfillment, peace of mind, family, careers, and wild dreams. Not alone, but in the company of friends. Not as an isolated moment but as the culmination of the past and the anticipation of a new future. And purpose is not learned by revelation—by being told—but by living itself. In "Barometer Soup," Buffett invites his audience to follow in his wake, a call to try a way of life that involves both work and a joyous turn, "a barrel-roll into the sun." "You've not that much at stake," he sings, because the waters you will travel have already been plowed, opened by his passing, and the troubled waters smoothed.

Instead of being given a purpose, Buffett and those that follow in his wake are "constantly searching . . . for more than just thrills." And what one finds is not a set of purposes, laid out in chapter form, but moments of experience suspended between lusting for the future and treasuring the past. It's not that a porpoise-driven life denies the existence of God or spirituality; it's rather that whatever purpose we have is more likely to be found in actually sailing the waters. "Go fast enough to get there," he sings, "but slow enough to see." Slow enough anyway to watch for the porpoises that might play in your wake.

The authors of this book all have a relationship with Buffett's music and writing and have themselves integrated some of his lessons into their own lives. Here you will sail on your own adventure and explore Buffett's writing and life as a guide to living an interesting life of your own; you'll experience his music and concerts as an opportunity for self-exploration; and you'll encounter new perspectives on what it means to be a dedicated Parrothead or a more casual fan.

Buffett's work does indeed pass Dewey's test of a successful philosophy. It does "end in conclusions which when they are referred back to ordinary life-experiences and their predicaments, render them more significant, more luminous to us, and make our dealing with them more fruitful." Buffett develops his philosophy out of his life and continues to live his life by that philosophy. For, as Buffett says, "You know I can't but be / Part of my own philosophy."

Coral Reefer
Reason

1
A Pirate Looks at 400 B.C.E.

AARON L. PRATT

> I know not how to conceive the good, apart from the pleasures of taste, sexual pleasures, the pleasures of sound, and the pleasures of beautiful form.
>
> —EPICURUS

I want you to picture yourself shoulder deep in an ocean of forty thousand Hawaiian shirt-wearing people, all simultaneously holding their hands palm to palm above their heads, swaying back and forth, their voices joining in a roar of "Fins to the left, fins to the right." The air is heavily laden with the smells of tequila and body odor as the crowd works itself into a frenzy that's been building since the first margarita was downed sitting on a tailgate in the parking lot hours ago. The guy next to you is wearing a coconut brassiere, and when he grabs your arm to tell you for the tenth time that he hopes they do "Cheeseburger in Paradise" you become keenly aware of the fact that this fifty-something-year-old man is as slammed as a freshman frat brother on a Saturday night.

You return your attention to the stage where the band looks like they're enjoying the party just as much as their none-too-sober fans are. The somewhat diminutive lead singer (it may just be that he's barefoot) strums a guitar shaped like a shark, bouncing around the stage as the piano player hammers out a rhythm and bluesy sounding solo. Eventually hopping his way back to the microphone at the center of the stage, Jimmy Buffett, dressed in Hawaiian print shorts and a bright yellow t-shirt that make him seem like just another Parrothead there for the show, opens his mouth and yells for the crowd to join him on the chorus one more time. The arms go up again, and your coconut clad neighbor slurs out "and you're the only bait in town" right in time with Jimmy and the Coral Reefers up on stage.

At this point, you have a choice: either you make your hands into a fin above your head and sway along with your newfound brethren of tropical-themed drunks, or you claw your way desperately through the dense crowd in a beeline to the nearest exit in hopes of escaping the encroaching contact high. Your decision depends a great deal on how you evaluate the behavior of the people surrounding you: you may be right at home, in which case kudos to you, but if you're more of a symphony or opera enthusiast, you no doubt find the behavior of the legions of Parrotheads completely unacceptable for a concert-going experience, or for that matter, for any sort of human interaction. In the example of your coconut-brassiered neighbor alone you are made keenly aware of the affront to countless societal taboos; his crimes against culture include cross-dressing, being completely shit-faced in public, and behaving like a kid one-third his actual age (he should know better!). What's worse is that this man probably has an important job and a family to take care of, but instead chooses to spend his Thursday night in a stadium bouncing a beach ball across the crowd as Jimmy launches into another verse of "Off to See the Lizard."

Philosophizing in 3/4 time

The Parrothead Nation condones and is, in fact, defined by these socially unacceptable attitudes and activities; how could any self-respecting individual justify falling in with these miscreants? These are hard-working, civilized Americans who are behaving like nineteen-year-old lightweights on their first bender, and they should be ashamed of themselves.

But before Parrotheads hang their heads (or roll their sleeves up for the bar brawl that's brewing), it seems worth noting that getting in touch with basic human nature and the pleasures the world has to offer is not necessarily a negative psychological regression.

Well over two thousand years ago some of the greatest philosophers of the ancient world prescribed precisely these actions. The philosophical schools of Cynicism and Epicureanism, developed in ancient Greece during the fifth and fourth centuries B.C.E., were grand departures from the mainstream ethics of their day. The founders of these two schools taught new ways of conditioning a person's mind so that their experience of the world, throughout their lifetime, would be as full as possible. These ways of thinking fall under the nomenclature of "graceful life" philosophies. The Cynic philosopher Diogenes of Sinope, the most famous of the Cynics, taught by example, breaking Athenian society's conventions by giving up all his possessions and living in the streets. Diogenes's philosophy was the original "back to basics" plan for human kind. Epicurus, founder of the philosophy that bears his name, also taught that people should disassociate themselves from the arbitrary roles and regulations imposed by society and that they should only submit to one ethical commandment: experience pleasure, avoid pain.

Diogenes of Sinope, Epicurus of Athens, and Jimmy Buffett of Key West. While it may seem like a strange grouping, it's actually an appropriate one. The Parrothead King, both in his own life's story and in the songs he's created, has become a part of this philosophical tradition that comes down to us through much more than two millennia's worth of human history. These graceful life philosophies are revolutionary ways of thinking that defy the traditional ethics of societal duty and moderation in an effort to get people to indulge one hundred percent in the "high life."

A Pirate Looks At 400 B.C.E.

Unacceptable behavior is the hallmark of Cynical and Epicurean philosophy. As we learn in Diogenes Laertius's *Lives of Eminent Philosophers* (Heinemann, 1925), for Diogenes of Sinope, the best promoter and example of Cynicism, that meant doing things like sleeping in a tub in front of the gymnasium in Athens, walking around town with half of his head shaved clean, and sitting down in the middle of the marketplace to eat his breakfast. He didn't recognize propriety in anything he did, saying that polite speech was like "honey used to choke you" (p. 53). He despised the conceit of the wealthy and loved to put those people in their place: once, when he was invited into an ornate mansion for dinner and told not to spit on the floors, Diogenes, after taking a quick glance around, hocked a loogie right in his host's face, telling him that there was no "meaner receptacle" available (p. 35).

The origin of his antics was his hatred for the pattern he saw the Athenian people's lives taking. "He would say that men strive in digging and kicking to outdo one another, but no one strives to become a good man and true" (p. 29). It was not just the pursuit of wealth that contaminated people's capacity for good, but also their willingness to be ignorant. Diogenes saw the conditioning of an individual's mind as the only real way of leading a good life, saying that to live well a person needed either "right reason or a halter" (p. 27). Diogenes saw those who clung unthinkingly to cultural conventions as being willingly led around by their empty heads, something that was intolerable to a man of such extreme wittiness and intelligence. Diogenes himself tried to exemplify all he taught about the supremacy of reason by ridiculing other philosophies and their proponents. Plato, even though he was one of the most well respected thinkers of his time (and ours for that matter), was Diogenes's favorite victim; he used his quick wit to show-up Socrates's most revered student at every possible opportunity. In one of their more amusing encounters Diogenes demonstrated the flaw in Plato's definition of man ("animal, biped, and featherless") by presenting a plucked chicken, saying "Here is Plato's man" (p. 43).

Diogenes proposed an alternative to the typical lifestyle by advocating a total break from the duties and demands of society. "Accordingly, instead of useless toils men should choose such as nature recommends, whereby they might have lived happily. Yet such is their madness that they choose to be miserable." In a tone that is unmistakably reminiscent of our modern American ideals, Diogenes stated that he "preferred liberty over everything" (p. 73).

Cynicism is about knowing what you want and then going out and getting it. It demands you look within yourself, blocking out the white noise of society, seeing what it is that jives best with your nature as a person, and then doing precisely that.

Of course, upon realizing what it is that you're all about, you might just realize that you don't fit in quite as well after all. Diogenes certainly didn't; he got beaten up a lot, though he did know how to fight back. He recognized that, while it was easy to agree with his principles, it was much harder for people to actually walk the walk of a Cynic: "He described himself as a hound of the sort which all men praise, but no one, he added, of his admirers dared go out hunting along with him" (p. 35). Most people were, in the end, too afraid to leave their comfortable position in society for the freedom of the Cynical counter-culture because they either didn't recognize their situation as one of misery (which Diogenes certainly believed it was) or didn't really want to spend their lives sleeping in gutters.

The vagrant lifestyle of the Cynic was one of the philosophy's primary drawbacks; how could anyone be happy if they had to wear rags instead of robes and sleep on the streets instead of in a bed? It was a way of thinking about yourself and your place in the world that required an incredible amount of devotion and discipline, and those of you who are weak-willed would never have been able to pass as a Cynic. But just as Diogenes had left the philosophical scene (he died in 323 B.C.E.), a new radical philosopher was coming into his own with an ethical philosophy that is so simple it makes Cynicism's chief commandment of "do what comes naturally" look complex.

Epicurus of Athens was a prolific thinker, crafting philosophical theories and maxims that were wide-ranging and far-reaching, yet all of his more complex ideas stemmed from the simplest observation on the true purpose of life: pleasure. That's right all of you drunken Parrotheads, now you have a friend amongst the ancient Greeks, one who believes that the chief goal in life is attaining pleasure and avoiding pain. And just as Diogenes taught by example, so too was Epicurus the model for the ethic he proclaimed. He was described as being in incredibly poor health, probably due to the fact that he was so fat that for a long time he couldn't even get out of a chair without assistance, spent vast amounts of money on food and drink every night, threw up two times a day from overeating, and was well acquainted with most of the Athenian courtesans. Because of the simplicity of his philosophy and his "indecent" conduct, many of his fellow philosophers absolutely despised Epicurus, just as they had Diogenes.

Yet why should Epicurus care? He was having one hell of a good time, and so were his followers. With life's most important purpose being manifested in good music and hot sex, how could anyone *not* have a blast?

It wasn't all just screwing and drinking, though. As we learn in Epicurus's "Letter to Menoeceus" (*The Stoic and Epicurean Philosophers*, Random House, 1940, p. 32), the main goal of Epicurean practices is "freedom from pain in the body and from trouble in the mind." Unfortunately for those Parrotheads who latched onto Epicurus's mandate for indulgence with too much vigor, this means avoiding hangovers and syphilis. "For it is not continuous drinkings and revellings, nor the satisfaction of lusts, nor the enjoyment of fish and other luxuries of the wealthy table, which produce a pleasant life, but sober reasoning, searching out the motives for all choice and avoidance, and banishing mere opinions, to which are due the greatest disturbance of spirit." Epicurus is essentially arguing both for people to enjoy themselves, but not to do so in ways that are counterproductive for their souls. So while drinking, partying, and fornicating are fun, one must remember that "the greatest good is prudence," which is the avoidance of overindulgence. In addition to this, Epicurus believes that one of the primary pleasures of the world is seeking knowledge, which means subjecting oneself to a study of (gasp) philosophy! Yet Epicurus states that "prudence is a more precious thing even than philosophy." The need to be temperate and have control over one's actions, especially when it comes to indulging in sinful pleasures of the flesh, is equally as strong as the motivation to go out and seek pleasure in the Epicurean ethic.

Finally, Epicurus joined Diogenes in advocating a break from cultural norms in his philosophy, and not just those that would have kept him from overindulging and putting on a few extra pounds. He stated that "we must release ourselves from the prison of affairs and politics" (p. 43). Epicurus, like Diogenes before him, saw the duties and roles that society roped people into and insisted that they free themselves from these in order to pursue what they really wanted to do. The main difference between Epicureanism and Cynicism is that the Cynics chose destitution and self-discipline as their way of leaving society, while the Epicureans choose indulgence and self-gratification instead. To the Epicurean, it is human nature to enjoy everything that a person can, just so long as you don't get hurt in the process.

The Person Your Parents Warned You About

The philosophy of "island escapism" that Jimmy Buffett has been teaching from stages across the United States and around the world is one that finds itself in the newest section of a long line of dissent. Counter-cultural philosophy is as much an institution as traditional philosophical values. The reason these anti-establishment philosophies aren't widely known is because most of these revolutionary thoughts have been incorporated into the mainstream; for example, the ideas of a democratic society or racial integration both started as radical ideologies only to be adopted and normalized later. Those philosophies that haven't, such as Cynicism and Epicureanism, suffer from a lack of publicity; most people wouldn't expect anything so exciting from a bunch of toga-wearing moldy-oldies. Luckily for us, these special ways of thinking were resurrected by Jimmy Buffett who, like those that came before him, taught us by example just exactly how we should be living.

Since it's unlikely that Buffett ever came across the ideas of Diogenes or Epicurus through personal study (he says in "Cultural Infidel" that "Philosophy is not for me, laughin' is my game"), it would seem that they are all more of kindred spirits in the sense that all three of these philosophizers set out on lives that would naturally go against the grain. For Jimmy Buffett, his anti-establishment mentality came from two main sources: his family, and his birth date. In *A Pirate Looks at Fifty* we learn that Buffett's father, J.D. Buffett, once told his son that he had decided to become an airplane mechanic when he joined the Navy "because it was what I wasn't supposed to do." Then, he remarked to Jimmy that it "looks like you have made a career out of that, doing what you're not supposed to do" (p. 153). Buffett not only created a profession of doing and singing about things that the more up-tight side of American society would despise him for, but he has lived his songs as well, starting at an early age and continuing to do so as he enters his sixties.

Growing up where he did, Jimmy Buffett was raised on Mardi Gras, where his parents would cut loose and act just as crazy as the kids, and on the beach, where the call of the ocean was ever-present to him from a minuscule age. His love of scuba diving, surfing, and sailing kept him on or in the water and away from the boring lives of other people who spent their days playing football or running for class president. Simply being at sea became an anti-societal jab: "When you spend a lot of time on the water, you lose touch with what's happening on the land" (p. 162). His idolization of pirates instead of Civil War generals also went against the cultural norms of the South in the mid-twentieth century.

And then of course there were the Sixties. Jimmy's date of birth put him in a prime state to be fully immersed in the greatest counter-cultural revolt to happen in America since we got tired of the monarchy from across the pond in the late 1700s. To Buffett, the Sixties were totally embodied in the movie *Easy Rider* in the scene where Peter Fonda and Dennis Hopper, sky-high on marijuana, dance to "Like a Bird" under the moonlight with a bunch of naked hippie chicks. "Role models for an entire generation went from presidents to gypsies." It was during this drug-addled time that Buffett learned how to "live for the day," making the most out of whatever life presented him (p. 69).

The United States of America was rocked during the 1960s by a massive counter-cultural assault. It was a movement that was centered on the principle that people should be independent and free: free to go where they wanted, free to do whatever drugs they desired, and free to have sex with whomever they could. Some call it the height of American hedonism; for Jimmy Buffett, however, it was inspiration. It was the Sixties that verified for Buffett that this was how he wanted to live his life: one day at a time, enjoying every second, whether it's standing on a beach wiggling his toes into the sand, kicking back under a mango tree with that frozen concoction he loves so much, or launching into the last chorus of "Fruitcakes" in front of forty thousand fans. In his own words: "I had always promised myself that I would not grow old like the majority of the people I see, working their asses off until their late sixties or early seventies and then retiring and going on a cruise, wondering how they let the good things in life pass them by. That was not going to be me" (p. 53).

So Jimmy Buffett's personal philosophy became that of making the most out of every opportunity he had to have a good time. Like Diogenes and Epicurus both, he dedicated himself to making sure that he lived his life the way he wanted it to be, and he taught his fans this philosophy through his music. In "That's What Living Is to Me," Buffett lays it out plainly for his students to take in: "Be good and you will be lonesome / Be lonesome and you will be free / Live a lie and you will live to regret it / That's what living is to me." Diogenes couldn't have said it any better himself. Being true to one's own self is the key to Cynicism, and, despite the fact that it is lonely to be outside of the influence of society, it is the ultimate liberation, and the ultimate freedom to do exactly what you want.

Wisdom Under the Mango Tree

> If you're looking for a quote from me, I'll be under the mango tree.
> —Jimmy Buffett

The Parrothead philosophy's key ingredient is "island escapism," the special brand of travel information that has come along with

Buffett's music since the beginning. While Epicurus may have advocated the pleasures of food, drink, and sex, he also wanted his followers to enjoy the wonders of the natural world. For Jimmy Buffett and his Parrotheads, the best place to fulfill their enjoyment of the natural world is on a sunny beach in the Caribbean. The appeal of the laid-back tropical lifestyle is only surpassed by the desire to experience the beauty of the southern latitudes, and this is the subject of many of Buffett's songs. But it's not just the enjoyment of being in a beautiful place: by leaving the hectic world of the USA behind and traveling into the realm of the tropics, Parrotheads are once again defying the norm by *relaxing* instead of *working*. To his critics, he simply responds "I Don't Know and I Don't Care," a song that overtly states his support of heading south to "sandy beaches in distant reaches." Buffett recognizes that these subversive acts beg the question "Is it ignorance or apathy? The worried will all disagree." Leaving behind the world of the "worried" and trading it in for a nap under a palm tree may not sound fair to those who insist on spending their lives working above the Tropic of Cancer, but it is an option that Jimmy Buffett is avidly recommending to anyone who will listen. It seems that, like Diogenes, Buffett just can't understand why people would want to live miserably, and he's not exactly interested in hearing their lame justifications.

With the backdrop of the Caribbean, Jimmy Buffett sings songs that entice his followers to relinquish the flat screen HD televisions and fancy cars that are the trademarks of an empty life in exchange for simple pleasures, the kind that provide genuine enjoyment. In this sense Buffett is like both of his Greek predecessors, but only because the society he's revolting against, American pop culture, is so materialistic that the only way to be counter to that is to be just a bit old fashioned. In his song "Tonight I Just Need My Guitar," he warns that "Need is a relative thing these days / It borders on desire. / The high tech world is full of bright shiny things / We think that we really require." In this facet of Buffett's philosophy we find ourselves in a gray area between Cynicism, which prescribes giving up material possessions, and Epicureanism, which teaches that indulgence is just fine, especially when it comes to buying new toys. However, this song in particular acts as a reminder to Parrotheads that not only must we invest in the pleasures of a new ski boat or a five-thousand-dollar ergonomically correct lounge chair, but also experience the simple pleasures, like strumming a guitar or taking in a sunset. These are often just as rewarding, if not more so, than the ones that cause a serious hurt on the wallet.

Still, getting what you want is the central theme in a lot of Buffett's songs, and nowhere is this better exemplified than in "Cheeseburger in Paradise," the ultimate song about knowing what you want and getting exactly what you need. Parrotheads the world over know that this song is not just about eating a good burger, but it's about tasting the proverbial "forbidden fruit." In the song, the narrator begins by saying that he's been on a vegetarian diet for the last seventy days, and that every night he is haunted by the dream of this delicious cheeseburger. Buffett lays out exactly what it is that he wants in the bridge, shouting "I like mine with lettuce and tomato Heinz Fifty-Seven and French friend potatoes. Big kosher pickle and a cold draft beer. . . ." Later on in the song he mentions how sailors in the old days had to eat the same thing every day, but when they got into port, they knew just where to head to find that perfect burger. Both the diet-breaking and the shore-leave craving in this song demonstrate that if you know what you want, then it's "Worth every damn bit of sacrifice / To get that cheeseburger in paradise!" When the goal is ultimate satisfaction and a great deal of pleasure, Jimmy Buffett exactly restates what Epicurus advocated more than two thousand years ago: go get it.

Having said that, Buffett does include disclaimers in some of his songs. Just as Epicurus warned about weighing pain against pleasure when deciding whether or not to do something, making sure that the pleasure you'd receive isn't overshadowed by the pain of getting to it, Jimmy warns of the hazards of overindulgence to the point of ruin. In "Margaritaville," for example, the protagonist is literally "wasting away again" after a wild season of partying. When the fun is over and the hangover has set in, the Parrothead King wants his subjects to remember: "Some people claim that there's a woman to blame, / But I know it's my own damn fault." One must remember that a Parrothead devotee must be self-sufficient, which includes taking responsibility for doing stupid things, and must maintain the Epicurean ethic of prudence, especially when not heeding this warning leads to the downward spiral Buffett describes in "Margaritaville."

Jimmy Buffett never strayed far from his roots in Cynicism and Epicureanism. He managed to incorporate these two philosophies by advocating indulgence, but always with a nod to caution and the simple pleasures, and a sharp break from society. His songs range from the blatantly lewd ("Why Don't We Get Drunk [and Screw]"), to tender ("Come Monday"), to thought-provoking ("Coastal Confessions"), and each serves its purpose of filling the Parrotheads' ears and minds with a way of thinking and living that Jimmy is positive will help them to live a good life because, hell, it sure has worked out well for him.

That's His Story and He's Stickin' to It

The philosophy of Jimmy Buffett and the Parrotheads is one of the great counter-cultural ways of thought in our society today. While most of Parrothead Nation is aging Baby Boomers who are, like Buffett, hanging on to the feelings of liberation and freedom that were sparked in the Sixties, these people are bringing the next generation (or two) along with them, introducing them to Buffett's vision of the world through his music. While this is exposing an entire new generation to the benefits of liberated thinking and action, there are implications that are a bit foreboding.

Picture a world full of Parrotheads unaware of their philosophical history. On every street, at all hours of the night and in the daytime as well, drunken gangs of youngsters dressed in full Parrothead regalia stagger around the streets belching out the only line they can remember from "License to Chill" over and over again. There are no policeman out to take these punks to jail so that they can sleep it off; they're all at home, where the blender has been going strong all night whipping out frozen concoction after frozen concoction. You'd find that the further south you travel the more and more you find sun drenched, crowd-laden beaches filled with people that look like cookies that were left in the oven too long. No one goes to work, no one goes to school, and the only remaining industries are sport fishing and tequila manufacturing. It's a world where innovation has been replaced by inebriation, duty to others replaced by do it yourself, and mainstream culture undone by a Gulf Stream mentality. Counter-cultures like island escapism are meant to rip apart the fabric of the every day world and replace it with something new and different, but do we really want this taken to its logical extreme? Diogenes and Epicurus both argued greatly in favor of a disassociation from society, but was it really their belief that society had to be disintegrated? Is it Jimmy Buffett's?

Thankfully, the graceful life philosophies of Cynicism, Epicureanism, and Parrotheadism all have built-in safety features to prevent such a catastrophe. The first, and most important of these, is that these revolutionary ways of thinking demand exclusivity and division from the masses. To be a Parrothead means to be an out-cast, someone whom others will find strange. If dressing in grass skirts and foam shark suits suddenly becomes an acceptable means of dress, there will no doubt be many people who don't think that dressing up like a fish is such a hot idea. If the counter-culture were ever to find itself in the mainstream, it would immediately come up against a new counter-culture. History has taught us that no matter how far you go back (even all the way back to the ancient Greeks) there were and will always be those who simply do not see their society as the right one.

The second self-correction that will keep Parrothead culture from becoming the mainstream is its reliance on society, and all of the things that society brings with it. While being a loner who hangs out on the beach all day may be fine for some, it's certainly not a truly acceptable way to live for all people. In this way, indulging in the good life of a Parrothead must be tempered by life back in the "real world." Even Jimmy Buffett, the best example of island escapism the world has to offer, has a wife and kids, works diligently at his job for most months out of the year, and is respon-sible for entertaining and enlightening thousands of fans every time he steps onto the stage. In the same way, Parrotheads everywhere have careers and families that demand their attention most of the time. The built-in safety net of mainstream society demands the prudence that Epicurus expects of his followers, and that Jimmy embodies for his fans.

While Epicureanism and Cynicism never really became main-stream, these two schools of thought both contributed to future philosophical ideas; the former was revived by Jeremy Bentham in his Utilitarian ethic of the late 1700s, and the latter began a long tradition of skeptical philosophy that, for the most part, has been limited to the academic realm. These ways of thinking were not able to be widely accepted simply because they were unable to be applied to *real* human society, as in a culture where people have to rely on others for things. Sustaining a life of pleasure or of skep-tical inquiry is nearly impossible unless you happen to be heir to some vast oil conglomerate, and so the individual is required to find a job to pay the bills, restricting their fun to weekends and holidays. The trick, however, is to remember the advice of Diogenes, Epicurus, and Jimmy when choosing a vocation: you have to find a calling that fits your natural abilities, it has to be enjoyable, and you must be just as passionate about it as you are about your leisure time.

The graceful life philosophies of Cynicism and Epicureanism ran against the grains of their societies, not because they were being difficult and wanted a fight, but because they saw that people were approaching the question of how to live their lives from the wrong direction; instead of seeing themselves doing a job well and enjoying it, people were taking whichever job was thrust upon them by familial or societal pressure. Those who were able to find a calling that they loved lived happily, and these Diogenes and Epicurus applauded.

In our modern day and age, Americans are among the hardest working people in the world, taking very little time off each year to relax and enjoy the pleasures that life has to offer. Our materialistic, profit-driven society hinders people from breaking away from the endless cycle of improvement in an effort to earn more money. But Jimmy Buffett threw a wrench into the cogs of that American culture, stopping the grinding down of the American worker long enough to show them what it would be like to indulge in the island life, one of rest and relaxation. And while that wrench will always be rendered flexible by the pressures of prudent living in mainstream society, bent nearly to the breaking point under the constraints of progress, island escapism cannot be destroyed, for in its philosophical teachings reside the hopes and dreams of the better life that all Americans strive for.

The concert is over, and you find yourself back at the nine-to-five on Friday morning, your head pounding, your eyes blurry, sporting a new tattoo of a name you don't recognize that is luckily on a part of your body that doesn't see much of the sun. You curse yourself for overindulging, you vow never to drink tequila again, and you happily put your nose to the grindstone once more.

But maybe one year later, when you overhear someone mention that Jimmy Buffett is coming to town again, you'll remember the feeling of freedom you experienced when you took control of your life just for one night and made it exactly how you wanted. Who knows, maybe you'll indulge again and find yourself that very next weekend, just for a few short hours, wearing a lei and a pair of oversized sunglasses, standing in the front row, your hands held palm to palm over your head, joining in with forty thousand people just like you and the man who started it all up on stage in singing it one more time: "Fins to the left, fins to the right, and you're the only bait in town."

2

Drinking the American Dream

DOUG ANDERSON

> But sometimes I still forget; Til the lights go on and the stage is set,
> And the song hits home and you feel that sweat.
> It's my job to be different than the rest, and that's enough reason to
> go for me.
>
> —"It's My Job"

> My teachers called me a daydreamer. They would write comments
> on my report card like, "He seems to live in a fantasy world and
> prefers that to paying serious attention to serious subject matters
> that will prepare him for life."
>
> —*A Pirate Looks at Fifty*

There's a common misconception that Stoicism—the philosophy
that followed Socrates's moral vision of controlling one's inner state
of being—entails passivity. There's a belief that the Stoic just "takes
it" because she can't do anything else.

Stoics *are* fatalistic in a way; they see us as born into a world
over which we have no significant control. However, the Stoics do
aim to control themselves even if they can't control the world—
their attitudes must fit their latitudes. But these latitudes also provide them with a job of work to do, whether as an emperor like
Marcus Aurelius or as a slave like Epictetus. These Stoics, and others like Cicero and Seneca, played important roles in Roman life.
They weren't passive folk—they didn't waste time. They came to
know their worlds and they came to figure out what their roles
were in those worlds. Seneca made clear that if we fail to find a

useful role, it's *our* fault not Nature's: "Life is long enough and our allotted portion generous enough for our most ambitious projects if we invest it wisely" (Moses Hadas, *The Stoic Philosophy of Seneca*, Doubleday, 1958, p. 48).

Jimmy Buffett, for his part, came to learn his own role—his job—in late twentieth-century American culture. His job was to *be* Jimmy Buffett. And part of *his* job has been to remind us in song that we should find our own. As he says in *A Pirate Looks at Fifty*, "My walkabout place cannot be yours. Your walkabout place cannot be somebody else's. You have to find your own" (p. 359). We're all engaged in finding and living an American dream.

Redreaming the Dream

Buffett's friend and fellow traveler of the banana republics, Hunter S. Thompson, said that by the 1960s the American dream had become twisted and was on its way to going belly up. He was talking about the post-war American dream of the 1950s—a house, a few kids, a dog, and upward economic mobility. Thompson, like Buffett a pop figure of the 1970s, checked himself out of the human race a few decades later. That's a key difference between him and Jimmy Buffett. Thompson was a Cynic; Buffett a Stoic; one chose death, one chose living. Very different American dreams! If Thoreau was right, the American dream is *always* in danger of dying. That's because it's not an end state we reached in the 1950s that has since dissipated or self-destructed; it's an ongoing dream that lives only when *we* dream it. That's the optimistic American stoicism of Buffett—Margaritaville is everywhere and nowhere. It's up to us. But let's back up a minute.

Most of us don't *know* Jimmy Buffett; for us he's a sound, a spirit, and an energy. He's a symbol we embrace, ignore, resist, or enjoy. One vision of Buffett-being is Key West party boy for whom "life is still high school" ("Last Man Standing"); this Buffett still sings "Why Don't We Get Drunk (and Screw)?" and dances on stage with his hands over his head in "fins" fashion. The other Buffett-being is a successful American businessperson with a Margaritaville empire. He's a workaholic who covers all the angles. He posts set lists for concerts on the internet months in advance. He plays music, sells lager, builds casinos and restaurants, sells cheeseburgers, writes novels, and sells tequila, and in 2006 was judged to be the seventh richest music star.

In the final analysis, we presume he's both Buffett-beings. That's the trick of *his* American dream. It's also the heart of his American Stoicism, where one learns to live hopefully toward the future while remaining fully cognizant of the deadening influences surrounding us. One "gets by" only by controlling one's own world, not the whole world. The key is staying alive as the person you are. As Seneca remarked to his friend Serenus, "Carius Dentatus was right, I think, when he said he would rather be dead than a living cipher; the worst fate of all is to be stricken from the roster of the living before you die" (Hadas, p. 87).

For Thompson, the American dream of the 1950s itself had died on the vine in the turmoil of the 1960s—optimism had turned to cynicism. "Success" was the man in the gray flannel suit. It was indeed what T.S. Eliot had portrayed in "The Waste Land" and "The Hollow Men"—people living lives of wealthy boredom, overwhelmed by their success. How could one stay on the roster of the living when the dream itself had become identical with choosing a living death? The answer, and this is what I think eluded Hunter Thompson, was to re-envision the American dream, not as the static end-state of home ownership, job status, and family reputation that Hunter believed it was, but as an ongoing process of staying on the roster of the living in the fated historical setting of American capitalist culture. This, I think, is akin to Jimmy Buffett's implicit story of the American dream. He sang that he'd rather die when living than live while he was dead!

As Buffett records in *A Pirate Looks at Fifty*, he began in the margins, engaged in folk and quasi-country music, and made his way toward the mainstream of pop music. But he did so on the basis of one major hit, "Margaritaville" in 1977. The rest he accomplished on the coconut telegraph; he built an enormous international following one listener at a time. But, in any terms of American life, he *succeeded*. In the 1970s it was a short trip for him from that success to becoming a role model for the "yuppies"—post-political, business savvy hippies, the hippies who had become the young upwardly mobile residuum of the Woodstock generation.

The yuppies seemed to return to a new end-state version of the dream—an update on the Fifties' version. Their motto: "He who dies with the most toys wins." The same game as the 1950s but stated with the irony of self-awareness. Buffett did not relinquish the competitive side of this aim, but he acknowledges that he did learn from what he had written and sung in the preceding years:

one must learn to "live" even while one competes and "succeeds." In the absence of such "living," our success quickly becomes hollow and tedious. Our achievement becomes one of wealth and mediocrity—we just live in the high rent district of Malvina Reynolds' "little boxes made of ticky-tacky."

Competing: American Stoicism

Buffett never relinquishes—in life or song—the key process of living an American dream; that is, he engages in hard working and productive living. He's recorded dozens of albums and CDs, he's written several best selling books, and he performs extensively every year. As he says, "I don't sleep late in the morning, I've worked since I was thirteen and I've done a lot of manual labor" (Matt Luna, "Margaritaville is Jimmy Buffett's Empire," www.iht .com/articles/2007/07/06/business/wbspot07.php, p. 2). But Buffett also knows that not all hard work is manual labor. Earth-Firsters are often tremendously hard working; music performers travel and perform relentlessly on "tours"; actors work long and difficult hours; and, as Buffet learned the hard way, novelists and autobiographers undertake an absolutely daunting task in every book they begin.

Buffett entered the competition on the American music scene, one of the most brutally competitive sites in American industry. But he also took up sales and marketing in developing Margaritaville Holdings into an extremely successful global business. In business, as in partying, Buffett is a competitor and sets out every time to be "the last man standing." Parrotheads recognize this side of Buffett and, seeing their own lives in light of it, generally applaud it. They are not the dullard washouts that they denigratingly refer to as the "parakeets." They are successful mainstreamers of several generations who live intense lives in a work-driven corporate America—doctors, plumbers, lawyers, ski slope groomers, and accountants who see in Buffett's music a way of staying alive.

Some who see his competitiveness and success in the music business want to discount his music as too pop, too easy, too happy, and too successful—he's dubbed a "sell-out." I've played in bar bands for years, and one of the biggest struggles I've encountered is that musicians who, driven by unwarranted arrogance, believe they are 'better than that', refuse to play Buffett songs because it will mark them as unsophisticated. Buffett just isn't counter-culture enough to be taken seriously by 'real' musicians—

or 'real' philosophers. Instead of drugging himself to death, he became an American success. But here's the irony—Hunter Thompson, counter culture's poster child, was every bit as competitive as Jimmy Buffett. His letters and practices clearly reveal a man committed to winning—by his own rules of Gonzo—in the competitive world of journalism and publication. Indeed, one reason he maintained for continuing to live on speed rather than switching to the tamer influence of marijuana was that it kept him alert and gave him a productive advantage, a *competitive edge*. *Rolling Stone*, after all, didn't remain a newspaperish rock'n'roll rag—it became a glossy, glitzy, and highly successful portrayal of the pop music world even as it retained its leftish style.

We may pretend otherwise but every musician in the game, from Kurt Cobain to Keith Richards to Lucinda Williams, aims for the kind of notoriety Buffett has achieved. Buffett cannot be discounted on this score; *he* is the one without pretension; he's the one who has achieved some semblance of self-awareness in an insane world. Like Seneca, whose boss Nero's perverted escapades, from executing his mother to putting on extravagant bloody gladiatorial shows, make American capitalism's excesses look extremely tame, Buffett has adjusted his attitudes to his historical latitudes and found a way to stay on the roster of the living.

Such simple honesty of the sort Buffett projects is, for Seneca, extremely healthful for the Stoic life. "The practice of maintaining a careful pose and never revealing your natural self to anyone," he said, is a "considerable source of anxiety" (Hadas, p. 103). Buffett doesn't hide from his audience. In his lyrics and his writing he's upfront—he tells us of his foibles and his failures. And frankly, it's the honesty of Buffett's songs that make them, contra the 'real' musicians, meaningful to several generations of listeners and a hell of a lot of fun to play in bars and on back porches.

As American Stoic, Buffett has acknowledged his fate. Born into a world of political freedom and economic competition, he needed to find a way to live. Unlike the Cynics, he opted not to 'drop out' and snipe profitlessly at the culture from the margins. Nor did his fatalism lead to a deadening inactivity. Jimmy Buffett engages in slow social transformation. He, as Stoic, doesn't try to be a social radical like Hunter S. Thompson. For him, some cultural change can be brought about, but always slowly under the larger powers of the cosmos to which each of us is but a small contributor. And though initially tempted by the toys he was collecting, Buffett came to see that their value was ultimately dependent on his attitude—on his having a sense of self-worth. We must find a useful life in our fated world.

This was Seneca's advice to Serenus when Serenus found himself in a general malaise while living in the midst of the wealth of the Roman Empire: "For when a man's declared object is to make himself useful to his fellow citizens and to all mankind, he will exercise and improve his abilities by participating fully in demanding activities, serving both public and private interests as best he can" (Hadas, p. 83). The trick is to find one's useful role without cynicism and without sliding into a life of quiet desperation.

One dimension of this Stoic survival story was to keep one's spirit, energy, or *thumos* engaged—as Thoreau might have put it, we need to keep our wildness in play even as we live in civilization. Seneca offered Serenus several points of practical advice including the need to dream and to drink on occasion. "It is important," he maintained, "to withdraw into one's self" to avoid the tensions of our public lives. Moreover, in general "the mind must have relaxation" so that it can "rise stronger and keener after recreation" (Hadas, p. 104). Such dreaming and relaxation occasionally might require a catalyst.

Thus, Seneca argued, sometimes we must enjoy a generous wine and "on occasion we should go so far as intoxication" because "drink washes cares away." The usefulness of drink does not end with the washing away, but also has a positive dimension: "Bacchus, who invented wine, is surnamed Liber, not because of the license wine gives the tongue, but because it liberates the mind from its bondage to care and emancipates it and animates it and gives it greater boldness for any enterprise" (Hadas, pp. 105–06). Buffett pursues his own version of this ancient Stoic story, creating an Americana dialectic of dream and drink. At fifty, he argued, "it's even more important to throw a few curveballs at my metabolic clock and ward off the horrifying thought, God forbid, of a routine life" (p. 334). For Buffett, we must, as in "Five o'Clock Somewhere," drink the American dream of a "Jamaican vacation," and, as in "Margaritaville," we must dream the American drink.

Dreaming the Drink

Rodney Crowell's song "American Dream" which appears on Jimmy Buffett's set lists and recordings begins with an awakening. The protagonist has been dreaming and opens the song with a question: "I beg your pardon, mama, what did you say? My mind was drifting on a Martinique day." It's been long months, if not years, of work in Augusta, Georgia, and it's a time of life when Augusta's "just no place to be." However, since it's not actually possible for most working folks to get to Martinique, the key to leaving Augusta is to dream oneself away:

> Dream Jamaica in the moonlight,
> Sandy beaches, drinking rum every night
> Got no money, Mama, but we can go,
> Split the difference, go to Coconut Grove.

The song establishes the dialectic that is at the heart of Buffett's Stoicism and his version of the American dream: a dialectic between dreaming and drinking.

Instead of dreaming of success in a mid-level management position, we dream of a night of drinking to fend off tedium. I can dream the escape from my living death, and the dream itself will entail or involve drink which will further the dream. And so, in "Five o'Clock Somewhere," the lunch break "hurricane" leads to an afternoon of drinking and dreaming that will prevent one from accosting one's boss and losing one's job. The Stoic element is fairly clear. We can't outrightly change the necessity of our working and living in America's competitive culture. Even if we "take this job and shove it," whether as a laborer or as an accountant, we will soon need to find another job to shove. What we *can* do, as the Stoics emphasize, is to change our attitudes and our outlooks to meet the latitudes in which we find ourselves. If we can lose ourselves in Buffett's rock'n'roll—in dreaming and drinking—we can not only wash away cares and tensions but refresh ourselves for a new and living adventure in our work.

To dream is to envision ourselves beyond where we are both physically and mentally—it is to improve our spiritual situation, one might say. We have all experienced the deadening effects of work, even if we otherwise love the work we do. When I worked farms, factories, and sawmills, the weekends bore the meaning of cash, freedom, and fun. Everybody's aim was a "Livingston Saturday Night," a clean pick-up, American beer, hot country music, and dancing til the early hours. We daydreamed about it all week. Now that I work at a university, I still dream that end-of-term breaks will bring party time. However, I usually end up listening to Buffett as I work. A variety of Buffett tunes thematize this fact; he knows and expresses how *we* feel. An extreme version appears in "The Weather Is Here, Wish You Were Beautiful" whose opening line sets the stage: "He worked hard all year, just wanted a few weeks alone." These few weeks, we know, can be fatally difficult to find—something always "comes up" as we say. The subsequent lines reiterate the "needs" established by this business partner's hard work and relationship tensions—the need for "a well-deserved overdue binge" and the need for a "time to play."

Dreaming lays the groundwork for serious attitude reorientation. It yields imagined possibilities of enjoyment, relief, and wildness. "Tin Cup Chalice" exemplifies Buffett's dreaming:

> I want to go back to the island,
> Where the shrimp boats tie up at the pilin'.
> Give me oysters and beer for dinner every day of the year,
> And I'll feel fine, I'll feel fine.

The dreaming opens doors to our sensuous being, the very being we routinely close off in our competitive working lives. Buffett rethinks the American dream, then, not as an accomplished state of affairs, not as a paradise at which we ultimately arrive. He's satisfied with a "happy ever after, every now and then."

The dream is an ongoing activity of *dreaming*, of envisioning our lives outside their actuality, aimed at opening spaces and possibilities for staying on the roster of the living. His dreaming is a cathartic escapism. We dream to escape the deadening influences, but only to return to that life alive, refreshed, energized, and wilded. If we can't learn to dream and to laugh, the Stoic educator would say, we might all go insane. Buffett is a master educator in the guise of a songman; he has been attentive to his own existence and this allows him to represent ours. His concerts become sites of the sort of escape he recommends—a dream-like time-out from worldy pressures. Likening his concerts to Woodstock, he says,

> That's what happens at our shows as well. They've always been known as opportunities to escape for the evening and just have fun, but you should see what happens when it rains. You would think that a driving thunderstorm would send the crowd to the parking lot or back to the warmth and shelter of their homes in droves, but not so. They yell louder. . . . I call it the Woodstock connection. Somehow the

rain connects them to the images of that landmark event and to that thread of uninhibited, childlike celebration. (pp. 154–55)

Escape, wildness, freedom from inhibition; Buffett's "job" is, as Stoic educator, to help us recover our balance in life.

He knows that at some level he loves his work, including the freedoms it buys him, and he knows the markers of desperation and oppressive stress. But he never forgets the catharsis and conversion of his day at the Coconut Grove bar with Jerry Jeff Walker. The experience "produced a basic [and Stoic] revelation that changed my whole way of looking at who I was and where I was going. My worries were somewhere else, and my tropical soul had finally come home to the sun. . . . my tropical resurrection revealed who I was. I could not be someone else" (p. 236). And so, in "License to Chill," he is able to sing for us as Seneca wrote for Serenus and as Epictetus wrote for his friends:

Livin' for the weekend,
Jumpin' off the deep end,
With just enough money to buy
A license to chill, and I believe I will.

Drinking the Dream

Ralph Waldo Emerson (1803–1882), influenced by neo-Platonists and Stoics, was a popular songster whose work of "raising and cheering" American culture served as a model for Walt Whitman, Emily Dickinson, Jack Kerouac, Allen Ginsberg, and, I think, Jimmy Buffett. He acknowledged the importance of dreaming, but he didn't think we were all naturally good dreamers. Many of us require poets and singers like Buffett to incite our own dreaming. And the poets sometimes need inspiration from outside their daily routines.

Emerson states in plain terms and without apology that poets often seek catalysts to find their natural dreams and to express their *natural* selves, not their overly-enculturated and overly-civilized selves. "The poet," he said, "knows that he speaks adequately, then only when he speaks somewhat wildly, or, 'with the flower of the mind'; not with the intellect, used as an organ, but with the intellect released from all service, and suffered to take its direction from its celestial life; or, as the ancients were wont to express themselves, not with the intellect alone, but with the intellect inebriated by nectar" (*The Collected Works of Ralph Waldo Emerson*, ed. J. Slater, Belknap Press, 1983, p. 16). It's no mistake that "Changes in Latitudes, Changes in Attitudes" begins with Buffett running into "a chum with a bottle of rum" and ends up with them "drinking all night." The catalyzing of wildness and a momentary authenticity is, says Emerson, "why bards love wine, mead, narcotics, coffee, tea, opium, the fumes of sandal-wood and tobacco, or whatever other procurers of animal exhilaration" (p. 16).

Buffett agrees that his own life's work was occasionally inspired by such nectars, but he pushes farther in the direction of Seneca's advice, suggesting that the liberating intoxicants are, to a degree, good for all of us. The central case of "Margaritaville" is a good place to begin. First, it's not a happy song on the face of it— guy loses lover, guy gets "wasted away," wallowing in his sorrow. And so the margarita is initially a deadener of pain and useful enough in that capacity. It can, as Seneca claimed, wash cares away. But notice that the song moves from the cliché of blaming women in general to an honest acknowledgement of the singer's own "fault" in the affair. The margarita thus liberates the singer to a moment of honesty that is in itself liberating—this is a persistent theme of both Stoics and Buffett. Life is too short for dishonesty. "Live a lie," sings Buffett, "and you will live to regret it, that's what living is to me" ("That's What Living Is to Me"). The joy of the public performance of the song lies not just in sharing a having-been-there moment, but also in the liberation of tequila and truth working in concert.

When Buffett anticipates writing the memoirs of his romantic's life when he is in his eighties, he admits that one of the conditions will be to "ship in a good supply of rum and red burgundy" (p. 5). We all stand in need of liberation: "Drive-In, Guzzle gin, Commit a little mortal sin, It's good for the soul" ("Grapefruit-Juicy Fruit"). The need for some inebriation-liberation is a part of our natures and, in Stoic fashion, Buffett recommends that we not fight our natures. Take, for example, "Why Don't We Get Drunk (and Screw)?" The cultured and the civilized take the song as a mark of Buffett's depravity. But it's a pretty damn honest song. And every highbrow with a bottle of expensive Bordeaux or a bottle of high end scotch has the same damn thing in mind; they either remain blind to it or think that their version of getting drunk and screwing is of a more sophisticated sort. When we cut the pretense, the liberating moment is the same for them as for the singer who has just bought a brand new waterbed. It doesn't make much difference what nectar inebriates us. Whether it's margaritas, spliffs, rocky mountain highs, rum, or the ocean, the key is that the "tiki bar is open," as John Hiatt puts it. The inebriation permits liberation, fights routine, enables creativity, and fends off stagnation—it allows the dreaming we need to both find out and help make us who we are. "Thank God the tiki bar is open; Thank God the tiki torch still shines; Thank God the tiki bar is open; Come on in and open up your mind" (J. Hiatt, "The Tiki Bar Is Open").

Banana Republics: Excesses in Paradise

As much as Buffett's songs honor dreaming and point to its cathartic virtues, he is well aware of its depraved side. As Seneca warned, "in liberty moderation is wholesome" (Hadas, p. 106). Those who mistake the dream for a curative end state and don't see it as a revitalizing process will most often find themselves lost and adrift and, ultimately fully disillusioned. Such dreaming to the point of excess, as the early Stoics well knew, becomes pathetic. The changing of attitude does *not* change the basic facts of our fated situation. And so Buffett, as Stoic educator, points out to us the dangers of excess.

The wise dreamer in "American Dream" "splits the difference" and heads to an ersatz Carribbean bar named "Coconut Grove." The hard core dreamers, thinking they have found the answer in "hopin' to have some fun," head instead to the banana republics. Their motivation is to ex-patriate, to leave behind their deadened lives in some northern working town. They are "trying to find what is ailing, living in the land of the free" by setting up shop in the islands (Steve Goodman, "Banana Republics"). But they are cynics, not Stoics; like Thompson they want to escape the whole mess instead of just taking time to regroup. But the joke is on them—the emptiness of life returns in their paradise escape home. The Stoic knows the encultured latitudes of history cannot be escaped in any permanent way; we can only find means of adjustment. The Stoic is not surprised when the "expatriated Americans" wind up "feeling so all alone, telling themselves the same lies they told themselves back home." The folks in the tropical republics have *their own* lives, latitudes, and burdens; they haven't time for whiners from the land of the free:

Down to Banana Republics
Things aren't as warm as they seem
None of the natives are buying
Any second-hand American dreams.

The expatriates have mistaken the dream for an end-state goal instead of a cathartic process that one adopts knowingly and without pretension.

Similar excess is of course available on the drinking side of the dialectic as well. If taken over the long haul, we call it alcoholism or addiction—an attitudinal orientation that precludes finding any role in a culture. It becomes a form of deadness worse than the deadness from which one was escaping. In *A Pirate Looks at Fifty* Buffett notes his own encounter with excess when "at some point in my late thirties, I realized I had advanced along the time line far enough for hangovers to have taken on the characteristics of recuperation from major surgery" (p. 252). The upshot was an exercise in self-control: "Fifty years of planetary occupation does not come without its share of bumps and bruises. Like most other survivors of the sixties, I traded my drugs and bad behavior for sleep, stretching, and physical activity" (pp. 205–06). Instead of going to rehab he changed his lifestyle. The Stoics' enduring claim is that they can control themselves—not the universe.

In the short run, we are given hints of the excesses made available by the intoxicants that in proper doses are useful. Buffett understands that his insights can be shared by the addicted—he knows that he *and* the wino "know." Similarly, in "Bank of Bad Habits," the protagonist distinguishes himself from a barfly but notes his proximity to the drunk: "The wrong thing is the right thing until you lose control." And this emanates into a concern for sexual excess and its issues:

you have to keep your head,
Or trouble is what you will find
Inside some stranger's bed.

The American Stoic must drink and dream without the excess; self-control must know its role in the revitalizing process of attitude adjustment. When instead one pushes the "Fool Button," the dangers of excess appear and one enters a world worse than the one from which one was running:

waking up in a strange room,
weird paintings on the wall
And mirrors on the ceiling,
I bolted for the door.

Too Much Tequila, Or Not Quite Enough

Buffett's American Stoicism places us in a mid-world. It's a border-land between the deadening acceptance of our habits and routines, living our lives in quiet desperation, and the killing fields of excessive wildness and dreaming: "too much tequila, Or not quite enough" ("Semi-True Stories"). Somewhere between God's own drunk and the CEO of Margaritaville we find Jimmy Buffett, American Stoic, doling out wisdom to us all in musical epistles—in what he calls "song lines." Although he claims that philosophy is not for him, he remains a "Cultural Infidel" not unlike Cicero:

Someone's got to talk about accountability,
Someone's got to raise some hell,
It might as well be me;
I'm a cultural infidel, believe in common sense.

The common sense he pitches us has power because, like Seneca, he understands *our* experience and is able to speak the language of adjustment that we can hear and appropriate. He sings the dialectic of dreaming and drinking—effectively but moderately. The common sense seems "common" because we "get it"—this has been our American fate. But Buffett's American common sense is, philosophically speaking, a Stoic take on the universe and our place in it. It's a "semi-true story,"

Well, the things that I've lived, and I've dreamed,
And I've seen, and I've heard
You take the good with the bad
And be glad to have every word. ("Semi-True Stories")

3

Martin Heidegger in Margaritaville

DREW M. DALTON

I had the distinct displeasure of residing for a few years of my life in what has got to be the coldest, rainiest and darkest of northern European countries—far from any coast-line, sunshine or fishing line. There, in the cold dark nights, huddled beneath a slate gray sky of low-lying clouds, I would sink into a funk deeper and heavier than even the funkiest baseline.

And so a ritual was born. On December 21st, the shortest and gloomiest day of the year, my expatriated friends and I would throw a party. We'd crank up the radiator heat in my little apartment as high as it would go, break out our Hawaiian shirts and Tommy Bahama shorts, throw some margarita mix into the blender (especially ordered from the States for the occasion) and crank Jimmy Buffett on the stereo. There with boat drinks in hand singing "Twelve Volt Man" at the top of our lungs, a small cadre of Parrotheads lost in Europe, we'd shout our defiance at the cold darkness and dream of a small strip of paradise somewhere "southeast of disorder" where we could spend our days just wasting away.

It was from these little vacations, these imaginary escapes to Margaritaville that we found the strength to push through till spring. Of course, I think it's precisely this kind of revelry that Buffett has in mind when he writes his music. Isn't this, after all, what a song like "Boat Drinks" is all about—a little "something to keep us all warm" in the winters of our life? Over the course of his career Buffett has fashioned himself as a kind of musical shaman offering his listeners transport to another realm. In this regard Buffett can be seen as a kind of uncanny hybrid, a curious cross

31

between a troubadour and a travel agent as much in the business of selling escape as in the business of making music. Buffett himself has repeatedly admitted as much. Take, for example, his October 6th, 2004, CBS interview where he told Correspondent Steve Croft that "I sell escapism," or again his 2007 Q&A in the swimsuit edition of *Sports Illustrated* magazine where he confessed, "I'm just doing my part to add a little more escapism to an otherwise crazy world."

"Havana Daydreamin'": The Value of Escapism

Escapism is the heart and soul of both Buffett's persona and his multi-million dollar empire. Whether through his music or his frozen-food dinners (which promise in their own way to transport our kitchens from the monotony of suburbia to the mess halls of "St. Somewhere", Buffett is in the business of selling escape. It's the centerpiece of his records and the main plotline of his two novels *Where is Joe Merchant?* and *A Salty Piece of Land.* And it is, moreover, what has attracted scores of fans for over thirty years now.

But why is this? What's so attractive about Buffett's brand of escapism that it has drawn so many for so long? What is it about the promise of escape his music offers that is so intensely alluring?

Buffett himself has offered an answer to this question. In the afterward to his 2004 novel *A Salty Piece of Land* Buffett makes the intriguing observation that ". . . now, more than ever, we don't just enjoy our escapism—we NEED it,"—we *need* a little break from the ordinary, a promise, however misleading, that somewhere out there, untouched by the disappointments of our lives, lies some release, some utopia where all our fears and anxieties will be wiped away. Escape is not merely superlative, Buffett seems to claim, it is not something extra or *en plus* which can be taken up or discarded at will, it is something necessary and integral to us—something that we cannot bear to live without. What makes the promise of escape so attractive, he seems to think, is that it is a vital element of our survival, as essential to us as sleep.

This claim, that we "need" our escapism, is more than it appears at first sight. Though on the surface nothing more than the banal assertion that it is pleasurable to escape and that vacations are fun, read literally, Buffet's claim seems to cut to the very core of what it means to be a human being. For beyond all possible banalities, the claim that there is some necessity to our escapism seems to assert that we as human beings fundamentally strive to be released from our selves, that we strive to be released from being itself—and this is a deeply provocative and somewhat troubling claim. For to claim that we *need* our escapism, that we instinctively strive to be released from ourselves, implies that there is something unpleasant about the nature of our being – that it is hard to be our being; and this is a claim that, by and large, the history of philosophy has been loath to admit.

"There's Nothing Soft" about Being

Since the beginning of philosophy, existence has almost always been associated with the good. While a seemingly esoteric claim at first glance, basically what has been claimed is that being, or existence, is something fundamentally worthwhile and worth preserving; that it is, in a phrase, good to be and always better to be than to not be. We should perhaps note here that philosophers have been struggling from the very beginning to define 'the good' conclusively. As a result a lot of disagreement always arises with any discussion of the good.

While some employ the term 'good' in a moral sense, using it the same way that we do when we say that someone is 'a good person', meaning that he or she is faultless or praiseworthy, others insist that the term 'good' implies only a kind of utility. These thinkers then only call something good that empowers action—something that does not impede our projects, but instead contributes to their successful completion. These thinkers use the word 'good' then in the same way that we use it when we say, for example, that a hammer or a shovel is good, meaning that it gets the job done, it does what it is supposed to do. Given the various interpretations of the meaning of the word good, it is clear that not all will agree on what it means to say that being is good. Very few, however, would disagree with the claim that it is nevertheless, in some sense, inherently good to be, however 'good' may be understood.

Though originally suggested by Plato, who is generally recognized as the father of western thinking, the argument that it is good to be is perhaps most articulately made by Saint Augustine of Hippo. In what is perhaps his most famous work, the *Confessions*, Augustine argues that it is always good in all cases to be, that is to exist, rather than to not be or not exist. Now this makes a lot of sense, after all almost all of us, given the choice, would prefer existence over non-existence, would prefer to go on living rather than be snuffed out. This is in large part why we don't all off ourselves at the first opportunity and why we try as best we can to continue our existence when it is threatened. This preference for existence over non-existence testifies, Augustine thought, to the fact that existence is a fundamentally good thing, that it is good to be, even if existence occasionally gives itself over to bad things, such as when you stub your toe or engage in global thermonuclear warfare, things we certainly couldn't do had we not existed. In fact, Augustine goes on to argue, if you think about it closely you'll discover that those bad elements of existence aren't a part of existence at all, but in fact the negation of it. Unjust excessive war, for example, is the attempt to annihilate existence. Evil, as the opposite of good, he concludes then, must be, likewise, the opposite of existence. It is, in a sense, the absence, negation, or deprivation of existence (*Confessions* Book VII, Chapter 12).

So it is that Augustine argued that being is a fundamentally good thing. This assertion, that it is good to be and bad to not-be, is not exclusive to early thinkers like Plato and Augustine. In fact it is maintained, if not overtly then at least as an underlying assumption, by a number of more modern thinkers. Take for example Gottfried Leibniz (1646–1716), who made it a central tenet of his thinking that we live in what he called "the best of all possible worlds." According to Leibniz, God, given his goodness, not only *would not*, but indeed *could not* have created existence in such a way that it is fundamentally bad. What Leibniz assumes then, is that existence is essentially good, even if bad things may be allowed by it. The goodness of existence has been a core conviction within philosophy. Even those philosophers who've sought to remain neutral on the value of being, thinkers like Immanuel Kant (1724–1804), would never have argued that just because being may not have a positive value that it is therefore something negative in value (*Lectures on Metaphysics*). Instead they would want to hold being as something fundamentally valueless, a mere condition for the possibility of both the good and the bad. On its own for them being remains something neither laudatory nor offensive—neither particularly uplifting nor particularly burdensome, but instead a purely empowering force, certainly not something heavy nor difficult to bear.

But if Buffett is correct and there is some necessity to our escapism, some irrevocability to our drive to be released from being, then there must be something good about such a release from being. After all, we couldn't need, nor even desire for that matter, something which we didn't perceive as somehow good. And, if it is good to *escape* from our being, then both the assumption of the goodness of being and the modern assumption of the neutrality of being must be called into question. And this is precisely what Buffett's music seems to do. For, if Buffett's is right, then some of the underlying assumptions of western philosophy must be rethought in such a way that the release from being or escape would be figured as good and being itself would be redefined as something if not bad, then at least burdensome—that is, as something we could want to escape. And, this reversal of the traditional evaluation of being seems to have some teeth to it. After all, if being were inherently good, why would we long so desperately to escape it? Why would Buffett's music and escapist image attract us so much? And yet, it does entice us—calling into question our relationship to our own being.

Think for example of a song like "Margaritaville." The depth of the escape sought in such a song is revealed through a relatively simple, albeit seemingly tangential, question: where is Margaritaville? This is a question which Buffett has been hounded by since the beginning of his career. It is one which he has nevertheless almost always answered in more or less the same way: "Margaritaville is nowhere." Margaritaville is not a place; it's a state of mind. But of course we all already knew this, there is no literal Margaritaville. It's not on any map. You can't get Mapquest directions for Margaritaville, because it doesn't exist.

And not just Margaritaville in its singularity, Shangri-La as well, all such utopias—they don't exist, they're merely fantasies. We all know that there is no actual "particular harbor" that will finally release us completely from the burden of having to be ourselves, the burden of having to be our being. This is part of what growing up and becoming an adult is all about, realizing that Never-Never land isn't real, that no matter how close we can get to such a paradise, we can never-never fully arrive there, never-never get far enough away from ourselves to fully be released from the occupation of having to be ourselves. As the saying goes, "no matter where you go, there you are,"—no matter where you go, you carry with you all of your worries and anxieties, the burden of having to be yourself. And this is no easy weight to bear. This is precisely why we must content ourselves with the fantasies offered us by "One Particular Harbor" and "Margaritaville"—they're as close as we'll ever come to a complete release from our being. For whether we're sitting on a beach in the Bahamas or drinking beer from a cozy in the parking lot of a Buffett concert in Boston, we are always plagued by some niggling worry or frustration—we always remain irrevocably attached to ourselves and our being and the myriad concerns and burdens inherent to our existence.

But knowing this, knowing that we can never fully escape and that there is no literal or actual Margaritaville, doesn't abate the longing for escape nor does it satisfy our hope and fantasy that somewhere out there lies the possibility of such a utopia. If anything, it only fuels it more, makes the desire to escape more poignant and more necessary. This reality seems to point to the fact that what we are longing for when we long for Margaritaville is not some actual release *within* being, say an even better or more relaxing vacation from the monotony of our daily lives, for example, or a better way of being ourselves, but something much deeper; an even more radical release and escape, a vacation *from* being itself, a break from the burden of existence.

Some thinkers, most notably the Roman Stoic philosophers, have interpreted this longing to escape as some sort of testimony to the goodness of death, arguing that only in death are we ever fully released from the grip of our being. But there's something unsatisfying about this interpretation as well, for when we long for Margaritaville it's not death that we want. Death is a frightening prospect, something we by and large strive to avoid. What we want is something other than death—something beyond even being dead.

Death, it seems to us instinctively, is just another way of being. A horrible way of being, no doubt, one not necessarily preferable to the way of being which we have now, but a way of being nonetheless. So it is that death does not seem to answer the kind of longing we feel with Buffett. Even when death is figured as non-being, as the end of existence as such, it still presents a problem for us. For that desire in our escapist flights of fancy is not simply to cease to exist in entirety; it is, impossibly, to exist somehow without being bound by the constraints of having to be—to be otherwise than how we experience being to be, as strange as that sounds.

What we want from our escape and what Buffett gives us a vision of is a way of being without being, as it were. Clearly this is a mind-boggling idea and something that needs more development.

Existence, Just Another "Tampico Trauma"

What the vision of 'somewhere' like Margaritaville promises is not merely some temporary release from our everyday worries, but a final release from being as such, from having to be at all, all the while paradoxically promising that we will still somehow "be" around to enjoy this release. It presents a vision of an escape not just from our temporary frustrations and concerns but from the possibility of having to be frustrated and concerned at all—from existence as a whole.

In Margaritaville, as a nowhere land, we catch a glimpse of a place where we can be no one, where we can be without being, as it were, and where the unruly freedom of chaos reigns, a freedom so profound it severs us from the constraints of being itself. Located, to use Buffett's phrase, somewhere "southeast of disorder," Margaritaville seems situated beyond the order and structure of existence, on the hither side of the organization initiated and maintained by being.

This desire for release evoked and expressed in Buffett's brand of escapism, as the desire to be released from being as a whole, seems to fundamentally call into question the traditional assessment of being as the good, as something inherently worthwhile. What the desire for escape articulated so purely in Buffett's music presents is the fact that we very rarely experience our being as something good, but more often than not experience it as something burdensome, weighty and difficult to bear. Those few moments in which we do experience it as a kind of levity occur only when we've managed to somehow nihilate its power over us through food, drink or drug—all acts which attempt to somehow mitigate the weight of being. What we strive for in a vacation, and what is expressed in Buffett's brand of escapism, is something of this nihilation.

This is, by the way, why vacations are never as relaxing as we think they somehow should be and why we inevitably come back thinking that we need another vacation to recover from the one we just took. What we strive for in vacation, and what we dream about while listening to a song like "Tin Cup Chalice" is a release so complete and a rest so deep that we do not even feel ourselves to be on vacation; indeed that we do not feel ourselves *to be* at all. What we long for in a vacation is to be severed so completely from reality that we cease to be entirely, which is, of course, impossible. As I mentioned earlier, even death does not necessarily promise such a release—there may, after all, be an afterlife, a hereafter in which we will continue to be, only not as we are now.

No matter how far we run, how much we eat or drink at the midnight buffet or how comfortable our hammock by the sea is, we are still burdened by the discomfort of having to be ourselves. And so even in Key West we still dream of Margaritaville—even while on vacation, we long for a more complete escape, one which carries us further afield than our own being.

This is the startlingly relevant and unquestionably profound philosophical assumption hidden within Jimmy Buffett's music: that it is hard to be one's being. That existence is not something light and easy, that it is not something necessarily good; but is in fact something difficult and burdensome to bear. From this we see that Buffett's music is only superficially about the joy of vacations and the pleasure of escape. On a much deeper level Buffett's music reveals itself to be driven by a recognition of the weight of existence and the necessity to somehow escape it.

But how are we to make sense of this recognition philosophically? If indeed, the bulk of the history of philosophy is established on the assumption that being is something good given the way it empowers everything we value about life, who can we turn to make sense of the sincere desire to escape being expressed in Buffett's music?

Freiburger in Paradise

German philosopher Martin Heidegger (1889–1976) saw his fundamental philosophical task as re-initiating what he called "the question of the meaning of being," and, in doing so, to call into question the assumed value and meaning of being, that it is good, for example, and try to understand it in a new light. In this regard Heidegger's work serves as the perfect lens through which to examine the way in which Buffett's brand of escapism seemingly calls into question the traditionally held philosophical assumptions concerning its nature.

Since the time of Plato, Heidegger claimed, the meaning and value of being has largely been taken for granted. We all naturally assume, for example, that being is good (that it is good to be), or if not good in its own right, then at least something light and easy to bear, something somehow empowering. We would certainly not consider it to be something burdensome or weighty. These assumptions, Heidegger claimed, are so much a part of our natural orientation to the world and our everyday discourse that were we to stop for a moment and inquire into the meaning of being we would be laughed at. "We all know the meaning of the word being," the response would inevitably come, "it's obvious—something either is or it isn't, it's as simple as that." And yet, thought Heidegger, the more one endeavors to think about the questions, the more he or she begins to realize that the concept of being is not as clear as it is generally taken to be. Think about it for a moment yourself, what precisely do we mean when we ascribe being to something? Can you define the meaning of the word being without invoking it somehow? As soon as we begin to ask these questions we quickly realize with Heidegger that as much as we use the word, indeed our language would not function properly without it, we have nevertheless somehow lost its meaning. 'Being', it seems, has somehow become an empty term for us. It is for this reason that Heidegger proposed to raise anew the question of the meaning of being, which he did most forcefully in his 1927 masterpiece *Being and Time* (Harper and Row, 1962).

Exploring the Tidal Pools of Existence

In *Being and Time* Heidegger proposed a novel approach to the question of the meaning of being. Being, he recognized there, is something which never appears without a specific context. It's not something we can somehow isolate objectively. We cannot investigate it as we could some primal element, like oxygen, devoid of a context, say in its appearance in the compound H_2O, or water. Instead, Heidegger argued, being is such that it always appears within or alongside some specific thing which *is*. Therefore, Heidegger proposed, why not investigate being as it appears in one particular formulation, namely the human being. Why the human being? Because, thought Heidegger, human beings are a peculiar kind of being in that they are the only kind of being to call upon its meaning—that is, they are, the only kind of being for whom the question of the meaning of being is an issue (p. 27); tables, for example, aren't concerned about the nature of their being.

This approach of course makes so much sense that it is almost banal: if we cannot get to being on its own, why not examine it as it appears to those beings which seem to have the most access to it. It's just like the beginning of a murder investigation; you interview those who knew the victim best. If the meaning of being has been somehow murdered over the course of western thought such that it now appears to be a dead and empty concept, to get back to the meaning of that being we should start by interrogating those who have had a particularly close relationship to it, namely human beings. So it was that Heidegger proposed to get at the meaning of being by investigating how it is that human beings experience being in general, but especially their own being.

But this is not as easy a task as it may at first seem, because human beings function generally and for the most part unaware of their own being. Instead they walk around, as Heidegger put it, "transcendent" to their own being, not concerned with the nature of their being, but concerned with those things which it allows them access to or the things it empowers them to do. So it is that for the most part human existence is lived beyond its own being, as it were, less concerned with its own nature than with whatever project it is engaged in at the time: working, raising kids, paying the bills, and so on. Heidegger thus proposed to investigate the meaning of the being of human beings via those moments in which these projects fail, those moments in which the transcendence empowered by being collapse, forcing human beings back upon themselves—that is, forcing them to reckon with the meaning of their being—moments like birth, death, and anxiety.

When we are born, Heidegger argues, we do not choose to be, but are instead "thrown" (p. 174) into our being and forced to tarry with this brute "fact" throughout our existence. Moreover, this existence, which we did not choose and which was forced upon us at our birth, is moved, from its inception, towards death (p. 279), a death which announces simultaneously the culmination and destruction of all of the possibilities offered by existence and which we therefore dread. These two titanic events are what define the nature of human existence, Heidegger claims. As such they hold a meaning that other events within human life do not. Death is not the same as a garden party or a car wreck; it has a special and specific meaning over and beyond any other such event. As a defining part of human existence, the meaning of events like birth and death thus help to define the meaning of human being.

According to Heidegger, the fact that we do not choose to exist nor do we choose the trajectory of our existence signifies that existence is for the human being something which cannot be freely taken up or easily discarded. Instead it is something which is forced upon us. It is a responsibility which is thrust into our hands and which we cannot easily shirk. Given the fact that being manifests within human existence as this responsibility which is forced upon us and which moves irrevocably towards a death we do not freely choose, Heidegger concludes that the being it defines should not be conceived of as something light and easy to bear, nor as something inherently good nor simply neutral and inoffensive, but in fact should be recognized to appear in its concrete manifestation as something burdensome and difficult to bear, as a weight. Being, thinks Heidegger, demands something of us, it demands that we take responsibility for it; and this is no easy task. For, how can one assume and take responsibility for something that they did not initiate. The sheer thought of it boggles the mind. And, yet it is precisely such a Sisyphean task, he claims, that our being calls us to.

Sure, being also empowers us to free action. It is the condition for all the possibilities of our life, what Heidegger in his enigmatic style names the potentiality-for-being of human beings (p. 183). Heidegger doesn't miss this fact. Quite to the contrary, it is in recognition of this reality that Heidegger claims that being as a whole, especially as it appears in human beings, should be more closely identified with the possibilities it presents than with how it actually appears; or, in Heidegger's words, "higher than actuality stands possibility" (p. 63).

So being is the foundation for all our experiences, both our pains and our pleasures. But more fundamentally, as this potentiality, as that which propels us towards these possibilities, being seems to place a kind of demand upon—it calls us to be responsible for those possibilities. Our being seems to compel and drive us, urging us forward towards the completion of those possibilities and potentials. This is why, according to Heidegger, we often feel guilty when we have failed to achieve all that we know that we are capable of (p. 314). Even in its function as that which empowers us, then, and makes possible all that we do and experience, being manifests as a kind of responsibility and burden. It is for these reasons that, according to Heidegger, anxiety, the fretful concern over the possibilities opened up by being, appears to be one of the primary modes in which we catch sight of the meaning of our being. In anxiety, Heidegger argues, we glimpse the nature of being, the weight and responsibility that having to be our being places upon us (p. 229).

Given its weight and burden, Heidegger goes on to claim, more often than not we choose to flee ourselves and our own being and act "inauthentically" by attempting in some illusory way to alleviate the tension of our existence (p. 220). This recognition prompted Emmanuel Levinas (1906–1995), arguably the most important and famous of Heidegger's students, and an important philosopher in his own right, to claim in one of his early works entitled *On Escape* that one of the fundamental ways in which we relate to our being is through the desire to escape it. What Levinas concludes from this, with Heidegger, is that being cannot be viewed as something inherently good or even valueless, but must be understood primarily as a kind of crushing weight and responsibility—a burden not easily born. As Levinas so wonderfully puts it, "it is precisely from all that is weighty in being that escaping sets forth," (p. 54).

This, for him, explains the kind of desire to escape which we found so clearly articulated in the music of Buffett—a desire which Heidegger might identify as somehow "inauthentic," given that the goal of such a desire is to evade the weight and responsibility of having to be oneself, but a desire which nevertheless appears to be integral to the human experience. Bear in mind that by calling such a desire to escape "inauthentic" Heidegger is not condemning it. Inauthenticity is not, for him, an evaluative judgment. Indeed, he forthrightly sets himself against such evaluations. Instead he sought solely to describe the way in which existence appears without reference to such ideas as the "ought" or the "should." By calling the attempt to escape inauthentic, then, Heidegger's only goal is to describe what it is that is striven for in such a move—in this case, the aim is to escape oneself and be another as indeed the word inauthentic denotes in its root, a negation of the Latin word for self *auto*—translating literally as being-not-oneself. What we long for in Margaritaville is a way in which we can be other than we *have* to be—a way in which we can be without having to be ourselves. In other words, what we long for in our escapism is a way of being freed from the burden and responsibilities of having *to be* ourselves—a way of being without the weight of being.

Jimmy Buffett: "Singer of Inordinate Tunes" and Heideggerian Troubadour

We see from this investigation that Buffett's music is more than merely a diversion. It is more than a banal assertion that sometimes it's good to get away. In his call to escape Jimmy Buffett seems to recognize a fundamental truth about the nature of being, a truth illuminated in the philosophy of Martin Heidegger and Emmanuel Levinas. Namely, he seems to realize that though our existence may indeed empower us to certain possibilities, this empowering is not something light and easy to bear. It's more than a mere condition for the possibilities of human life. Instead, it is a heavy burden and responsibility—one which presses down upon us at all times and drives us towards escape. So it is that we finally come to recognize the profoundly philosophic truth of Buffett's words that, "we don't just enjoy our escapism—we NEED it." We need to be released from the grip of being. As such, only such an escape, and not being itself, can be properly called the good. This is not to say that being is therefore something bad; but it is certainly not something merely neutral or inoffensive either. It is instead, as Heidegger shows, something which presses down upon us with a weight and responsibility—a weight and responsibility that we will inevitably long to evade quite possibly with the help of Jimmy Buffett and a good strong boat drink.

4

Licensed to Chill

PHIL OLIVER

I fully believe in the legitimacy of taking moral holidays
—WILLIAM JAMES

Well, it's only up to you, no one else can tell you to go out and have some fun . . . And take a Holiday. You need a Holiday.
—JAMES WILLIAM BUFFET

There are people who think they are, for whatever reason, *special*. When philosophers succumb to this conceit, they very often think they are special precisely because they *specialize* in some rare and—so far as the general populace is concerned—exotic, undusted corner of theoretic possibility. They presume to grasp something technical most of the rest of us cannot, and that very exclusiveness—they suppose—elevates and enables them as knowers of life's hidden secrets.

Open Court's *Popular Culture and Philosophy* series of books clearly does not subscribe to any such pretense, nor—*emphatically*—does James William *Jimmy* Buffett. In this Buffett shares more than nominal resemblance to the great American pragmatist William James (1842–1910). "The philosophy which is so important in each of us," he insisted before a 1906 audience of mostly non-academics, "is not a technical matter; it is our more or less dumb sense of what life honestly and deeply means." What's more, noted the professor, "it is only partly got from books; it is our individual way of just seeing and feeling the total push and pressure of the cosmos" (*Pragmatism* (Dover, 1995), p. 1).

Unsympathetic observers of the Jimmy Buffett world's peculiar brand of enthusiasm might be tempted to make hostile and obtuse mischief with James's 'dumb' remark, but they would be missing an elemental point: our moments of greatest elevation and insight defy verbal expression. They are had and enjoyed, and mostly *not* spoken, though they are sometimes sung. But these are songs whose deepest melodies must be hummed. They are "not a technical matter," but neither are they easy to put into words.

This is not to deride either James or Buffett as verbal simpletons. Those contemptuous critics, besides missing the point about deep non-verbal experience, would also be missing the bookish verbal facility of both Professor James and Crooner Jimmy. But knowing how to deploy words well, for both of them, is but half the story of their creativity. Both draw judiciously from well-springs of joy that need and know no words, though words may sometimes serve as helpful signposts to something we're called to discover in our own experience. In *The Thought and Character of William James* (Little, Brown, 1935), R.B. Perry notes that "There are occasional moments when experience is most fully tasted in the exhilaration of a fresh morning, in moments of suffering, or in times of triumphant effort, when the tang is strong, when every nuance or overtone is present. James would arrest us at such moments, and say, 'There, that is it. Reality is like that" (p. 371). And Buffett's songs can arrest us in similar ways.

Not only are James and Buffett open to non-verbal expression, but their enthusiastic receptivity to the delightful dimensions of life leads them both to embrace "moral holidays," occasions when we're most attuned to the bliss that carefree moments can deliver. Contrary to a popular misconception, however, care*free* moments are not care*less*. A moral holiday is not a holiday from moral responsibility and humane concern. More on this in just a bit.

"Growing Older But Not Up"

Specialized knowledge has of course been crucial to the progress of our species—we wouldn't have landed on the moon, or built a reliable bridge, or cured any illness, or mapped the genome without it. But we also need a broad acquaintance with topics of wider currency. We need to know how to have fun, how to be happy, how to live peaceably with billions of our fellow humans, and how to teach some of those lessons to our children. Such wisdom may often elude us, but it is not inherently elusive. It's of the first order of importance to us all to conquer the conditions of our own happiness, and it may be the single most important condition of our civilization's survival that our successors retain that ability.

If Buffett is a philosopher—and of course he is—he (like William James) is of the genus that aspires to speak to and for the many, not just a specialized few. Henry David Thoreau belongs to the same tribe. He said long ago that whatever splendor of purpose may accrue to the vocation of *professing* is due to the anterior luster of *living*: "it is admirable to profess because once it was admirable to live." Explaining himself to his flinty and practical-minded Yankee peers, Thoreau said he "went to the woods because I wished to live deliberately . . . not, when I came to die, discover that I had not lived" (*Walden,* Beacon Press, 1997, p. 85). In the same vein, I submit, Mr. Buffett pronounces in "Growing Older but Not Up" that he "would rather die while I'm living than live while I'm dead."

Living, as intended here, is a festive and a communal achievement not the preserve of secluded scholars or guardians of arcana. Thoreau was no Parrothead, and it's plenty amusing to picture him joining the chorus of "Why Don't We Get Drunk (and Screw)?" But the impulse to "suck the marrow out of life" is not at all hard for a Parrothead to appreciate—who in a complementary spirit may also relish sucking the zesty juice out of a lemon. And though the popular image of the Yankee hermit holed up in, or walking near, his hut speaks most distinctly not of community but of solitude, the testament of his solitary communion in *Walden* is an invitation to us all to find our quiet source and center and then to share and celebrate the news of what we find there. It's simply the next step to take our celebration to the beach, and to shatter the quietude with a chorus.

This is fundamentally the same demand for "life, more life" that William James identified as the driving engine of religion. By all accounts, James was (or more accurately, made himself) a more playful and convivial person than Thoreau. He overcame a life-threatening existential crisis of the spirit in his twenties. "I just about touched bottom today," he confided to his journal in the spring of 1870, before going on to proclaim a new-found confidence in his willful capacity to get on with living in a constructive and productive spirit. But subsequent journal entries and published reflections throughout the balance of his life documented an ongo-

ing and not always successful quest to subdue feelings that threatened to spoil his hard-won equanimity.

The Buffett worldview speaks as well to that gnawing, desperate feeling of existential angst that sometimes assaults those who
reflect on the inevitability of cosmic collapse and universal annihi-
lation, in however many billions or trillions or quadrillions of
earthly turns around the sun. Woody Allen's childhood alter-ego
Alvy Singer, in the film "Annie Hall," is so afflicted. His mother con-
sults "Dr. Flicker," whose wise counsel comes straight from
Margaritaville: we've got to try to enjoy ourselves while we're here.
Philosopher Bertrand Russell concurred: "Although it is of course a
gloomy view to suppose that life will die out—at least I suppose
we may say so, although sometimes when I contemplate the things
that people do with their lives I think it is almost a consolation—it
is not such as to render life miserable. It merely makes you turn
your attention to other things."

Russell goes too far, in denying that anyone ever loses sleep
over losing existence. But the sanity-saving turn of attention to
other things, the decision to enjoy and celebrate our passing
moments: this is not mindless hedonism. It *is* a form of humanism.
("Buffett-ism is a Humanism," Jean-Paul Sartre might have written.)
Richard Dawkins, too, the eminent evolutionist and ardent atheist,
humanely ponders: "Isn't it sad to go to your grave without ever
wondering why you were born? Who, with such a thought, would
not spring from bed, eager to resume discovering the world and
rejoicing to be a part of it?" (*Unweaving the Rainbow*, Mariner
Books, 2000, p. 6) Parrotheads are widely recognized for rejoicing,
perhaps less so for *discovering*; but the "conquest of happiness," in
Russell's happy phrase, is no small discovery.

There is a cosmic—or perhaps just a comic—tension between
the high-minded Victorian seriousness we associate with the nineteenth-century world of William James, and the attitude he himself
endorsed in the famous 1897 essay *The Will to Believe*: that there's
nothing so very serious, after all, about our conceptual gaffes if
we're prepared in good faith to learn from them. "Our errors are
surely not such awfully solemn things. In a world where we are so
certain to incur them in spite of all our caution, a certain lightness
of heart seems healthier than this excessive nervousness on their
behalf." Exactly so. Meta-physician, heal thyself.

It is at any rate a clear mark of our time that very many of us
habitually take seriously all sorts of things arguably not worth our

attention, things arguably not even capable of educating us at all in any significant way—among which might be listed our collective mania for sports and games. (But I would argue not, so long as they're *my* sports and games that we consider.) That is a subject for another day, perhaps a day falling between Super Bowl Sunday in January and the day a few short weeks later when pitchers and catchers report for Spring Training: delightful days both, for some, and unofficial holidays. (See and hear *Jimmy Buffett: Live at Wrigley Field*—a concert recorded on a fine Labor Day while the shock and trauma of 9/11/01 still resonated sharply and painfully for Americans—to explore the convergence of our games, our music, and our moral sensibilities for those who share the Buffett state of mind.)

"Always Take the Weather with You"

What can we learn from the huge corporate success of Buffett-mania? It's been reported that Buffett's far-flung branded enterprises including restaurants, beer, clothing, household items such as blenders (naturally), footware, novels, and (by the way) music—generate over forty million dollars in revenue annually. His namesake Warren might be envious of such a successful portfolio, and philosophers writing about it all are well beyond envy. Obviously, Buffett's a savvy businessman. But the more telling lesson is that he strikes a chord among millions, not only those in his peer demographic of aging boomers but among everyone who feels lightened and restored by the "license to chill" that is his brand's happy dispensation. They respect and enjoy his artistry, but more than that they revel in his attitude and wish to borrow it. "There is something extra-musical about the whole thing," commented one observer who then went on to speculate about what he saw as the near-universal fantasy of running away to a tropical paradise, drinking margaritas, chucking so-called civilization and leaving it behind for good ("Parrotheads Rule," *Nashville Tennessean*, December 30th, 2008).

Well, maybe. But an even more universal aspiration is to bring the spirit of paradise into our days and lives without sacrificing the treasures we already hold. You don't have to leave town to enjoy a moral holiday. You don't even have to leave the office. This is one clear message to take away from a song like "Trouble on the Horizon," with its wise admonition to "always take the weather with you" wherever you go, even or *especially* when we find ourselves beset by "roadside bombers and tsunamis'" and floods and famine. We need our fun, never more than in a hostile environment.

Scholars of the Spanish-American philosopher George Santayana may recall that he once said a similar thing. Santayana's great problem, according to Henry Samuel Levinson,was "how to display suffering's meanness and then transcend it by celebrating passing joys and victories in the world" (*Santayana, Pragmatism, and the Spiritual Life*, University of North Carolina Press, 1992, p. 12). Moral holidays are precisely those times when passing joys and victories present themselves for celebration, whether quiet and restrained or loud and boisterous—as in the company of Parrotheads, for instance. Such vacation-like states of mind may last for days and weeks at a time, but more typically extend only for hours, minutes, or even moments. But they can be repeated, and cultivated, and made habitual. They can become constructively, *positively* addictive.

"I fully believe in the legitimacy of taking moral holidays," James wrote in *Pragmatism*, meaning those marvelous respites from care and concern and struggle, typically coincident with the aggressively pursued leisure we call "vacation" (and the English call "holiday"). A moral holiday, then, is a vacating, an emptying, a withdrawal from the daily grind and the daily hand-wringing, when we tell ourselves that it is truly morally acceptable just to relax, not only our bodies but especially our consciences, with regard to the world's (and our own) panoply of worrisome and regrettable facts; to accept ourselves and the world for awhile, despite our flaws and its corruptions and depredations; and so, to renew ourselves for the return to the fray.

"Moral" may seem misapplied in the description of a deliberate period of neglect toward issues of the greatest moral gravity, but James denies any contradiction here. Our world is the scene of every kind of event, from joyous and ennobling to perverse and profane. In such a world, moral holidays are not merely tonic; they are probably essential to our sanity and, viewed in evolutionary terms, to our survival.

Most of us find at least a week or two out of the year for this kind of renewal, but we allow ourselves to believe that time for renewal year-round is unthinkable. Apparently, we prefer to collapse into our vacations than to take them more nearly as needed, tonically and often. James contrasted our busy-ness with the artful approach to life practiced elsewhere, inviting us to consider "the shopkeeper in Germany, who for five or six months of the year spends a good part of every Sunday in the open air, sitting with his family for hours under green trees over coffee or beer and Pumpernickel, and who breaks into Achs and Wunderschons all the week as he recalls it." His "contentment in the fine weather, and the leaves, and the air, and himself as a part of it all" is a springboard of renewal that propels him cheerfully back to work, back, as we say, to "reality." But he knows that his recreation is at least as real as his work (which would suffer as surely as he would without his springboard). Perhaps the shopkeeper knows something we do not, or have forgotten.

The Jewish-Texan musician-cum-gubernatorial candidate Kinky Friedman, in a review of Buffett's *A Salty Piece of Land* (*New York Times Book Review*, November 28th, 2004), detected in Buffett a strong affinity with the adventurous spirit of the sea-going tales of Robert Louis Stevenson. William James was also a Stevenson fan, echoing the sentiment that "To miss the joy is to miss all." Most of us are good at catching those forms of joy that are surrounded by ritual and the stamp of our culture's habitual approval; but so many of life's potential golden moments are small, unmarked, and uncelebrated. Buffett and James are collectors and celebrators of golden moments.

"That Frozen Concoction"

Some might be inclined to hear in Buffett's tunes a tone of stoic consolation or old-school Epicurean detachment, settling for whatever small and secure satisfactions we can manage and repeat (cheeseburgers, blended beverages, pleasurable parties, the occasional water-borne escapade) but not ever expecting to soar. This would place his mark just a notch above resignation but well short of joyous affirmation. But that's wrong.

Buffett does offer consolation, but not in the form of any mere consolation prize. He's not just *settling*, he's sailing and seeking, changing attitude with latitude. He's glad he doesn't live in a trailer, but it's clear he's after more than just a shabby roof over his head— especially one subject to one of those ruinous Florida gales that sweeps everything away. Again, his is the voice of a risk-running celebrant and hunter of gold: We may not know where we'll be when the volcano blows, or the ship starts to sink, or the economy tanks; but we sure won't be fretting and cowering in a corner. While we live and breathe we'll settle for nothing less than our full entitlement, our happiness.

One of the bigger risks Buffett explores is the Russian roulette of alcoholic consumption, particularly of those fabled frozen concoctions. Do they help a Buffett-styled hero hang on, or do they keep him hanging just beyond the point of return to solid and stable ground? William James also meditated on the mystical and medical properties of alcohol and other perception-altering ingestibles. This famous passage from *The Varieties of Religious Experience* captures a plaintive mood of honest ambivalence that may also be heard in Buffett's music:

> the sway of alcohol over mankind is unquestionably due to its power to stimulate the mystical faculties of human nature, usually crushed to earth by the cold facts and dry criticisms of the sober hour. Sobriety diminishes, discriminates, and says no; drunkenness expands, unites, and says yes. It is in fact the great exciter of the Yes function. . . . Not through mere perversity do men run after it.

And "it is part of the deeper mystery and tragedy of life that whiffs and gleams of something that we immediately recognize as excellent should be vouchsafed to so many of us only in the fleeting earlier phases of what in its totality is so degrading a poisoning" (p. 307).

The catalytic poison in this instance is alcohol, but James's gleaming, fleeting "excellences" may arrive through many and various portals of experience. What is the strange, wonderful, darting mysterium we recognize but cannot hold? No very precise answer is possible for James, of course, or there would be more than a "whiff" to inspire us. Evidently, though, he intends not intoxication, as such, but whatever it is about this state that leads one to affirm and embrace the world even while recognizing its deficiencies.

The pedigree of such exalted states, and their sustainability amidst all the other obligations and relations of a healthily-social life, are suspect; but like James, Buffett is willing to admit the intrinsic good of the states themselves, the way they "unite and say '*yes!*'" to life and connection and hope. Set apart from their wider implications and effects, they promise "more life." But alas, they can only be set apart in imagination. The real lives we must lead require us to sober up and get serious.

Alcohol, then, and other psycho-active substances that interfere with our capacity not merely to establish social connections but to

---

[1] Authors, respectively, of *Flow, Authentic Happiness, Stumbling on Happiness, The Happiness Hypothesis, The Science of Pleasure,* and *The Happiness Myth.*

maintain them steadily and responsibly, are not the most reliable catalysts of our moral holidays. For some, they are just too dangerous to play with. There may be Parrotheads of whom that is true. One hopes they will all find alternative pleasures to set in motion the holiday state of mind.

Fortunately this is a topic that has lately come in for much, and much overdue, attention. The literature of happiness in the modern world has found its scribes in Mihaly Cskikszenmihalyi, Martin Seligman, Daniel Gilbert, Jonathan Haidt, Paul Martin, and Jennifer Michael Hecht, to mention only a few.[1]

"People are shouting too many philosophies of health and happiness at us" (p. 321), observes Hecht. She doesn't shout, but urges us to get intimately in touch with our own personal needs and dispositions and live by our lights, into the light. Martin offers a similar prescription, noting the different strokes that free different folks to slip the noose of daily toil and stress. Among some of his own favored humble pleasures: walking, gardening, cooking, fishing, napping, sitting in silence, having lunch. Nothing Dionysian or debauched, it is reminiscent, in fact, of the deceptively banal wisdom dispensed by the sagacious *Monty Python* troupe in *The Meaning of Life*: try and be nice to people, avoid eating fat, read a good book every *now* and then, get some walking in, and try and live together in peace and harmony with people of all creeds and nations.

Walkers, apparently, shall inherit the earth: "Give me the blue sky over my head, and the green turf beneath my feet, a winding road before me, and a three hours' march to dinner—and then to thinking!" wrote English essayist William Hazlitt in 1822 ("On Going on a Journey," in Aaron Sussman and Ruth Goode, *The Magic of Walking*, Simon and Schuster, 1967, p. 227). This sentiment will need to be re-calibrated, since some of us (part of the time) and all of us (some of the time) find *not* thinking the greater pleasure. But the point here is that most Buffett fans are much more content with innocent pedestrian pleasures, figuratively or literally understood, than is widely admitted. And they're more thoughtful. *And*—this brings us to the most egregious misunderstanding surrounding the whole "moral holiday" idea—they're good people.

"Trip Around the Sun"

It's a cultural habit, and a common one, to equate moral holidays with amorality (at best). The carefree, pleasure-seeking, happiness-indulging mood is casually conflated with the *careless* indifference of those who are indifferent to the well-being of their fellow humans. But this is itself a careless mistake. Nature may be indifferent to human concerns. But we all know enough caring humans to recognize that *human* nature cares.

Friedrich Nietzsche said in *Birth of Tragedy* that if we listen too intently to the world's "innumerable shouts of pleasure and woe," we will be overwhelmed. The daily newspaper, "pumping its inky current of despair" (James Wood, "Holiday in Hellmouth," *New Yorker*, June 9th, 2008) and now its cleaner digitized stream of sadness via the Internet, constantly and vividly reinforces the perception of a world spinning chaotically out of control. It also records the shouts of pleasure, of course; but they may become harder to hear, or harder to credit, in a time of war and economic collapse.

The temptation to detach oneself from the Information grid and the news cycle altogether, to go "on holiday" from bad news and negative feeling, and so to recover at least an illusion of personal security and a prospect of happiness, is strong. It's surely one of the great perennial motive forces behind the religious impulse, as mirrored in the familiar scripture: "His eye is on the sparrow, and I know He watches me."

But this attitude and the impulse driving it find expression not only in the voices of those possessed of a conventionally-religious sensibility. As noted above, in the second of a series of acclaimed 1906 public lectures that would become *Pragmatism*, James turned to the question of moral holidays and suggested that they *are* for everyone—no less than philosophy itself. Josiah Royce and F.H. Bradley, James's favorite contemporary metaphysical antagonists, had championed our right as humans "to take a moral holiday, to let the world wag in its own way, feeling that its issues are in better hands than ours and are none of our business." Royce and Bradley thought it a signal merit of their Idealism that it conveyed and philosophically rationalized such a right, and a disturbing deficiency of James's "radical empiricism" that it did not. James's answer to this charge betrays an air of disdain for any merely theoretical imperative: "I just take my holidays," metaphysical necessity or its absence notwithstanding.

A world whose total structure and determination was foreordained would be one in which, on the Idealist view, "the individual members may relax their anxieties occasionally, in which the don't-care mood is also right for men, and moral holidays [are] in order" (Pragmatism, p. 29). A pluralistic, open, unsettled universe such as James describes, on the other hand, seems to demand our unflagging vigilance and seriousness, on pain of permanent setback. We won't feel free to relax and release our care, the Idealists implied, if it is a controlling condition of progress in our world. So long as we hold the lever of incident and accident, we must stand fast and steady. James often recurs to nautical imagery to communicate this sense of "shipwreck" as one of life's looming, ineliminable features. Relaxing our steerage may run us aground.

Jimmy Buffett has also given vivid expression to a naturalized form of the "moral holidays" idea. This "son of a son of a sailor" is also drawn to the sea, whether in quest of earthly paradise or in lament of missed or misnavigated life-passages. For legions of Buffett's fans, something like the "moral holiday" idea (though usually inchoate, and not identified by name) supports an expansive and inclusive worldview—a "license to chill" for which, as the eponymous song makes explicit, "we're all qualified."

The song urges us to "let the rat race run" while we "roll around in the sun." In the fade-out of this tune we hear a fleeting acknowledgment that such dogged commitment to one's own hedonic gratification might strike some not merely as self-indulgent but even "mentally ill" and morally abject. Finally, a terminal invocation of "Dr. Phil" suggests that self-seeking retirees from the rat race may place themselves crazily out of touch. And the singer's plea to "leave me alone" will sound irresponsible to those who consider it a human obligation to run life's race whether we enjoy it or not.

In "Trip Around The Sun," the singer-philosopher's commitment to enjoying the race and relinquishing responsibility is re-affirmed:

> I'm just hanging on while this old world keeps spinning
> And it's good to know it's out of my control . . .
> . . . Yes, I'll make a resolution
> Then I'll never make another one.

William James defends moral holidays, as he defends ideas generally, in terms of their usefulness or "profitablility" to our lives. But he also insists on the resounding importance of returning from our holidays and re-entering the race. His presumption is that "letting go" is intermittently useful and even delightful, but not permanently advisable. He did not enjoy contemplating the thought that "it wouldn't change a thing." That very thought was, in fact, a source of profoundest distress to the young William James who, if we are to trust the intimate confidences of his diary, rescued himself from suicidal indecision and despair only by persuading himself that exertions of will (and the willful redirection of one's attentive engagement with life) changes everything.

The concept of a moral holiday is widely misconceived, and not only among undergraduate philosophy students weighing (say) the seductive temptations of Platonic invisibility per the "Ring of Gyges," or Nietzschean non-accountability ("beyond good and evil"). *Time* magazine once casually regarded "the moral holiday, when the rules are suspended and one is transformed into anything one wants"— think Mardi Gras or Club Med (www.time.com/magazine/article/0,). One benighted blogger, perhaps a *Time* subscriber, misidentifies "what William James called a moral holiday, the occasional moment when the rules of decency do not apply" (www.cultureby.com/trilogy/2007/01/). Another insinuates lax conduct involving "a moral holiday in Mexico with an American woman" (http://islandgrove-press.blogspot.com./2007/10/moral-holiday-in-mexico-with-american.html). Still another wonders: "Is it ever justified to take a moral holiday . . . to allow yourself to be immoral" (http://pjw-truth .blogspot.com/2007/03/ moral-holiday.html)?

But James's holidays were never an excuse for indulging fantasies of indecency or amorality—a claim possibly not *always* applicable to *Jimmy*—but always a plea for sane self-preservation in a daunting world. "A breathing space in the purposefulness of the earnest," as one newspaper account of James's time put it, lets us relax and re-generate, and then return to the fray.

If a moral holiday is taken to imply that we can ever entirely abjure our responsibility to acknowledge the reasonable claims and to respect the reciprocal humanity of others—let alone act in blatant violation of their status as our social equals—then none of us is entitled to one. But that clearly was not William James's meaning, nor is it quite implied by Jimmy Buffett's characteristic invitation to "chill."

But yoking a high-minded New England Age of Victoria philosopher with a free-spirited beach bum remains a challenge. With the foregoing discussion of James's nuanced disdain for the disease of alcoholism (which consumed his brother), perhaps we can temper Buffett's anthemic fondness for "booze in the blender" in Margaritaville and begin to hear it more as a paen to the "laid back" state of mind than as a literal hymn to drunkenness. Or we can hear it as a call to drink at a larger and more life-affirming, happiness-affording well. And then to get back to work.

Parrotology

5
Balance on the Water

AMANDA E. FELLER

As a pilot I know that if you are flying from point A to point B and a big storm blocks your way, you don't just barrel on through. You either land or do a one-eighty and go back to point A.

—*A Pirate Looks at Fifty*

A gap exists between Buffett the mirage and Buffett the life manager. An observer of the mirage sees Parrotheads, parties, and the "phlock." Phlocking is about migration to Key West as well as the creation of the Oasis in the desert. It's collectively creating and visiting a place that Buffett refers to on a live album as existing "at the bottom of a Cuervo bottle and the back of your mind." The official *Margaritaville* website defines the location as: "in the tropics somewhere between the Port of Indecision and Southwest of Disorder." The phlock seeks escapism and, on the surface, the Buffett musical experience seems to oblige.

In contrast, an observer of Buffett the life manager sees more than the archetypal beach bum. The "when life hands you limes, make margaritas" recipe of Jimmy Buffett's life has been a mix of success, hard work, complexity, faltering steps, life crises, and near misses. A close examination of Buffett's way of understanding, responding to, and engaging challenge illustrates the transformative process. As told in Buffett's songs, books, and interviews, this process is artful and complex. The process begins with disorientation, a familiar concept in Buffett's work and life.

For the novice, transformative experience is profound, often dramatic, involves hard work, and follows a four-fold process. For the more experienced, transformative process intuitively becomes a way of managing life; disorienting experiences are less dramatic and more easily addressed. Through repeated use of this process, Buffett has managed a balanced and flexible approach to life and its disorienting challenges. In this manner Buffett serves as a philosopher and guide to transformative process.

Beyond the phlocks, Jimmy Buffett has achieved success as a singer-song-writer, novelist, restaurateur, pilot, ecological advocate, and all-around explorer. Buffett directly attributes his legacy to his good luck that "a summer job . . . has lasted quite a long time" ("10 Questions," *Time Magazine,* July 16th, 2007). In an interview with *Page One*, a literary news website, Buffett explains that he leveraged this "luck" "to maintain that summer job as long as I can . . . it's exciting to be able to have the opportunity to do things I always dreamed of as a kid." Beneath the playful surface of Buffett's demeanor is a strong current. In October 2004, CBS's *Sixty Minutes* interviewer Steve Kroft observed, "the life [the fans] think you're living, doesn't seem at all like the life I see you leading . . . you're a workaholic."

This fits for a "pirate, two-hundred years too late"—a modern Mark Twain in a hyper-mediated WIFIed world, experiencing the world as an adventurer seeking new worlds, exotic ideas, and strange civilizations alike. Equally accepted are risk, danger, and uncertainty. It's a way of thinking from a time when travel was not tourism. As the great American intellectual Daniel Boorstin noted in *The Image, or What Happened to the American Dream* (Kingsport, 1961), "many Americans now 'travel', yet few are travelers . . . the experience has become diluted, contrived, prefabricated" (p. 79). Within the transformative perspective, the goal is not to find or escape to, in Boorstin's words, a "convenient, comfortable, risk-free, trouble-free" experience. Rather, encountering the inconvenient and the uncomfortable means to encounter something new about the self, most notably how one creates meaning.

As a storyteller, Buffett's lyrics and manner consistently embrace the highs and lows of mortal living. Buffett's "Caribbean drunken rock-'n'-roll" style goes well beyond the common narrative. A casual listener might think of the ever-popular "Margaritaville" as a song to induce escapism. Yet, just past the lost shaker of salt and mysterious tattoo, is contemplation and reconciliation. Buffett's collected works explain the transformative journey in ballad form.

Transformative Process: Changes in Attitudes

In transformative process the disorienting dilemma is the starting point for deep personal growth. The sudden circumstances which call into question one's way of thinking and being in the world are of greatest potential for personal growth. Such circumstances produce a feeling of disorientation where the compass seems to no longer function. Those who embrace a journey when faced with disorientation find recalibration and reorientation.

When the way is lost and personal truth disturbed—seemingly happily married friends get divorced; an adult child comes out of the closet; a member of a culturally protected family marries across an ethnic divide; a loved-one dies suddenly; a close neighbor or friend is revealed to be something other than expected; a seemingly secure career falls apart—the moment, however difficult, is an opportunity to reshape one's understanding of the world. Alternatively, the moment can pass, and deep attachment to an old belief continues. Old views are forced ill-fittingly into this new world and the moment is marked by denial and recalcitrance. Finding one's way again is not immediate or easy; time and space for reflection are necessary as is dedication to the journey. This isn't as simple as seeing a glass half full or finding a silver lining, attitudes more fitting to lesser challenges.

Buffett's life and music are built on navigational themes related to sailing and flying. Orientation and the loss of direction are dominant in his music and stories. Taking time to reflect and recalibrate the compass are also dominant themes. "Changes in Latitudes, Changes in Attitudes" is the most clear example, elegantly summarizing transformative process in six words. "Trying to Reason with the Hurricane Season" is another example. As a pilot and sailor Buffett naturally relies on the hurricane as metaphor, the ultimate disorientating circumstance.

The Adventurer: A Pirate's Life

When Jack Mezirow (*Learning as Transformation*, Jossey-Bass, 2000) the father of transformative learning theory, first witnessed disorientation as something produced by learning, he considered what he was seeing as something more meaningful than simple frustration. At the time, Mezirow was working with a group of women returning to college later in life. Through careful observation, conversation, and study, Mezirow found that the disorientation alone was not so unique; after all, much in life can leave us feeling out of step with those around us. He looked more closely at why the disorientation occurred, how it was treated, and if any meaningful change accompanied re-orientation. He saw uniqueness, not in the disorientation alone, but in the means used to make sense of the experience. He also found the destination point of the transformative journey surprising as did those who journeyed there. The learning taking place was much deeper and more meaningful than the classroom topics the women were studying.

Transformative learning theory is a specific understanding of what happens when disorientation is explored in particular ways and where such an exploration takes a person. If navigated carefully, an individual moves from feeling powerless to feeling empowered. Moreover, the process is not only about creating new understandings but also about a fundamental shift in *the way understanding is created*. In essence, transformative learning is an intense, specific exploration that yields new ways of making sense of and consequently navigating the world.

Transformative work is not therapy for clinical diagnoses. Nor is transformative work about generic change, such as dealing with moving to a new city or starting a new job. It is not about dramatic upheaval. Transformative work is a highly particular process and one that requires paying attention, dedication to process, being open to self-reflection, and a willingness to surrender "rightness."

Those who meet these conditions over time become more skilled at the process. The transformative process can become a habitual one—a way of thinking about and managing life. Higher awareness of the conditions which create disorientation yields overall more balance. Someone new to the process might appear as if in sudden free-fall. Whereas someone more experienced can appear more "together" when disorientation strikes, naturally following the exploratory process transformative process demands. Buffet's narrative provides guidance and insight into just such expertise.

Buffett's expertise as an adventurer mirrors his expertise at transformative living. In interviews and autobiographical works Buffett repeatedly defines his life's story in terms of voyage and exploration. Ports of call are selected for their easy access to the next. His preferred means of transportation allow for impulsive departure, encounters with salty characters, and adventures off the pages of Hemingway or Twain. For this reason self-piloted sailing and flying are desired over the more efficient means of commercial travel. Appropriately, a favored form of transport is that which combines sea and air—the flying boat. Throughout his writings, Buffett expresses a kindred spirit with early maritime adventurers as well as with his grandfather, a sea captain.

Exploration is a defining quality of Buffett's life. For the explorer, a willing heart and navigational mind are essential traits. The wanderlust heart knows that travel to destinations unknown means encountering the unexpected and participating in the story. However, one must not mistake haplessness for exploration and vice versa. Adventurers classically find their way by stars, charts, and properly calibrated tools. Being lost and unable to return to home port (or to any port) is undesirable, however romantic it might seem. Moving into uncharted waters or flying into unknown conditions is rarely a smart move. Together the willing heart and a navigational mind make for adventure.

In *A Pirate Looks at Fifty* (Random House, 1998) Buffett writes, "I have dodged many storms and bounced across the bottom on occasion, but so far Lady Luck and the stars by which I steer have kept me off the rocks" (p. 8). This generally positive assessment minimizes the storms of Buffett's life. What it does not minimize are the means by which he has maintained momentum. We all know people who never really survive unexpected upheaval and remain lost. Buffett's demeanor, like the surface of his lyrics, is casual and carefree. But a happenstance life, one without a deeper method, would make as much sense in Buffett's life as a rudderless boat. His life has been artfully, however intuitively managed. As an accomplished explorer, he embodies equally a willing heart and a navigational mind.

Set Adrift: The Disorienting Dilemma

Watch out for that gravity storm, It don't give no warning signs.

—*Gravity Storm*

Now on the day that John Wayne died I found myself on the continental divide. Tell me where do we go from here?

—*Incommunicado*

People are creatures of habit, moving to a certain rhythm. A sudden and unexpected change of rhythm often produces a feeling of suspended animation governed by mild shock or stunned silence. This event is a disorienting dilemma, an experience that creates awareness of flawed thinking. The assumptions governing how one sees the world, makes decisions, creates judgments, and approaches new experiences are, maybe quite possibly, substantially flawed. In this moment an individual is unexpectedly released from life's moorings. Before supplies such as instruments and sails can be inventoried, thoughts and feelings are stuck in a loop of being adrift.

The disorienting dilemma can be connected to something larger in culture or to something seemingly minor. It can be something as large as coming in contact with the devastating consequences of war, poverty, or climate change. It can be connected to some personal aspect with family, health, work, education. Regardless, as Mezirow observed, the dilemma penetrates core assumptions. The dilemma begins innocently as a competition between compelling new ideas and old ideas that have given shape to the world. The dilemma strikes more deeply because the individual is not only confronted with new ideas, but with the origin of those ideas. The new knowledge is difficult to accept because it challenges (1) old knowledge, (2) the people and institutions that did the teaching, and (3) the means of knowledge creation.

The human mind, psyche, and spirit cannot manage the threefold inquiry with ease. A cascade effect typically occurs where the deeply entrenched assumptions that govern one's life are collapsing. This is not to say that all of one's assumptions are invalid. However, the pseudo-logic at work is that if one part of the governance is flawed, then it all could be flawed. This is what creates stunned inaction in the transformative process. To be clear, this is not about physical and psychological trauma. These are categories of injury that require specialized treatment. Transformative process involves individuals who are living relatively normal lives and who experience a challenge to what generates "normalcy."

In Buffett's narrative, the lure of "Margaritaville" serves as an example. Indeed, urban legend would be incomplete without the story of the slightly weary individual inspired by song. The unfulfilled individual crosses paths with a particular Buffett song, usually while in a bar drinking or while driving (hopefully not in combination). Inspiration strikes! Singing "wasting away again . . ." is only interrupted by exclamations of *"Carpe Diem!"* and both accompany packing. From this inspired place the drive South begins. As one blogger writes (Cutter, "Two Tickets to Paradise," http://blog.thes-martspace.com/?p=19), "I was looking for something. I wasn't sure what, but I thought it probably had something to do with the ocean, sand, girls, and drinks with umbrellas. Most of all I thought it had something to do with having less responsibility, not having to have a plan . . . that happiness was there. That life would be different here. That I would be different there . . . I guess the moral of the story is that I should have listened to less Jimmy Buffett."

This is an important distinction in the Buffett narrative—a journey to escape is not a transformative one. While Buffett freely admits to selling escapism, it is often confused with a permanent state of being. This is a detail which separates those knowing that, like it or not, a transformative journey has begun from those who expect to be transformed by a simple change of venue. The explorer has a navigational mind, so regardless of the force—gentle wanderlust or overwhelming rip-tide—all is not lost. Those who react to an inspired moment as *the source* for a changed life will be disappointed.

An ignored dilemma means rather immediate disappointment, as with the blogger who thought he had listened to too much Buffett. The blogger's assumption is a common one, that a change of venue produces a change of self—a happier, more content, more satisfied self. This assumption is problematic. As the adage goes, no matter where you go, there you are; because no matter where you go, you take you with you. If a person believes, as did the blogger, that being on a beach and not in an office will yield a happier, more satisfied person then they are looking in the wrong place for transformative experience. In this case, the disappointment is rather immediate as the new location does not meet expectation. Our blogger seemed to find the beaches, women, and drinks with umbrellas, but not the expected prolonged happiness.

Escapism must not be confused with transformative process. Vacation must not be confused with everyday living. Temporary escape is energizing because it is in stark contrast to everyday life. Those who confuse or conflate escape with transformative process become increasingly resentful or lost in the party. The type is familiar—the person who just doesn't know that it is 3:00 A.M., the party is over, and the guests have all but gone home. Yet they hang on as if the party has just begun, making a spectacle of themselves and making others uncomfortable.

To some lifelong Parrotheads even the temporary escapism of Buffett is being lost to "parrot-keets," the younger generation seeking only a drunken party. Don and Sandi ("Indecision May or May Not Be My Problem," http://www.zimmoland.com/?p=89), two lifelong and slightly disgruntled Parrotheads reflect that "the lifestyle Buffett has sung about, that we tried to live by, has now became an excuse for the latest trend of Parrotheads to get drunk and screw . . . what they are going to drink at the next flocking, and how falling down drunk they got at the last one. . . . Have they experienced enough of life's struggles to know what it is to need an escape for a few hours?" This confusion between temporary escape and transformative process is something Buffet addresses in the *Sixty Minutes* interview: "I feel so privileged to have fans that are loyal, but on some days, I want to go to them and say 'Get a Life,' you know? It's just made up."

Accepting a disorientating dilemma as a starting point of an unknown journey is the first step to a difficult and rewarding experience. Imagine the blogger's response from a transformative perspective rather than an escapist one. Upon hearing Buffett the blogger begins a process of sorting through feelings of discontent. The song still inspires a journey, but one within the self rather than one to Key West. While a party on the beach sounds far more appealing than digging into life choices, the party is short-lived. Both have a place and serve different needs.

A particular memory in Buffett's narrative exemplifies the disorienting dilemma. When asked by *Sixty Minutes* what drives him, Buffett recounted, "the first thing that pops into my mind is I remember, years ago, seeing kind of a has-been country singer working—when I first moved to Nashville—in a bar in a Holiday Inn. . . . And it was obvious that it had been somebody that'd been there and come back down, and I never wanted to make that run back down. 'Remember me back in 1977? I had this one hit, "Margaritaville".' I did not want to be one of those people." The answer provides more insight than just explaining a minor disparaging reference to the Holiday Inn menu in "Cheeseburger in Paradise."

The dilemma was not the has-been country singer or the Holiday Inn, the dilemma was the future flashing through Buffett's mind. It was the possibility that his desired music career might be short-lived. The visualization likely conjured a decision matrix of life-style choices. What choices did the has-been make that Buffett could avoid? What choices and opportunities were missed? What made "Margaritaville" so popular and more than fluke? What if it were a fluke? What's the next project? How soon can some music be written and produced?! Whatever the visualization entailed, the nature of the encounter in 1970s Nashville served as a dilemma. This is in part evidenced in that it remains a strong memory, strong enough to find its way into interviews and song.

In a 2004 interview with *Rolling Stone* ("Sunshine Superman," September 2nd, 2004, p. 78) Buffett referred again to the Holiday Inn moment, when responding to questions of hard-partying, "I found myself in the horrible position of not giving my best onstage. And I felt very bad about that—the Catholic guilt welled up in me. I could have gone right down a predictable road, when you wake up and you're a has-been with nothing. But I woke up and said, 'You better straighten out, dumb-ass!' The thought of playing three shows a night at a Holiday Inn on Murfreesboro Road—that scared me." The Holiday Inn moment has obviously continued to serve Buffett as a point on the compass.

Interpreting the moment as a dilemma illustrates how those familiar with transformative process can use smaller moments to prevent becoming suddenly adrift. Rather than waiting for the reality of a career lull or fall, Buffett imagined the fall. The more the transformative way informs how one engages and manages life, the less the need for dramatic or targeted transformative process.

Disorientation: "I Don't Know Where I'm a Gonna Go"

I told them they should learn from us, I think I told them wrong.

—"The Missionary"

Some people claim that there is a woman to blame. Now I think, hell it could be my fault.

—"Margaritaville"

When experience deeply alters one's way of understanding and of being in the world, the realization settles in of being adrift and disoriented. Purpose and certainty have vanished. Familiar faces look different. Familiar voices speak as they always have and yet they sound like gibberish and babble. Above all, there is a palpable sense that *something is not right*.

One of Buffett's earliest songs, "The Missionary," captures this experience. In it the missionary's core values of faith are badly shaken. The cause is a contradiction—those who taught the missionary about turning "sword blades into plows" were revealed as the agents of war. As the missionary continues pondering the contradiction, another appears. In contemplating the jungle population, the thought occurs, "their nakedness was no disgrace" and "the population lived in peace." The teacher of morality becomes the student. As the missionary realizes that the "uncivilized" population has proven more peaceful and harmonious than that of home, only questions remain. The feeling of disorientation takes over, "I told them how they should learn from us, what should I tell them now?"

Disorientation is powerful. Physical, geographic, and transformative disorientation all generate similar feelings including panic, vertigo, anxiety, resistance, and confusion. The experience should raise questions rather than lead to knee-jerk action, problem-solving, or statements of certainty. It is a rule given in survival guides to stay put if lost. The chances of being found are much greater.

Imagine you are out walking a familiar nature trail. A flashflood comes rushing through. In the aftermath the landscape has been completely altered. The path leading back home has disappeared and the route forward is difficult to see—is there one easy way through or many? Which direction does each apparent way go? Which leads roughly in the right direction? What if the way that seems right abruptly turns ninety degrees? Is it better to go back? Are there even enough landmarks to be certain of direction? When disorientation strikes, the most important action is to stop moving and take time to begin asking questions and making assessments.

However, disorientation can be ignored and a way forward can be forced. The missionary could ignore the nagging doubts and return home with a general sense of dissatisfaction or perhaps shake off the experience as a quirk. Ignore disorientation and dissatisfaction multiples. This is clear when thinking about being adrift. A course is mapped predicated on the certainty of current location. But getting there from here can never happen because the primary assumption of location was wrong and the situation is now worse than it was.

Imagine the missionary brushing aside the nagging doubts and continuing instruction. "Nakedness" is treated as disgraceful along with all the other lessons, despite the missionary's deepening understanding to the contrary. The missionary returns home and is confronted more directly with peacekeepers acting as warmongers. Or perhaps the missionary later works in another location where life is far more tranquil and loving than home. Eventually the doubts resurface, enhanced and added to by similar experiences. Perhaps guilt is added to the mix—guilt for not changing course sooner and guilt for lost time.

Denying circumstances, the reshaped world, requires more energy than processing disorientation. Yet there are those who cling to old beliefs that no longer fit. The longer an old view is forced to work, the more problematic life becomes—the world just does not seem to work right. A common outcome is that the world and a majority of people in it are to blame and the person in denial sees him or herself as a victim. An unwillingness to deal with disorientation can fracture lives and relationships more dramatically than the disorientation itself.

This recalcitrance is not something commonly found in Buffett's works. Rather, a small example of well-managed disorientation is seen when Buffett is asked about his seeming party life-style. In his 1996 *Rolling Stone* interview Buffet comments, "I was [the biggest partier]! I had a great time! Then people started dying, you know. And having nervous breakdowns. And then you go, 'wait a minute here'." Another answer Buffett commonly provides to the question of giving up hard partying is "when hangovers began to feel like surgical recovery days".

A much larger example is Buffett's near-death experience. In 1994, Buffett made a solo day of flying and fishing. As he began to take off his seaplane unexpectedly caught a wake resulting in a crash. The mental aftermath of such an experience is a landscape of competing questions, some more logical and coherent than others. In *A Pirate Looks at Fifty*, Buffett recounts the story, placing emphasis on his training as a pilot and on his willingness to reflect on lingering questions. In recounting a conversation with his friend Paul Tobias, therapist and fellow pilot (who also had a near miss), Buffett maintains a balanced perspective, "we were not terminally unique in our near-death experiences. Hell, in this age we were just two of a thousand people a day who experience the same thing . . . it was life throwing a hundred-mile-an-hour fastball at your head that barely missed" (p. 62).

During the immediate hours and days following the crash Buffett reflects on life, plays tennis, experiences flashbacks, and combats physical pain with Advil. A few days later something meaningful shook loose. Despite nasty weather Buffet recruits friend Charlie Hergrueter to go fly-fishing. The morning is a bit rough and when Charlie suggests calling it a day, Buffet resists, "I was lost in a mental fog. It seemed like I had lost connection to the ocean, and something inside me said I couldn't go home again until I found out for sure" (pp.70–71).

Recognizing disorientation is tricky and the reason for it trickier still. On a boat or in a plane, instruments help. In life, recognizing disorientation is more challenging. Feelings of panic, anxiety, resistance, and confusion are unfortunately common in life. When feelings of disorientation take hold the main task is to address the reason for it. Is this a simple and temporary situation—an instrument that has failed or an unexpected change in wind leading one off-course? Or is there something more substantial happening? If the situation is not minor, then the search begins. In the transformative journey disorientation happens when what has served as magnetic North for one's compass has vanished.

Exploration: "Lookin' for Better Days"

He went to Paris, looking for answers to questions that bothered him so.

—"He Went to Paris"

I took off for a weekend last month, just to try and recall the whole year.

—"Changes in Latitudes, Changes in Attitudes"

Having acknowledged the circumstance of being adrift and disoriented, the exploration begins, seeking how one came to be in uncharted waters. The first part of the transformative process essentially involves awareness that the compass no longer functions and location is unknown. When one is bothered by questions—when the assumptions governing life have cascaded—the task is to sort through the remains. In the process, all assumptions are examined and assessed on a scale of reliability to disservice. In the process the mechanism—the way of thinking—that produced the now-faulty ideas is discovered. Transformative exploration is focused on being adrift as much as it is on the validity of the moorings—the mechanics of learning, insight, and meaning-making.

Introspection requires time and space. The opening line of Buffett's "Changes in Latitudes, Changes in Attitudes" is fitting to transformative exploration. Taking two days to inventory the other 363 is a tall order and yet it is well placed. Reflecting on one's past before moving into the future is a healthy practice for general living. Reflective practice is something that helps maintain balance of mind, body, spirit, and emotion. It is a conversation with the self about what is in order and what is amiss, and whether the course is true.

Buffett illustrates how in everyday life, reflection is more within reach than often assumed. It is not some wacky Age of Aquarius notion that must be added to an already full schedule. Reflective practice uses everyday activities in a mindful way. These can include sleeping dreams; free-form writing; journaling; prayer or meditation; meandering thoughts while walking or driving; sharing stories; playing sports; and much more. Such practices engage the mind, body, spirit, and emotion in various combinations. Without reflective practice in everyday life, two pitfalls await: intensive off-the-charts disorientation and escapism masquerading as transformation. Both are increasingly likely with the ever-growing wired world.

Written years before the invention of the Crackberry, Buffett's narrative spoke to the speeding up life's pace in "Trying to Reason with Hurricane Season," "And now I must confess, I could use some rest, I can't run at this pace very long. Yes, it's quite insane. I think it hurts my brain." Later, in 1996, the lyrics of "Holiday" more specifically linked technology with too rapid a pace, "You're caught in the Internet. You think it's such a great asset. You're wrong, wrong, wrong." Ten years later the lyrics of "Everybody's on the Phone," capture what has become of the technology and pace: "Everybody's on the phone so connected and all alone. . . . You're loud and clear but I don't understand."

The more society pushes a 24/7 world, a WIFI tether, and an insane work-week, the less healthy and productive it becomes. Individuals become off-balance, too mind-only, and focused on a never-ending to-do list. Failure to create balance eventually leads to highly dramatic and intense disorientating dilemmas. Absorption in technology and eighty-hour work weeks means less awareness and consequently minor course corrections are never made. In contrast, the individual leading a more balanced life, one familiar with transformative process, seldom experiences a disorienting dilemma of off-the-charts magnitude.

Who imagined that forty-plus years after its creation by Dr. Timothy Leary (*Flashbacks,* Tarcher, 1983) the concept of "Turn on, Tune in, and Drop out" would still be desperately needed? "In public statements I stressed that the . . . process must be repeated if one wished to live a life of growth. Unhappily my explanations of this sequence of personal development were often misinterpreted to mean "get stoned and abandon all constructive activity" (p. 253). The misinterpretation is akin to mistaking escapism for transformative practice, believing location, not introspection is the key to happiness via growth. Indeed, the more life becomes compressed the louder the Sirens' call becomes, luring us into escapism. To avoid either the temptation of escapism or the consequences of dilemmas ignored, the increasing demands must be resisted. "Unplug to reconnect" might be the millennial update to Leary's slogan and might reflect Buffett's expertise as a guide.

Transformative exploration cannot happen without reflective practice. Yet, lives cannot be suspended—families, employers, bill collectors would be less than understanding. Within the constraints of practical life, space must be created. Withdrawing from life's routine is common during the first stage of exploration. Unplugging from technology, delegating tasks, and disengaging some from people creates space to go within. Buffett's lyric, "if the phone doesn't ring, you know that it's me," provides both permission and advice on withdrawing. Putting down the Crackberry is a good first step. Driving the car without the radio on or making dinner without background noise is a simple way to unplug. The idea is to not fill every waking moment with the thoughts and noise of others.

To regain bearings when magnetic North has disappeared takes thoughtfulness. For the exploration to be conducive to transformative process, activities are not hapless, selected arbitrarily. They go beyond the everyday reflective practices of quiet walks and artistic creation. The reflection must be framed and purposeful. The dilemma created disorientation because some part of operating in the world is at odds with the world. As with Buffett's near-death experience, the important questions must be separated from the incidental ones. For example, a common reaction is, "Have I spent enough time with my family or have I neglected them?" If given a choice, we want to spend more time with those that we love. But given this, are there regrets? Buffett has given no indication in his book or interviews that such a question lingered.

In contrast, questions connected to the disorientation take more time to surface. In Buffett's case, this was not family or aging or too-full-a-plate. The deeper assumption that needed exploration, as indicated in his recounting, was the confidence in his relationship with the water and the confidence is his piloting skill. As Buffett and Charlie continued fishing in less than ideal conditions, the weather changed. Buffett catches and artfully releases a small bass. "As I watched the little striper glide away from my hand to the security of the deeper, darker water, I thought back to the crash, when I was the one scrambling out of the water in search of safety. As the equatorial Africans say, 'down is up and up is down.' . . . The morning was complete. . . . I had rediscovered my saline psyche. Two days later, I climbed back into the left seat of a De Havilland Beaver and went flying. . . . I had been given another shot, and I intended to learn from it. . . . And it all began with one small bass" (*A Pirate Looks at Fifty*, p. 72).

Buffett's near-death experience illustrates four aspects of critical reflection; two emerge directly from the small bass story. First, reflection must investigate much more than the obvious. A critical question is, "How did I come to falsely believe X?"—a question which penetrates personal narrative and life experience. Exploring this singular question over days, weeks, and months can reveal layer after layer of insights. Through the exploration other assumptions are reformed. Eventually, new knowledge and new ways of thinking about knowledge replace the old.

A second aspect of critical reflection found in Buffett's small bass story is the importance of exploration using all the senses. Buffett's insistence on staying out in nasty weather was not formed at the mental, conscious level. Mind, body, spirit, and emotion are four elements of self that are often out of balance. Mental exploration is not enough to sort through a dilemma, the foundational assumptions that have been challenged, and the means by which the assumptions were formed. Instinct and intuition are manifestations of the less conscious self, and not easily explored through conscious mental effort. When Buffett recounts the days that follow the crash, a majority of the story is about everything but the mind.

An aspect of mind, body, spirit, and emotional exploration is that they are used in various combinations. As shared in *A Pirate Looks at Fifty*, Buffett decided to save his marriage when a day of surfing finally made it "click" for him. Intense physical activity paired with attention to emotional states is an example of how to explore. Another is to pair overt thinking about assumptions with an artistic activity. Writing or conversing about the governing assumptions involved in the dilemma might happen just before a solid night of sleep. The brain is hard at work while consciousness sleeps, especially processing the most recent conscious work. The pairing is important because it is within the less conscious self that assumptions can be exposed. If the conscious mind were capable of such work, there would be little need for transformative process.

The third aspect of critical reflection Buffett's experience illustrates is about expertise in transformative process. The adventurer with his willing heart and navigational mind manages the near-death experience with relative ease, at least as he tells the story. Not everyone manages similar experiences so well and so quickly. Some never really overcome such an experience, becoming defined by it, either going too far into self-doubt or going too far into risk-taking. To manage the experience as part of the story and not *the* story, takes dedication to process. To do so almost seamlessly, takes expertise with the process. The more one adopts transformative process into everyday living, the less startling and dramatic dilemmas become. The investigation of assumptions and the process which creates them is habitual. Throughout the larger Buffett narrative sailing, surfing, fly fishing, and airboat flying are discussed as enjoyable hobbies and metaphors of balance. Each is a mixture of art and science and therefore of mind, body, spirit, and emotion.

The fourth and final aspect of critical reflection Buffett's experience illustrates is the role of others in the process. Quiet space is needed for critical reflection, especially at the start of the exploration. As the important questions rise to the surface and as deeper exploration yields uncertain treasure, others can assist. In addition to understanding the need to withdraw, others can take an active role in the exploration. When Tom Freston, co-founder of MTV Networks, was fired in September 2006 he seemed, according to the *New York Times* ("From Hollywood to Eternity," May 20th, 2007, p.1), "to exemplify that search for a compass, . . . globe-trotting like a young backpacker." At one point during the trek Freston traveled with friend and ideal facilitator of exploration, Jimmy Buffett.

Others can ask probing, thoughtful questions. They can listen to stories of assumption formation. As partners in exploration, they can reflect and paraphrase these stories, separating out the intervening thoughts and emotions—thoughts which have a way of adding meaning and clouding insight. These partners can share in artistic play, walkabouts, or a day on the water surfing or sailing. Buffett emphasizes that he and his friend Paul, the therapist, spent time talking about their near misses in the language of pilots. And Charlie, the fishing guru, was sought out as a kindred spirit, someone that understood the water. In this way old friends fill a new role.

Re-Orientation: "Wonder Why We Ever Go Home"

For I have plowed the seas, and smoothed the troubled waters, come along and let's have some fun, the hard work has been done.

—"Barometer Soup"

Follow the equator, like that old articulator. Sail upon the ocean, just like Mr. Twain.

—"Take Another Road"

When in unknown waters exploration yields a sense of direction and a recalibrated compass. On the other side of disorientation is re-orientation. This part of the transformative journey is marked by a sense of momentum and equilibrium. This confidence in balancing on the water can be found throughout Buffett's narrative.

Harnessing this energy is important. New ways of seeing the world and making sense of experience have replaced the old. These new ways need to be tested. Whether living in our familiar lives of work and home or living in some new version (new job, new city, new home, new relationship), the life being lived is altered. Relationships and human activity are interpreted in new ways. Because experiences are interpreted differently, one moves differently through life than they did prior to the disorientation. Consequently, the course now charted is new.

A challenge then is that the new compass functions differently than others'. A new, alternative perspective on the world in a world that is largely the same can tempt vulnerability. Knowing about and adventuring on a round, not flat, Earth is feasible. Convincing others to come along or to at least be supportive is not so simple a task. The pressure to recant can be intense. Yet, transformative process cannot be undone because the fundamental means of interpreting life experience have been altered. Re-orientation can take time and patience is required.

As a result, the tension between a new perspective and an old life can be a prolonged or second-tier transformative process. Time may be required either to help others understand the new self or to transition to a new social group. The time allocated may feel a bit like a disorientating dilemma—frustration or disappointment that others will not or cannot travel the same path. It is a realization and sentiment expressed somewhat in "I Can't Be Your Hero." While the lyrics are firm and changes for the better have occurred, the tone carries an element of sadness—that roles once played are retired. However, this sorting out of who is onboard and who is not may have happened in the exploration phase. If others were invited in and willing to assist in the exploration, the re-orientation process may be quite smooth. If others are unable or unwilling to be involved, then the re-orientation process may be difficult and relationships will be strained.

The major pitfall of re-orientation is in believing that it is absolutely accurate. The dilemma and the disorientation have vanished, so it is easy to consider the self *transformed*. Yet, there is no true completion to the process. This is an important understanding of transformative process. The world and all its circumstances are ever-changing. The self is part of that dynamic process. "Transformation of self" is an error in thinking and can lead to over-confidence. If one well-processed disorienting dilemma is treated as a singular life event, then the next one will be just as troublesome if not of a larger magnitude. Alternatively, if transformative thinking is accepted into everyday life, then growth is more steady and pleasant.

"Livin' It Up"

When he yelled from the drive, my heart came alive, "Jimmy boy come along." It's time to see the world.

—"Pascagoula Run"

Bend a little, one way or the other. You got to leave your mind open to discover. Seems I've been fightin' it all along.

—"Bend a Little"

Exploration is not hapless, it has a purpose. Adventure is not guaranteed to be safe. However, a wanderlust heart combined with a navigational mind can weather storms and take advantage of clear skies. Experience is about both the journey and the destination. Both are about the stories and the characters on which they are built, "the place where the fantasy seems to be dwindling is with the people; we have more tourists than travelers running around the world. I run all over the country and all over the world, and still find spots that just take my breath away. As long as you're in motion, life is an experience and it's meant to be lived. Fortunately, I come from a family of gypsies and sailors." These are lessons and inspirations from the narrative of Jimmy Buffett ("About Jimmy," www.margaritaville.com//index.php?page=jimmy).

Beyond inspirational stories, quotations, and songs is a narrative of a life well-managed. To the casual outsider Buffett's life appears carefree, an easy cruise on a perfect day. To them the music sounds as it once did to music columnist Ben Wener, "laidback, drink-up, Key West-rules attitude, as if nothing mattered in the world except where to get another case of Coronas and a really juicy lime" ("A Non-Parrothead Looks at Jimmy Buffett," *Orange County Register*, April 24th, 2000).

The music requires more than a surface treatment. Wener who married into a phlock, recounts his long weeks purposefully dedicated to the entire Buffet collection and chronology. Throughout those weeks flashes of insight and respect were mixed with annoyance. Once finished with the task of exploring Buffett's work, however, Wener conceded appreciation, "I'm forced to admit I like some Jimmy Buffett—a matter underlined the farther I journeyed through his impressively lengthy career. . . . Buffett proved himself to be the best sort of troubadour: a trusty one who tells the truth as best he knows it. . . . he digs deep enough into himself to really get at something amazingly universal—and it's usually autobiographical." Upon such consideration even the ever-popular "Margaritaville" is understood as more than a hair-of-the-dog quest. It tells the story of certainty ("I know it's nobody's fault") turned inquiry ("hell, it could be my fault") to insight ("I know it's my own damn fault").

Those that look closely at Buffett's life can find a similar treatment of certainty. He handles challenges and disorientation with seeming ease. The examples of near-divorce and near-death are both avoided and well-handled. The former is treated with willful diligence, however delayed the insight. The later, occurring further on in life, is treated quickly and intuitively. Moreover, both called for and held Buffett's attention, but not in an all-consuming narcissistic manner. What appears as a carefree attitude is actually an expertise with transformative process. As is the case with experts, they make overwhelmingly hard work look easy.

Balancing on the water is not easy. Together, the workaholic and the beach bum pursue a life of adventure; one cannot live without the other. The Buffett narrative exemplifies transformative process. In this, Buffett serves as guide to living life as transformative potential, "you have to challenge yourself. I still fly airplanes for the same reason. You have to keep yourself on the cutting edge" (Craig Wilson, "Five Questions for Jimmy Buffett," *USA Today*, May 8th, 2008).

May the summer job long continue.

6
Meeting a Salty Piece of Land

CELIA T. BARDWELL-JONES

I lived in the U.S. Virgin Islands on a tiny island called St. John for four years after graduating from college and working a summer on a tender boat in Alaska. This tiny island (or rock, in my most desperate hours) was only nine miles long and three miles wide. While it represented my desire to become displaced and detached from everything familiar to me, it also became my first experience in yearning for a sense of community, a sense of belonging, or to put it simply, a home.

It's not to say that Los Angeles (where I grew up) or even the place of my birth, the Philippines, did not register any meaning of home or family commitments for me. However, living on St. John provided me my first glimpse of choosing and cultivating my own sense of belonging to a very special community, a very special island. I could not help but recall this experience as I began reading Jimmy Buffett's books and listening to his music. A true wanderer! But a wanderer who finds that the desire to escape inevitably leads one to find a home.

On a less bright note, my recollection also could not help but associate Jimmy Buffett with the negative practices of tourism. Living in St. John on a sailboat afforded me a perspective on tourism in the Virgin Islands. Jimmy Buffett is no foreigner in these parts as his musical legacy has inspired many Parrotheads to find Margaritaville in the paradise of the Caribbean. It's not unusual to see Buffettesque businesses emerge as his fans seek that cheeseburger in paradise on their week of vacation. Working in the food service industry as waitress, bartender, and wine steward, I couldn't help but observe the decadence, the meaningless mantras fueled by rum at various watering holes on the island, the cultivated ignorance of St. John's rich historical sites, and finally the trash left at the heels of mass-market tourism run amok.

I'm not suggesting that Parrotheads, or even Buffett himself, are solely responsible for the tourist culture on St. John. However, in an age when our travels and mode of traveling are defined by tourist destinations created by global capitalistic markets, the question that becomes pertinent for any traveling Parrothead is "Am I a tourist or something else?" Given Jimmy Buffett's implicit message about journeying on the road less traveled, it seems consistent to think that Parrotheads should be more aware of their modes of traveling.

Isn't the nature of a Parrothead opposed to that of the tourist? Authentic Parrotheads—to be consistent with Buffett's sense of adventure—should be opposed to being simple tourists in their encounters with culturally different others. Rather, these encounters should be seen as ethical contexts requiring moral reflection. But who wants to think about such things on vacation? Doesn't Jimmy Buffett demand escape from concern and reflection? It seems to me that this moment of encounter between culturally different others is central to Buffett's philosophy.

In a globalized age where tourism will not go away, it becomes a crucial activity in examining how we come to know ourselves as genuinely culturally diverse human beings. In light of Jimmy Buffett's commitment to the road less traveled, we can ask: How is Parrothead tourism possible?

"All the Tourists Covered with Oil"

As travel becomes a more pervasive feature in our contemporary lives, we might consider the ethical implications associated with this activity. In his essay *Perpetual Peace* (Hackett, 1983), Immanuel Kant thinks that world travel might help to ensure the possibility of peace. Since the surface of the Earth is the finite and common possession we all share, we need to be able to tolerate the presence of each other. "Hospitality," says Kant, "means the right of the stranger not to be treated as an enemy when he arrives in the land of another" (p. 118). Kant defines clearly what good behavior the host country is obliged to practice, namely hospitality to the strangers who visit their homeland. Yet Kant does not reveal the good behavior the traveler must maintain to facilitate peace.

One might imagine that the reason the tourist visits another country is to exchange ideas, learn about other cultures, and make meaningful relationships with culturally different others since we all live on the same planet. To dominate, colonize, or destroy the toured culture's values and ways of life would be antithetical to the tourist's duty. However, I'm not sure that Kant was ready to deal with the devastating effects of contemporary mass-market tourism.

Jamaica Kincaid's powerful critique of the tourist culture in Antigua depicts some of the frightening realities of global capitalist culture. In *A Small Place* (Farrar, Straus, Giroux, 1988) Kincaid describes the tourist this way:

> an ugly thing, that is what you are when you become a tourist, an ugly, empty thing, a stupid thing, a piece of rubbish pausing here and there to gaze at this and taste that, and it will never occur to you that the people who inhabit the place in which you have just paused cannot stand you, that behind their closed doors they laugh at your strangeness (you do not look the way they look). (p. 17)

Kincaid's perceptive analysis of the tourist becomes relevant today as tourist markets continually expand on a global scale. The World Tourism Organization anticipates over a billion international tourist arrivals by 2020. Tourism will not go away anytime soon.

What makes Kincaid's criticisms of tourism relevant in an increasingly tourist-driven global economy is the reality of the effects of tourism upon those who live in these toured landscapes and sites of escape. The tourist is ugly in two ways from the perspective of Native Antiguans. First, the tourist sees the "native" of the host country as a thing, a souvenir to purchase for the purposes of the temporary enjoyment of the tourist. The assumption here is that the "native" does not *travel* during this encounter. Second, the tourist's failure to acknowledge the natives' perspective causes the native to see the tourist as unable to understand and therefore 'stupid'. If tourists won't engage the world-view of the locals, the tourists remain ignorant about the reality of the place they visit. If the purpose of travel is to learn about other countries, then the tourists' concern with their own pursuits of leisure and pleasure is not enough.

I recall a day when I was hitchhiking on the island of St. Thomas and a local picked me up. A Jimmy Buffett song came on the radio and with hateful scorn the driver immediately turned it off. We ended up talking throughout the twenty-minute ride about how Buffett's legacy affected the island. Echoing many of Kincaid's criticisms, the driver expressed concern about the visitors' irreverent disregard of the island's cultural histories. This cultivated historical amnesia produced tourist landscapes that fancied escape and getaways rather than cultural enrichment. The islands were regarded as a playground for the upwardly mobile mainlanders, rather than a place where local inhabitants lived out their lives. My distraught driver claimed that the consequences of Parrothead tourism made many locals cynical, distant, and mistrustful of tourists. Tourists interact with locals in ways that demean the island and its people. While they may seem like Parrotheads—listening to "Margaritaville," covered with oil (or at least some appropriate sunscreen)—Buffett himself seems to call these tourists to task in "The Ballad of Skip Wiley," who recommends: "Lock the tourists up in theme parks and zoos."

So how do these tourists do it? How do they travel and what are they thinking? According to cultural tourism analysts, McKercher and du Cross (*Cultural Tourism*, Haworth Hospitality Press, 2002), most tourists risk excessive behavior they would not exhibit at home, including excessive alcohol consumption and flamboyant sexual behavior. McKercher and du Cross explain how these activities utilize the dichotomy of "strangeness versus familiarity," which privileges the familiar over the strange. In order to avoid extreme and sometimes dangerous behaviors, tourist managers try to ensure a level of interaction comfortable enough that the tourist will not experience the culture shock that leads to problematic behavior. So an environmental bubble is formed by and for the tourist. She seeks a "safety blanket," a familiar social and cultural environment within the foreign country she visits, "enabling the person to sample the unfamiliar while not being overwhelmed by it" (p. 117).

Consequently, tourist managers who want to maintain the economic viability of the tourist industry in a particular country encourage the host country "not to be so damn foreign" to the tourist. Certain tactics the host country can employ are encouraged. Here are some of the aphorisms the tourist industry promotes: "Mythologize the asset," "Build a story around the asset," "Emphasize its otherness," "Show a direct link from the past to the present," "Make it triumphant," "Make it a fantasy," "Make it fun, light, and entertaining" (p. 128).

Modern tourists seek safety blankets, environmental bubbles that prevent them from interacting meaningfully with the toured other. The need for a safety blanket can be understandable in contexts where the toured culture might be radically different from our own. Eating cobras in Vietnam may not be desirable for a Western tourist, which may lead her to find other more familiar meals. However, what makes the environmental bubble problematic in the context of mass tourism is its attempt to fossilize the environmental boundary to the point where the mass-market tourist habit of interaction with others becomes 'natural'. The boundary this creates excludes the experience of the foreign influences and so cultivates a single model of tourist experience. When this process of naturalization is further cultivated in global tourist economies, it encourages tourist habits Kincaid calls "ugly and stupid." In an era of mass-market tourism, tourist managers avoid cultivating tourist interactions as specific encounters with the cultures they meet.

Highlighting the uniqueness of touristic encounters would go against the very grain of tourist management since there is less control and more risk when the environmental bubble is shattered. This would just lead to more excessive behavior. The tourist and the toured must be domesticated in order to prevent culture shock and a bad vacation. Unfortunately, the result is a narrow conception of the tourist as one who is enclosed within familiar boundaries of home and never leaves a space of comfort. The toured culture becomes an object to consume, fossilized in time and space, whose contact with tourists only serves to mystify the background enough for the tourist to have a good time. As a result, mass-market tourism does not lead to genuine encounters with the strange, unfamiliar toured culture.

Anchors in Experience: Encountering A Salty Piece of Land

Buffett's stories of adventurous meanderings may appeal to those of us who cannot escape the banalities of our monotonous lifestyles. In reading his novel, *A Salty Piece of Land*, we live vicariously through Tully Mars's laissez-faire attitude, openness to adventure, and amazing network of friendships that span the rugged territories of Wyoming and across oceans to the Pacific Islands. This is certainly a book of travels and traveling.

The novel follows the meanderings of Tully Mars, a character from Buffett's previous book, *Tales from Margaritaville*, a cowboy from Wyoming who's running from bounty hunters hired by his former employer, Thelma Barston. After learning that the ranch where he worked would be herding poodles instead of cows, he threw a massage table through the window. Following this act of vandalism, Tully becomes a cowboy in search of escape as he travels to the coast of Alabama, Key West, Mexico, Belize, and the Caribbean. Eventually, he ends up working as a fishing guide with a Mayan shaman named Ix-Nay. Having lost his sense of home, and caught up in the moment of travels and adventures (too many to list—you have to read the book), Tully meets Cleopatra Highbourne, a one-hundred-and-one-year-old woman who is captain of an illustrious schooner called *Lucretia*. Upon meeting this high queen of the seas, Tully's life begins to change. Cleopatra is on a mission to find a rare "bull's eye" lens for her lighthouse on an island called Cayo Loco—the salty piece of land. Through this relationship with Cleopatra, and his active participation in finding the lens, he also becomes able to find meaning in his life. In effect, he is able to cultivate a sense of home.

I understand much of what the protagonist Tully is seeking as nothing more than a sense of home, a sense of place. It seems that this desire for connection within the context of travel challenges the environmental bubbles crafted by tourist capitalist economies, bubbles which create rigid and mystified limits around the common Parrothead tourist. Unlike such tourists, Buffett encourages us to escape, but also to stay grounded. He persuades us to embark on our boats and seek the song of the ocean, but to also have on board good anchors in order to meet that salty piece of land.

Buffett's notion of agency, when seen within the context of our desire for travel and adventure, as well as our yearning to remain connected and anchored within meaningful social relationships, is important. There are three salient aspects of Buffett's notion of agency and boundaries. This analysis underscores the importance of boundaries as sites of appreciation, as potential contexts where fruitful and meaningful cross-cultural relationships can form and thus can direct us to better modes of travel.

First, it is important to understand the meaning behind the metaphor of the ocean and its relationship to a salty piece of land. What is it about the ocean that represents our need to escape? Tully literally escapes from the landlubber reality at the ranch and finds himself on a shrimp boat heading to Mexico. Feeling like a "pirate," he describes his experience on this boat heading out to sea as "tasting the first bite of a new world that was to become a steady diet in time" (Buffett, p. 23). Unanchored, the boat offers a liberating view of the world. The possibilities for one's future are endless. The unanchored feeling displaces Tully's previous sense of home, since he is most concerned with escaping entirely from his former life (the bounty hunters don't help either). The song of the ocean represents that desire to pick up anchor and push the boundaries of the self to wider places.

In the lyrics to "A Salty Piece of Land," Buffett highlights the "meeting" of the song of the ocean with a salty piece of land. Thus, the song of the ocean requires a stopping point, a place to drop anchor for a while and find oneself. In this sense, the self cannot remain unanchored, free-floating and unconnected to relationships. The project of finding oneself manifests within relationships, with others. Tully's transformation takes place because of his encounter with Cleopatra and his commitment to find the lens for the lighthouse. As her death approached, this purpose became an essential project for him. Even though our desire to escape our place of familiarity conditions our departure from home, it is also important to recognize a yearning to anchor ourselves within experience, within meaningful relationships. The moment we drop anchor, we have made an effort to become part of a social experience that is not conditioned solely by us.

Second, Buffett recognizes through the apparatus of travel that agency is everywhere. Tully can be taken up by the winds of fate or the agency of others (Cleopatra Highbourne) and embark on a journey of self discovery. Yet it is not a one-sided process; he also recognizes that he has something to offer to his relationship with Cleopatra, namely his contacts with Willie, who eventually finds the bull's eye lens for her lighthouse.

While the expansive territories he covers in the book seem outlandish and surreal, the idea that emerges from this apparatus of haphazard traveling is the relatedness that spans the world. Networks of relationships chart Tully's eventual meeting with Cleopatra and that encounter leads to a transformation of the self that occurs throughout the book. Tully cannot escape these relationships because, as an agent, he participates willingly in a world. Tully's unassuming character develops a tolerance of difference and creatively embraces the continuity that connects the world through networks of travel.

Third, Buffett emphasizes the nature of boundaries as possibilities where critical self-reflection can take place. Tully Mars is the survivor who emerges as the type of agent who walks on a precarious edge and must do so alone. The choice he faces presents itself this way, according to Cleopatra: "On the one side is your ability to be comfortable in a world inhabited only by yourself. And on the other side is your desire to share your time with others. How do you balance?" (p. 418). At the boundary of self and others, the survivor embodies a choice, a willing act that encourages the crossing of that which separates the self from others. An isolated self can never achieve self-fulfillment. She or he is a "free-floating" and ungrounded wanderer, lacking any real meaning in life.

This is the self that Cleopatra hoped Tully would avoid and so fired him in order to help him find meaning in his life. Through this act, Tully claimed that Cleopatra indirectly saved him from himself. In his song, "A Salty Piece of Land," Buffett laments the state of the survivor as one infused with terror. "Survivors seem to function best when peril is at hand." The nature of this peril involves an ultimate assault on the ego, destroying boundaries of the self that would continually construct artificial barriers to others. Self-awareness emerges as one's song of the ocean—one's creative desires for adventure—co-mingles with one's yearning for connection with others, for meaning, for a salty piece of land. "Still I search the constellations," Buffett sings, "And the tiny grains of sand / Where the song of the ocean Meets the salty piece of land." It's the meeting that counts.

"When the Coast is Clear"

Can the Parrothead tourist be saved from herself as Tully was? If so, how one refigures the boundaries calls upon both ontological and ethical strategies. If we examine Kincaid's criticism earlier in the essay closely, we see that the ontological strategy she implicitly suggests is that we take seriously the realities of boundaries between the tourist and the toured other. For the tourist to become less ugly and more self-reflective, and hence have better access to truth, the tourist must comport herself differently at the boundaries of the encounter with the toured other. What might this strategy look like?

It would entail a sense of agency that suggests new articulations of how one might perceive the "Natives" of a culturally toured country. Rather than viewing the culturally toured as fossilized in history and space, passive and waiting to be consumed by the tourist, the culturally toured are in fact agents in creating the experience of travel that is experienced by more than just the tourist. Travel becomes a bi-directional activity that emphasizes participation by both the tourist and the culturally toured.

Following Kincaid, a tourist is ugly and stupid when she lacks a correlative recognition of the experiences of the culturally toured. The consequences of this detached perspective are the tourist's unfamiliarity with the real living conditions of Antiguans: the bad roads, poor health care and education facilities, and the history of oppression in Antigua. Because the realities of the experiences of culturally different others are concealed within a language of escape and privilege, cultural difference becomes a touristic product to be consumed rather than understood. To visit Antigua would be to engage the local inhabitants in order to understand their lives. Knowing this reality would affect one's experience of travel.

The activity of travel is an apparatus that is open-ended and can serve many purposes depending on the traveler's (agent's) purposes and desires. The activity of travel, in fact, can generate particular instances of wholeness that can facilitate the creation of cross-cultural relationships without leading to a homogenous collectivity. Moreover, from Buffett's perspective, travel is an apparatus that can potentially bring us out of the rigidity of our lives and bring us into relation with new experiences. Understanding travel as an apparatus that is open-ended challenges the construction of bubbles that hide the local environment for the purposes of comfort and exclusion. In fact, we might see the environmental bubble as an apparatus that speaks to a certain tourist desire and is not dictated by the nature of travel itself.

The tourist need not think that interacting with culturally different others can only occur within service-driven contexts. The tourist can make a choice to craft their environmental bubbles in ways that cultivate self-reflection and growth. With the rise of travel in the industry of mass-market tourism, there is a potential for more boundaries to emerge, thus inviting new forms of intra-action with culturally different others. And finding oneself on the edge as a survivor cut off from familiar places and ways of life might encourage the Parrothead tourist to see the plastic limits of Buffettesque tourist ventures and embark on more boundary-crossing contexts on their holidays. In "When the Coast is Clear," Buffett himself seems to reject mass-market tourism as a kind of circus that blocks reflection and transformation. "The tourist traps are empty / Vacancy abounds / Almost like it used to be / Before the circus came to town."

Understanding the constitutive force of boundaries in experience underscores the ethical aspect of travel and tourism. In this sense, tourism, understood as an apparatus, can be re-figured from an individual activity of escape to a more Kantian sentiment of meaningful exchange, which emphasizes the value of learning from culturally different others in order to become better human beings. In this way, travel is a mode of activity that fosters a critical self-reflection on one's sense of belonging in relation to others. The responsibility of the traveler is to pay attention to the boundaries that condition reality and the choices that are made within intra-action with others.

Reading Buffett's sense of travel as an apparatus allows us to see this activity as providing opportunities for ethical reflection. While engaged within a language of escape, Buffett's notion of travel co-mingles with a desire for connection, a desire for meaning, in effect, a desire for home, which can only be achieved within relationships. To be consistent with Buffett's philosophy of travel, Parrothead travelers, especially the ones who distinguish themselves from tourists, must see this tension and conflict within their own travels. In an early song, "The Stories We Tell," Buffett asks whether traveling is really the answer:

> Talkin' to myself again
> wonderin' if this traveling is good
> Is there something else a doin'
> We'd be doin' if we could?

But in "Off to See the Lizard," he decisively replies that travel, not mass-market tourism, opens up possibilities and puts one on the edge, not by giving answers, but by raising doubts.

> I'm turning off the waterfall the tourists can go home
> Feel its time to travel, time to write a poem
> Time to seek some therapy
> I'm goin' walkabout
> Answers are the easy part, questions raise the doubt.

In this sense, travel elicits a deep urgency in us to engage in self-reflection. This kind of reflection requires an attention to the boundaries of our encounters with culturally different others when on vacation. However, seeking the salty piece of land within an ocean of touristic environmental bubbles might prove to be difficult, especially if one's choice of a holiday might be in a country where cobras are eaten. Nevertheless, it is best to understand Buffett's message as continual and often slow efforts to assault the boundaries of the self. It's through this state of peril within encounters with culturally different others that the Parrothead tourist can truly be saved from herself.

Piratology

7

Jimmy Buffett, Pop Prophet

CHRISTOPHER HOYT

Altered Boy

Jimmy Buffett begins his memoir, *A Pirate Looks at Fifty*, with a four-hundred-word synopsis of the major themes and events of his life, the first line of which reads, "I broke out of the grip of Catholicism and made it through adolescence without killing myself in a car." Further references to his "escape" from Catholicism abound in the book, and in any number of passages he variously refers to the sea, to fishing, and to music as his true religion.

To understand Buffett and his art, we must take these pronouncements seriously. That's not because Buffett's work is covertly religious or anti-religious, but because his songs and stories—and indeed the persona of *Jimmy*—are expressions of someone seeking the meaning of life in a modern, secular context. The first track on Buffett's first album is "The Christian," an uncharacteristically biting song that chastises religious hypocrites with lyrics like:

> Could you really call yourself a Christian
> If charity costs half as much as beer?

Signaling the direction his own life and art would take, the last song on the album, "Truckstop Salvation," tells the story of a traveling hippy who shows up in a two-bit town where he is misunderstood by the locals, harassed by the sheriff, and harangued by the preacher. The chorus protests:

> He's what they've tried to kill
> With their Bibles and their stills

But he's not weird
Just a man that's bein' free

From "Truckstop Salvation" (1970) to the story of Tully Mars told in
A Salty Piece of Land (2005), Buffett has consistently sung and written about characters who reject conventional values and lives to
seek meaning and happiness on their own terms, most of them in
the tropics.

In Steve Eng's *Jimmy Buffett: The Man from Margaritaville
Revealed* (St. Martins', 1996), we learn that Buffett has said many
times that his concerts are meant to recreate the spirit of Mardi Gras
(pp. 37–38). Some people may mistake that for a pledge to sloth and
drunkenness, since that is all that many people see in Mardi Gras.
For Buffett, however, it's something much more substantial. In his
memoir, Buffett describes how as a boy he recognized that despite
"all the frolicking and carrying on, there was something spiritual
about Mardi Gras" (*Pirate*, p. 37). What particularly caught the young
Buffett's attention was the ritual parade wherein Folly chases Death
out of town, walloping him on the behind the whole way. "Forty-
five years later, I still vividly recall that first encounter with Death,
and learning that Folly was the only way to deal with it. You know
that Death will get you in the end, but if you are smart and have a
sense of humor, you can thumb your nose at it for a while" (p. 39).

Buffett's response to the ritual is remarkably sensitive. The practice of "carrying out death" has been part of the celebration of Lent
in Europe for many centuries, and has taken numerous forms at
various time and places. Its varieties are famously documented by
James Frazer in *The Golden Bough* (Gramercy, 1981, originally published in 1890), but Frazer says too little about its meaning, and
suggests only that its function is essentially magical, that it is meant
to ward off plague, pox, and other life-threatening illnesses for the
coming year (pp. 257–276). The philosopher Ludwig Wittgenstein
criticizes Frazer for his reduction of this and other religious rituals
to magical incantations, and urges us to see them instead as expressions of a spiritual attitude towards events and aspects of life that
are profoundly important to us, events such as birth, death, fire, the
similarity of people and animals, and more ("Remarks on Frazer's
Golden Bough," in *Wittgenstein: Philosophical Occasions* (Hackett,
1993), pp. 119–155).

Buffett's reading is right in line with the sort that Wittgenstein
has in mind. Buffett describes his "irreverent" attitude towards

death as a façade rooted in his experiences at Mardi Gras, and it is that façade which largely defines *Jimmy*. His fun-loving attitude is not rooted in aimless hedonism, but in the idea that to thumb one's nose at Death is simply to embrace and enjoy life.

Buffett describes playing music, fishing, surfing, and a few other ordinary activities as potentially religious experiences. In each case, what he has in mind is that they make him feel alive, present in and part of the world. Each seems to be a way of thumbing his nose at Death just a little while longer. Witness how, in *A Pirate Looks at Fifty*, he describes a simple moment of catching and releasing a striped bass:

> [The fish and I] were connected by more than the monofilament line that had brought him into my hands. I had used all of my modern material and primeval stalking to fool him and catch him, and then I held him by the tail and moved him back and forth in the water so that the motion would return to his gills . . . I let go and he was gone. (p. 72)

Buffett's connection to the world through music would seem to be stronger yet. In his memoir, he describes how he likes to visit places where the people treat music as "almost religion" (p. 368), and one of the most striking scenes in the book is his account of visiting Trinidad, where, he says, "music is as much nourishment as food or water" (p. 389). He writes:

> If you are a Christian or a Jew, then Bethlehem is your place. If the steel drum is your baby, then Laventille is the cradle . . . The history of Carnival in Trinidad is full of confrontations with the colonials, who banned the fiesta on numerous occasions. But it still went on in Laventille in open defiance of the oppression of fun. (p. 397)

Buffett is enamored with the steel drum because it is the sound of fun in defiance of authority, of joy in defiance of Death. *Jimmy* brings steel drums along to recreate Mardi Gras wherever he goes—to encourage a Love of Life, not besotted sloth.

Why Don't We Get Drunk . . . in 1973

Buffett never says just what he finds lacking or distasteful in religion, but it is essential to see that a large part of his appeal lies in the fact that he models an alternative vision of meaning and purpose to which many people respond. Buffett's appeal and success center largely on his construction of the persona of *Jimmy*, who we might consider a kind of alter ego to the real Buffett. Speaking of *Jimmy* that way is not meant to be disparaging or disrespectful. Buffett himself speaks of the "myth" of *Jimmy,* and the matter of how that myth meets up with reality is what we're looking at here. *Jimmy* is ideally laid back, and apparently devoted to an easy life of margaritas on the beach with pretty women. The most naive reading of *Jimmy*—the view of him held by lots of casual listeners and a few Parrotheads as well—is that *Jimmy* is perfectly content to be wasted away again in Margaritaville. Now, that's certainly the wrong way to understand Buffett.

In a 1983 interview, Buffett says that while he's glad to have people let loose at his shows, he hopes that "the rest of the week they are providing for their families and working hard" (Eng, p. 191). Buffett himself is a notoriously hard worker who played live concerts well over a hundred nights per year for two decades, and really only slowed down substantially when he redirected his attention to the development of his commercial empire, Margaritaville Holdings. The company oversees a record label, two restaurant chains, a line of merchandise, and soon, a casino. *Jimmy* is the guiding spirit and spokesman for the whole thing, attracting many hundreds of millions of dollars per year in sales to his magnetic image. Buffett, on the other hand, is supposedly a terrific and quite serious business manager with a hand in every pot. So is the persona of *Jimmy* nothing but a put on? No, but it takes a while to explain why not.

To understand *Jimmy* and his allure better, it helps to place him in his historical context. Buffett is a product of his times and, because of his fame, he's now a symbol of them, too. Born Christmas Day, 1947, he's part of the generation defined by Viet Nam and the social upheaval of the 1960s and 1970s that saw any number of iconoclasts more radical than he. Seen against the backdrop of Malcolm X, draft dodgers, Timothy Leary, and Jefferson Airplane's "White Rabbit," Buffett's objection to hypocritical Christians, his preference for margaritas on the beach, and his infamous use of the word "screw"—in the song, "Why Don't We Get Drunk (and Screw)"—look like pretty tame stuff. *Jimmy* became popular at a time when dropping out of the stilted, stifling mainstream for a life a sex and drugs and rock'n'roll was a pretty easy sell.

Part of *Jimmy's* staying power derives from the fact that he has managed to carve out an identity and an ethos in the absence of formal religion or any other source of absolute beliefs, unlike many hippies who faded into the void they created. The social radicals of Buffett's generation did a lot of good: they made ground in the fight for civil rights, environmental responsibility, opposition to unjust wars, social programs for the needy, and more. But they also cut themselves off from the anchors of established values and mores, leaving some feeling not free, but frighteningly adrift. One of Buffett's close friends in Key West was the writer Thomas McGuane, who shared his fondness for heavy drinking, libertine society, and the pirate past of the place. The two would go on to live, travel, and work together for years to come. They have also been related since 1978, when McGuane married Buffett's sister, Laurie.

When they met, McGuane was working on *Ninety-Two in the Shade* (Penguin, 1973), a novel whose plotline mirrors many of Buffett's own stories; the young Thomas Skelton seeks to restart his troubled life in Key West, where he arrives with nothing and soon takes work as a fishing guide. But while Buffett's hero, Tully Mars, follows that plotline to a happy end with a wife, child, and mansion on Key West, Skelton is so profoundly alienated from his own feelings and values that he botches his life and finally walks deliberately and coldly into his own murder. Skelton's demise is rooted in his inability to find his bearings in a social milieu that values little else but freedom and pleasure. In one scene, not only does Skelton find his girlfriend, Miranda, in bed with another man, but must suffer her account of the spectacular orgasm she had. Of course he feels jealous, but worse still is the shame he feels for being jealous. He is ashamed that he cannot live up to the ideal of free love that gripped so many of his generation. After pages of Skelton musing on his anger, jealousy, shame, and self-loathing, the scene comes to a close when he and Miranda express their respective views on how one is to respond to the ultimate pointlessness of life:

SKELTON: It's just that when you realize that everyone dies, you become a terrible kind of purist. There just doesn't seem to be time for this other business.

MIRANDA: But darling that's all there's time for. (p. 22)

The characters say no more and thereafter go their separate ways, presumably because their differing views of how to face the meaninglessness of life are irreconcilable. But notice that these characters swim in the same soup as do Buffett's. In fact, they swim in the same soup as Buffett and McGuane themselves did in 1972. But neither *Jimmy* nor his fictional heroes suffer the doubt and self-loathing of Thomas Skelton. Indeed, Buffett's laid-back, upbeat response to life in a world devoid of absolute values would seem to lie near the heart of his persona and near the heart of Buffett's songs and stories.

Another Page in History, a Stepping Stone for You and Me

To really understand *Jimmy's* place in our culture and our time, however, we need to situate him and his generation in a much broader historical context. To most people who lived through the social revolution that began in the 1960s, it felt radical. Suddenly, men grew their hair long and women cut theirs short, people quit their churches and took up paganism, shacking up and free love supplanted marriage, and so on. The truth, however, is that the 1960s were merely an intense moment in the evolution of Western Civilization away from a religious worldview to a modern, secular worldview. The philosopher Friedrich Nietzsche published his infamous proclamation that "God is dead" in 1882, just before the start of the Twentieth Century. He didn't mean that a superbeing had expired, of course, but rather that modern peoples were in the midst of constructing a worldview and social order in which religion would play a drastically diminished role.

To appreciate his point, we need to consider the radical changes that were mounting in the West for several centuries, and apparently coming to a head in Nietzsche's day: the invention of the printing press in the fifteenth century began a gradual shift of knowledge away from a once uniquely literate clergy, thus preparing the way for secular rivals. Two and a half centuries later, the Age of Enlightenment took hold in earnest, and rationality supplanted Church dictate as the ideal of knowledge. Scientific explanations of natural phenomena proliferated, and by the mid-nineteenth century, even human life seemed rationally explicable. Darwin published his famous theory of evolution, and

Virchow proved that electrical stimulation can move muscles, thereby eliminating the need to posit the mysterious extra-physical energy of *vital force* (roughly, spirit) to explain how bodies are animated. Moreover, the rapid rise and obvious power of industry seemed to prove that science and technology were the right tools by which to master the world. Meanwhile, European monarchs were murdered or neutered by angry masses across Europe and the colonies, thereby undermining the longstanding idea that political and social power are divinely granted and maintained. Religious people today may take umbrage at Nietzsche's heretical ideas, but no honest thinker can deny that the Church and religion simply do not occupy the pre-eminent social positions that they held four or five centuries ago.

In Nietzsche's day, the dominant view of the coming secular age was optimistic, to say the least. Utopians ruled the day. Democracy was expected to give power to the people and let them take control over their own lives. Medicine, which was just beginning to trade shockingly crude and ineffective methods for proven techniques, was expected to help rid the world of disease. Industry was expected to produce goods in such abundance that there would be no want in the world, and workers might expect to have leisure time where machines effectively replaced them in the workplace. And of course, in a world controlled by a populace in want of nothing, there would be no wars. What would anyone fight for?

Such utopian fantasies began to slip away in the early twentieth century when greedy industrialists like Rockefeller and Carnegie—the so-called "robber barons" of America—lived extravagant lives while the working class lived in squalor. Then came the two World Wars, when technology proved man's bitter enemy. In World War II, the horrors of war were graphically and gruesomely on display for everyone in the advanced world via newsreels shown in the movie theaters. Nietzsche's pronouncement of God's death took on new resonance in a world with such obvious and extreme injustice. Many people began to lose faith in what Jean-François Lyotard calls *metanarratives*, or ways of understanding the universe under a single scheme or principle. The world suddenly appeared cold, uncaring, and unprincipled.

By World War II, there were countless signs that people were struggling to understand their place in a universe that seemed devoid of God and purpose. In Europe, existential philosophy gripped the imagination of philosophers and laymen alike. The philosopher, Sartre, rose to the status of a celebrity in Europe based on his seminal explication of existentialism, a philosophy rooted in what it means to live in a world without a God. Sartre explains the slogan of his philosophy—existence precedes essence—this way:

> What do we mean by saying that existence precedes essence? We mean that man first of all exists, encounters himself, surges up in the world—and defines himself afterwards. If man as the existentialist sees him is not definable, it is because to begin with he is nothing. He will not be anything until later, and then he will be what he makes of himself. Thus, there is no human nature, because there is no God to have a conception of it. Man simply is. ("Existentialism Is a Humanism," in *Existentialism from Dostoyevsky to Sartre*, 1989)

In short, we have to define ourselves and determine what the aim of our lives should be, since the universe simply exists, without purpose or values.

In America, the absence of God suddenly showed up in the movies, in the guise of *film noir*. Hard boiled detectives like Phillip Marlowe and Sam Spade led audiences into the underworld of crime and debauchery that lay just beneath the veneer of proper society, but they were unlike the good guy heroes of 1930s films. Marlowe and Spade were morally ambiguous characters themselves, comfortably carousing with shady characters, and sometimes making pretty shady deals. *Noir* heroes sometimes lost, and villains saved themselves through murder, luck, or corrupt dealing. The days of white-hatted good guys and black-hatted bad guys were over. Buffett and his generation might have felt like radicals when they cast off God and church and set about defining the meaning of life in secular terms, but they were part of a much larger historical trend. Most ironically, they were actually following the cynical lead set by their parents' generation, who invented and embraced characters like Marlowe and Spade, along with the dark and godless worldview they represented.

Let the Rat Race Run Roll Around

The great danger for us moderns adrift in a world without purpose or values is that we will become alienated from ourselves and others. The concept of alienation is most closely associated with Karl Marx, who is best known for writing *The Communist Manifesto*.

Marx argues that capitalist economies force workers into jobs that are deeply impersonal, and thus alienating. Factories, for example, are specifically designed to produce exactly the same product again and again, irrespective of the particular workers on hand. Unlike farmers, say, who must invest their expert knowledge and care to maintain healthy crops, or artisans whose products immediately reveal their taste and skill, factory work eliminates the worker's personal investment, and thus threatens to leave her feeling disassociated from her labor and its product.

Of course, a lot of modern work leaves little more room for personal expression: data input, warehouse management, and fast food preparation are obvious examples. Even many high paying jobs held by lawyers, software engineers, and managers are so rigidly structured as to eliminate the personalities of the people who do them. Capitalist culture also encourages people to sacrifice their values to economic prosperity. Students who really love poetry or history might major in accounting because they believe it will help them get a "good" job after college. Unfortunately, if you find accounting classes unrewarding, then accounting jobs are likely to prove no more satisfying. A person can only absorb so many choices that do not reflect her feelings and values before her life will feel like someone else's, that is, before she ends up alienated.

Any number of factors beyond our control can force us to live lives not of our own choosing, and thus they threaten to alienate us. Wars, economic depressions, hurricanes, disabling diseases, the deaths of loved ones, all can quickly redefine what we do and ultimately who we are. We have no control over whether we're born into rich or poor families, whether we're short or tall, and with or without the basic intelligence necessary to prosper in school and in many modern careers. Two college basketball players of equal ability might head down very different paths after they graduate, one into photocopier sales and the other into the NBA, only because one is six feet two inches and the other seven feet tall. One will live his adult life as a salesman who once played college basketball, the other as a privileged celebrity.

Our life narratives are a way of making sense of who we really are, and what our real values are in a world where so many of the facts that define us are beyond our control. A young ROTC student may not fully identify with being a soldier, and telling the story of how she joined the military in order to pay for medical school may help her stay connected with her deeper values during military training or combat. Life narratives also help us make better choices in the future because they remind us of which aspects of our lives we don't really identify with, and which ones we do. Our life stories both define and affirm our place in the world, and keep us connected with our values and feelings.

People who live lives constructed around values that are too shallow or not genuinely their own soon find themselves lost in an alien narrative. On the rural campus where I teach, I sometimes see white kids raised in Appalachian towns and comfortable suburbs mimicking the thug life they see in movies, ads, and music videos. They blast rap music from their SUVs as they drive slowly around campus slumped low in their seats. Surely they're not worried about being shot, but only mimicking people who (supposedly) are. Of course, some of them might go on to carry guns or deal drugs. If they do, how should they tell their life narratives? Are they really thugs, or only mimicking thugs? Where does reality end and fantasy begin in such a case? Part of the appeal of thug life is its supposed gritty reality, one that contrasts sharply with the insipid world of shopping malls and look-alike housing developments. The irony is that media images of gangster life are almost all phony, most of them contrived specifically to appeal to people bored by the numbing artificiality of their own environments. The plight of those who mimic unreal lives is usually a grim one. All too often, they end up living inauthentic lives, alienated from themselves.

Far from being the story of a shallow rake, the myth of *Jimmy* describes someone who manages to be wholly authentic and fulfilled despite living in our modern context. *Jimmy* won't put up with the alienating tedium of work in a factory or office cubicle. He would sooner bum around beaches, smuggle marijuana, work a fishing boat, or busk on street corners. *Jimmy* lives the fulfilling life we moderns crave but seem unable to achieve. Of course, a misguided Parrothead might fall into the trap of merely mimicking *Jimmy*, the way foolish teens mimic music video stars. But that would only be to misread the myth. In his memoir, Buffett tells us that he has new adventures ahead of him, new songlines to follow, but . . .

> I won't put them in this book, because then I might set out on my journey and find you at the end, waiting for me with a margarita and a hundred questions. That's not how it works. Fun is about as good a

habit as there is, especially when your search for it becomes tempered with the wisdom of time on the water. The destination is not that rewarding if you have not had the experience of the journey. My walkabout place cannot be yours. Your walkabout place cannot be somebody else's. You have to find your own. (*A Pirate Looks at Fifty*, p. 359)

For those who understand it, the myth of Jimmy outlines a path of authenticity in our modern world. But anyone who merely mimics Jimmy or wastes away his own life in Margaritaville will have missed the point. To interpret the myth correctly, we need to develop a deeper understanding of the vocabulary in which it is told, and the elements of which it is made.

I Don't Go to Church and I Don't Cut My Hair But I Can Go to the Movies and See It All There

We might say that Buffett and his generation openly embraced the idea of a world without absolute values or purpose, and thereby the project of establishing new values and new social ideals based on new principles. But where were those principles to come from? Both Sartre and Nietzsche essentially throw up their hands and admit that all values are simply chosen by a sheer force of will that cannot be justified.

A century earlier, Mill and other leading philosophers of the Enlightenment were committed to principles supposedly grounded in human nature, and especially in our natural capacities for pleasure and suffering. The good and the right are those things that promote human happiness, they said, the bad and the wrong, those things that promote sorrow and suffering. Buffett comes closer to the latter view, but the fact of the matter is that he sets forth no systematic theory of values. Like most moderns, Buffett simply pieces his view together using various principles that strike him intuitively using the vocabulary of our day. In other words, Buffett conjures an ethos from the ephemeral, fantastical world of pop culture.

The character of Tully Mars is another alter ego to Buffett, someone a lot like *Jimmy*. Mars, who is first introduced in *Tales from Margaritaville* (1989) and who makes a return as the hero of *A Salty Piece of Land*, is a cowboy who leaves Wyoming behind to seek adventure and happiness in the tropics. In a telling passage near the beginning of "Take Another Road," the short story introducing Mars in *Tales from Margaritaville*, Buffett draws Mars's character in revealing terms:

> [The owner of the ranch where Tully worked] Mrs. Barston reminded Tully a lot of Cora Brown, an ex-beauty-shop-operator-turned-cattle-baroness from Schenectady who he'd seen in a movie called *Rancho De Luxe*. The film had been shot fifteen years ago up in Livingston, Montana. Tully had ridden his horse all the way through Yellowstone park up to the film location just to get a look at his hero, Slim Pickens, the man who rode the H-bomb in *Dr. Strangelove.*
>
> Tully wound up working six weeks as a stand-in. The director said he bore a striking resemblance to Jeff Bridges, the star of the movie. He also had his first real affair—with the set designer, a beautiful lady from Maui. She tried to get him to come to California, but Tully knew this was as close to Hollywood as he ever wanted to get. . . .
>
> He hadn't a clue as to where his fascination with the ocean came from. When he was a child, he had practically memorized *Treasure Island* and never missed an episode of "Adventures in Paradise" on the old black-and-white TV—watching Gardner McKay steer the schooner *Tiki* through the South Pacific.
>
> When the movie *Donovan's Reef* came out in 1964, he hitchhiked all the way to Denver, which was the closest place it was showing. For two days he watched John Wayne and Lee Marvin swagger through French Polynesia, fighting, loving, and drinking Tahitian beer from giant brown bottles. (pp. 14–15)

Buffett's use of references to movies and television is striking in both its rapidity and its variety of purpose.

First, we're told that Tully makes sense of his world via references to actors and screen characters: his boss reminds him of the fictional Cora Brown, his hero is an actor, and his fascination with the ocean was fostered by television and movie adventures. Second, notice how Buffett establishes the character of Tully Mars by relating him to movies and television. We see what sort of a man he is via his being star-struck by Slim Pickens and *Donovan's Reef.* Lastly, notice that he places Tully Mars on the set of *Rancho De Luxe*, a film that Buffett scored and in which he had a cameo appearance. One might say that Buffett is doing little more than playfully hiding an Easter egg for Parrotheads to find in his text. Anyone who gets the reference is bound to chuckle. However, it's also fair to say that Buffett is deliberately crisscrossing fantasy and reality. This is a theme to which we will return shortly, but we need to explore the prominence of screen images in Buffett's life and art more thoroughly first.

Buffett's extensive references to pop culture are an honest reflection of how most of us today understand the world and our place in it. We live in an age when it is common for people to recite film and television lines from memory, and friends will often amuse each other by performing entire dialogues from their favorite scenes. So it's perfectly realistic when Buffett has Tully Mars and Archibald Mercer bond over their spontaneous recitation of a scene from *The Man Who Would Be King*. In this aspect, Buffett's fiction is both a product and a reflection of the artificial world we live in, a world in which Hollywood fictions define many of the cultural landmarks by which we orient ourselves in the world, and from which we derive many of the values that we live by.

Tully Mars leaves his home in Wyoming and his career as a cowboy to set himself adrift with little money, no plan, and no friends where he is going. What inspires him to take such a risky leap? It seems he has not got over his childhood fantasies of life at sea that were largely inspired by "Adventures in Paradise" and *Donovan's Reef*. That explanation is shown to be realistic in part by Buffett's own description of how he felt just like Gardner McKay, captain of the *Tiki*, the first time he sailed to St. Bart's.

Buffett's fantasies, his ideal of rugged men adventuring in the tropics with a devil-may-care attitude towards danger and retirement plans, appear to be lifted from movies and other pop culture. Near the beginning of his memoir, Buffett reflects on how he devised a value system when so many moderns seem unable to do so:

> It seems that here in America, in our presumably evolved 'what about me' capitalistic culture, too many of us choose the wrong goals for the wrong reasons. Today spirituality and the search for deeper meaning are as confusing as the DNA evidence in the O.J. Simpson case.
>
> . . . I saw more meaning in the mysteries of the ocean and the planets than in theology or religion. . . . My heroes were not presidents, they were pirates. Emerging from adolescence with a healthy 'lack of respect for authorities', and a head full of romanticism and hero worship, I was able to come up with an answer.
>
> Q. What are you going to do with your life?
> A. Live a pretty interesting one. (p. 8)

So the young Buffett gave up the ideals of the Church for the ideal of an adventuresome pirate.

The catch is that the sort of pirate that Buffett has in mind is obviously the swashbuckling rogue made famous by Errol Flynn and Disney, not the fantastically cruel outlaws who murdered innocent men, women, and children in the Caribbean for pleasure and profit. The lives of real pirates were more closely matched by Tupac Shakur than they are by Buffett. *Jimmy* might like to drink rum and sing merry songs with his mates, but I don't think he's game for cutting off a man's ears or keeping a woman enslaved to serve the crew's sexual pleasure. Buffett's ideal isn't the brutal world of gangsters, but the Island of Lost Boys, a paradise where men never lose their youthful enthusiasm for adventure that was first described in *Peter Pan*, and then later reappropriated by Buffett as a destination for Tully Mars in *A Salty Piece of Land*.

One might object that children always adopt overly simplified visions of their heroes, and that little boys everywhere idolize pirates without understanding what it really means to be one. Those points are valid, but they don't diminish the significance of the fact that many of Buffett's lifelong values, and the reference points by which he assesses his own life, are derived from movies, television, and other pop cultural products: He describes his wife as a cross between Catherine Deneuve and Mr. Spock (p. 14); his favorite planes are the Gulfstream G-IV and the Falcon 50, which he describes as being "as close to the starship *Enterprise* as we can get without going to the Paramount set" (p. 14); his seafaring grandfather was his "Long John Silver" (p. 15); he describes his attitude towards religion as a cross between Joseph Campbell, a real person, and Forest Gump, a loveable dimwit played by the actor Tom Hanks (p. 35). He seems to think about Bogart every time he steps foot on Key Largo, and his interest in the Caribbean island of Martinique was sparked by the film version of *To Have and Have Not* (p. 429).

Buffett is a child of the modern age, and thus his worldview and his art are infused with phrases, images, and ideals absorbed from movies, television, advertising, and other elements of pop culture. His first hit, "Come Monday," was initially given limited airplay in Britain because it contains the lyric, "I put my Hushpuppies on," a reference to a brand-name product. To abide by the BBC's sanction against advertising, Buffett released a version in which he sings, "I put my hiking boots on" (Eng, p. 158). He uses a line from the Brylcreem jingle, "a little dab'll do ya" in his song, "Pencil Thin Mustache." And he uses a slightly altered version of the line again in his memoir when he says that Matouk's hot sauce, "is the real thing, and just a little dab will do ya" (*Pirate*, p. 392). Near the beginning of his memoir, he's discussing the relatively serious matter of how one might approach one's fiftieth birthday, either with feelings of despair and mortality or with joy for having made it so far. "I instinctively chose door number two," Buffett says jokingly, alluding to the old game show, *Let's Make a Deal.*

The crucial insight here is deeply ironic: Buffett's incorporation of commercial slogans and Hollywood fictions into his understanding of the world is perfectly authentic. Pop culture provides all of us moderns many of the values that we guide our lives by, and many of the reference points that we incorporate into our narrative accounts of the world and our place in it. Thousands of people bought a .44 Magnum to feel more like Dirty Harry, and thousands of young people were lured into the military by ads showing soldiers battling dragons. The recent popularity of television programs featuring forensic scientists has prompted a surge in students majoring in the field. Anyone who leaves such pop cultural references out of his personal narrative is almost certainly the phony.

Semi-True Stories

Jimmy is himself a kind of pop icon, of course, and one of the most curious facts about Buffett's art is the way he works that image into his songs and stories. The result is to carry the reader into a fantasy world—Margaritaville, to be precise—that intersects with reality. Tully Mars is aided in his journey by characters named "Clark Gable" and "Captain Kirk." The characters of Margaritaville come and go between songs and stories, vanishing for years at a time only to reappear in a new piece. Frank Bama the hard boiled hero of *Where Is Joe Merchant?* (1992) pilots a plane called "The Hemisphere Dancer," also the name of one of Buffett's planes (p. 8). And in the short story, "Are You Ready for Freddy?" a character named "Buffett" meets up with an older rock star named "Freddy" who leads a band called Freddy and the Fishsticks. Parrotheads will know that "Freddy" is Buffett's pseudonym in real life, and Freddy and the Fishsticks his band. They will also spot that Freddy's biography in the story is actually Buffett's. Here again, the list could be extended a long way.

The story of *Jimmy* is undoubtedly doctored to promote the myth. For starters, Buffett is selective in the biographical details he emphasizes in his public accounts. Consider that his only memoir to date, *A Pirate Looks at Fifty,* centers around a playful excursion to the tropics in his quirky flying boat—not, say, the business dealings behind the Biloxi casino. Going further, certain details of the biography have the whiff of embellishment about them. After his plane crash in a Nantucket harbor, did Buffett really go to the movies and console himself with a Cherry Coke and Junior Mints (*Pirate,* p. 58) or is that just a jokey reference to his 1994 song, "Fruitcakes"?

Buffett's promotion of *Jimmy* is seemingly ceaseless. He describes leaving his tour guide in the Amazon Jungle (the Amazon Jungle!) with T-shirts and CDs to hand out to the locals because he liked "the idea of the myth taking hold in these parts" (p. 385). Buffett is constantly aware of the image that he makes, and seems to script his real life to look like the movies. In his memoir, he describes piloting his flying boat over strangers on a remote Caribbean beach:

> The faces looking back say it all. The best part of this old bird is the role she plays as a kind of prop to Caribbean life. A flying boat in these surroundings just can't help but conjure up dreams and visions of romance and adventure, but like our show on tour, it's more work than one might expect to keep it looking fun. (p. 409)

Buffett works hard to be the man who brings Mardi Gras with him wherever he goes—both on stage and in his private life. The lesson here is not that Buffett is a phony, even if *Jimmy* is a bit of a put on. The truth seems to be that Buffett himself isn't clear where the boundaries between his life and his performance lie. He even recounts a therapist saying to him, "Jimmy, your life is not a performance. Your performance is a part of your life" (p. 61). Still, Buffet's intent doesn't seem to be to hide or deceive, but rather to tell a story that is in some sense more authentic than any simple recounting of the events of his life. He expresses that view in the chorus of his autobiographical song, "Semi-True Stories" (1999):

> It's a semi-true story . . .
> I made up a few things
> And there's some I forgot.
> But the life and the tellin'
> Are both real to me.

If Buffett means that the myth of *Jimmy* contains more profound truths than an accurate biography would, he might be right.

No matter how hard Buffett might strive to live authentically, to put the facts of his life in sync with his real feelings and values, the fact of the matter is that he—like all of us moderns—is thoroughly riddled with romantic Hollywood ideals that simply cannot be put into practice. Buffett sings that he was born two hundred years too late to be a pirate. But the truth is that the myth of the swash-buckling, fun-loving rogue established an ideal in his imagination that could not be lived in any time period. Yet that myth shaped Buffett's worldview and his life nonetheless. Ironically, Buffett might now be better able to represent his earnest attempt to live a life in synch with those impossible values through the myth of *Jimmy* than he could through a literal biography.

The Missionary

It's not such a stretch to say that the myth of *Jimmy* has religious overtones to suit our modern age. It's a story pieced together from the dreams and visions of Hollywood, yet aiming for something deeper. It's the myth of a man striving after a spiritual connection with the world and others in the absence of systematic religion, and told in the vocabulary of pop. It's full of contradictions and at least a few fabrications, but it speaks to our longing for meaning and ful-fillment in an era when both seem all too elusive. If Buffett's first album foretold a life in search of meaning in the absence of formal religion, his latest album, *Take the Weather with You* (2006), con-firms that having fun continues to be his spiritual ideal. The album is mostly covers, but he did co-write "Hula Girl," the tale of a "Guardian Angel" who goes unrecognized, despite the spiritual message she brings:

> With hidden wisdom to impart
> In a world that needs more dancing
> She's a hula girl at heart.

The world needs more dancing, more joy, more days of Mardi Gras. It needs Folly to give Death a swat on the rump. The hula girl—hardly more than a symbol of exotic sexual allure in popular culture—might be a guardian angel pointing the way to a spiritu-ally rewarding life. And Buffett himself might be a kind of prophet who, through the myth of *Jimmy*, helps us see what it means to live authentically in our commercial age. Compromised as he is by his impossible Hollywood values and dreams, *Jimmy* models vitality and spiritual fulfillment in a form and a vocabulary that moderns can understand. His story is an odd one, since it speaks of authenticity in the inauthentic vernacular of pop culture. Still, when all is said and done, the myth of *Jimmy* addresses the spiritual needs of many Parrotheads more deeply than formal religion, and may in fact outline the sort of myth that we need now, here in late modernity.

8

Buffett the Ironic Pirate

ADAM GLOVER

Philosophers don't usually talk about pirates. If they do, it's probably only in the context of a more general discussion of the ethics of theft—or else in their course syllabi. For, as the great English lexicographer Dr. Samuel Johnson (1709–1784) once told us, pirates are basically plagiarists. They take something that isn't theirs and use it as if it were. And that's immoral. Just as theft short-circuits the market by allowing some individuals to benefit illegitimately from the work of others, so plagiarism short-circuits the point of university by allowing students to get academic degrees for something they didn't do.

Many philosophers, then, would tend to agree with Charles Johnson (*A General History of Pyrates*, 1724) that piracy is "the great Mischief and Danger which threatens Kingdoms and Commonwealths," though they might replace "Commonwealths and Kingdoms" with something like "Morality and Academic Integrity." At any rate, it seems that the most you can say philosophically about pirates is that they're bad and that you shouldn't be one.

Jimmy Buffett, on the other hand, talks a lot about pirates. And doesn't just *talk* about them; he seems to *like* them. Buffett once told an interviewer that pirates were his "heroes," and went on to explain that "when everybody else was studying generals and American war heroes, Jean Lafitte was my hero. . . . Everybody else was building battleships, I was building the Black Falcon [Laffite's ship]" (interview with *Literary One*).

My favorite Buffett song, "A Pirate Looks at Forty," makes this theme explicit. That song is framed on either end by an invocation of "Mother, Mother Ocean" and split down the middle by the singer's plaintive confession that he is himself a "pirate," albeit "two hundred years too late." The association of pirates and oceans— terms which, taken separately, are standard fare in Buffett—is as natural as it is problematic. Natural, because the traditional image of piracy is of a Calico Jack (or, more recently, a Jack Sparrow) perched proudly at the helm of an ominous ship rigged with foreboding black sails and a wind-whipped Jolly Roger. But also problematic, because pirates have an uneasy relationship with the ocean on which they seem so obviously at home. For pirates, by all accounts, do not really *belong* on the sea at all. They exist there derivatively, secondarily, parasitically, like a tick that grows fat and satisfied at the expense of its host. This is why honest sea-going merchants hate pirates as much as store owners hate petty thieves. In both cases, the former do hard work while the latter reap easy rewards.

So, both natural and unnatural, both obvious and problematic. As I've already suggested, however, Buffett further complicates this scheme by claiming not only that he is a pirate, but also that he (somehow) arrives "too late" to be a pirate. But how, exactly, does one arrive "too late" to be a pirate? This question becomes even more interesting when we note that part of what it means to be a pirate is *already* to have arrived too late. Pirates plunder others' vessels, search for others' treasure, burn others' CDs. They are never there at the beginning. They arrive after the voyage has begun and make off before it is over. In this sense, Buffett's claim to have "arrived too late to be a pirate" would signal a kind of double belatedness: too late to be an honest merchant *and* too late even to plunder honest merchants for their wares.

Let's take Buffett's song "A Pirate Looks at Forty" as the jumping-off point for an ethical and philosophical meditation on the themes of belatedness and piracy. I have already noted that Buffett links the idea of belatedness to the idea of piracy, and that he represents himself as somehow having arrived "too late" even to be a pirate. But a cluster of questions still linger. How to understand the notion of piracy? What would it mean to be a pirate? What would it mean to be in some sense "too late" for piracy? If Buffett thinks of himself as a belated pirate, how does he suggest that we order our pirate lives? Is there something like a "pirate ethics," a "pirate code"? And, perhaps most importantly for our purposes, how might we give these ideas philosophical content? To get a better angle on these questions I will link the notion of piracy, admittedly not a philosophical topic, with another concept that does have a bit of philosophical currency: intertextuality. The idea of intertextuality allows us to make sense both of the notion of piracy and of Buffett's claim to be in some sense a "post-pirate." It also helps us sort out the ethical implications of the "pirate's life."

"Who's Gonna Steal the Peanut Butter?": Intertextuality, or Taking What's Not Yours

Merriam-Webster Online tells me that, in its most basic sense, intertextuality has to do with the relationship between one text and another (http://www.mw.com/dictionary/intertextuality). The most obvious example, of course, is the citation, in which one text is literally inserted into another text. For instance, when I say, "The chorus of Buffett's 'Peanut Butter Conspiracy' begins, 'Who's gonna steal the peanut butter?'," I am practicing this most basic form of intertextuality, since I have placed a bit of one text (Buffett's) inside another text (mine). For the founder and principal exponent of intertextual theory Julia Kristeva (born in 1941), however, intertextuality is not limited to explicit citation. Instead, as Kristeva tried to show in a series of essays collected (in English) in her 1980 book *Desire in Language* (Columbia University Press, 1980), all language use is in some sense intertextual.

The basic point is that texts (novels, poems, philosophical essays, technical reports, and so on) are not independent, self-contained entities but are instead composed of words and phrases, thoughts and ideas drawn from previous texts. Put differently, any given text, from an intertextualist point of view, is not an original, unified whole, but rather, as Graham Allen (*Intertextuality*, Routledge, 2000) puts it, a "temporary rearrangement of elements with socially pre-existing meanings" (p. 37)—or, in Kristeva's words, an unwitting "mosaic of quotations" (p. 66).

In my experience, the easiest way to understand intertextuality is to think about the Internet.[1] Suppose, for instance, that you go to Wikipedia and search for the entry on, say, Henry Fonda. Now, at

---

[1] See Allen, *Intertextuality*, pp. 199–208 for more on this. Another extremely helpful discussion of the relationship between intertextuality and Internet technology is George P. Landow, *Hypertext: The Convergence of Contemporary Critical Theory and Technology* (Johns Hopkins University Press, 1994). I am deeply indebted to both of these.

first glance, Fonda's biography looks like a unified, self-contained text that begins with the actor's birth and ends with his death. But this is deceiving, since interspersed throughout the entry on Fonda are various *hyperlinks* to other texts: one to an article on *Twelve Angry Men*, another to an article on his daughter Jane, yet another to an entry on the Boy Scouts. And, what's more, all these hyperlinked texts are themselves composed of hyperlinks to other texts which are in turn composed of hyperlinks to yet other texts, which are in turn . . . such that with only three clicks of the mouse, I can get from Fonda's entry to an article on echocardiograms or ancient archeological artifacts. And so, despite appearances, Fonda's Wikipedia biography is manifestly *not* a self-contained text with a single, unified meaning, but rather exists within a potentially infinite intertextual web (pun intended) that has no obvious beginning, no obvious end, and no obvious center.

So that's the basic idea of intertextuality. Of course, much of this may seem either intuitively obvious or downright crazy—and, in either case, of little consequence. But for Kristeva, as well as for later theorists influenced by the idea of intertextuality, the idea that language use amounts to a rearrangement or reweaving of inherited words and ideas has profound philosophical implications.

In the first place, to say with the intertextualist that writing is a reweaving of different meanings rather than the *creation* of meaning is to say that the words I use do not originate with me and hence that I do not have control over them. Consider, by contrast, a traditional, commonsensical model of interpretation according to which the author determines the meaning of her text and the job of the reader is to discern that meaning. From an intertextual perspective, however, such a strategy is wrongheaded. To see why, consider an example. Suppose I'm feeling particularly narcissistic one day and decide to compose a Wikipedia entry on myself. In it I would want to include various facts—that I was born in Glasgow, Kentucky, that I have three siblings, that I play guitar, that I like to read poems, that I listen to Jimmy Buffett, that my favorite philosopher is Thomas Aquinas, and so on.

With a little work, I could produce an article a bit like Fonda's (though with some obvious differences—I, for instance, am *not* the sixth "Greatest Male Star of All Time"). And, at first glance, my entry, like Fonda's, would appear to be a self-contained text with a single, unified theme (something like "Adam's life" or "the essence of Adam"). But, again, this is deceiving, since, just as before, my autobiography will be interlaced with hyperlinks to other texts, which will in turn be hyperlinked to other texts, and so on.

Now this little thought-experiment suggests two things. First, it suggests that, even though I wrote it, I nevertheless cannot control the meaning of my text. This is simply because there is no such thing as "my text," since what *seems* to be my text does not exist as a unified whole, but rather as part of a vast web of other mutually interpenetrating texts. Indeed, the first line alone ("Adam Glover, born 1985, Glasgow, Kentucky") is already chocked full of hyperlinked, intertextual references: from the opening chapters of Genesis and the United Nations' International Youth Year (1985), to Scotland, the Loch Ness monster, and cryptozoology. The point, at any rate, is that while I seem to have "created" my text (and hence seem to have *authority* over it), I simply cannot regulate the way it is constituted by, and intermingles with, a vast array of other texts. It branches off in different directions and so acquires diverse shades of meaning and nuance that I could never have imagined.

But, and perhaps more importantly, the autobiographical exercise suggests not only that the meaning of my text is never stable and unified, but also that my own *identity* is neither stable nor unified. Of course, I believe intuitively that I possess something like a fixed "identity"—that something answers to the "I" of "I am Adam." You probably do too. What I discover by trying to write my Wikipedia autobiography, however, is that this apparently firm "I" is always already constituted by, dispersed among, and hyperlinked to a vast number of other texts. I find, in other words, that every attempt to describe myself, to fix my "self" in language, forces me to use phrases and ideas (e.g., guitar, poem, Thomas Aquinas) with socially pre-existent meanings and thus that the process of "composing my identity" amounts to little more than a reweaving and rearranging of these pre-existing phrases and ideas. If I think about this long enough, I may even begin to doubt the existence of a single, unified "me"; I may come to believe that the "I" of "I am Adam" is, from the beginning, nothing but a diffuse hodgepodge of pre-existing elements, that it shoots off in so many different and contradictory directions that there is no non-tongue-in-cheek way of talking about "who *I* am."

Intertextuality and Piracy, or Another Way of Taking What's Not Yours

By now the relationship between intertextuality and piracy should be reasonably clear. One way of summarizing it would be to say that from the point of view of intertextuality, all writing—all thinking, all believing, all anything—is a kind of piracy, since it involves the parasitic reweaving of already-existing words, thoughts, and ideas. Another way of making the same point is to say that to be a pirate is always to have arrived too late for meaning, to have missed the possibility of seeing things as a steady, unified whole. It's rather to be like me trying to "compose" my identity on Wikipedia only to find that the words and phrases I use are inevitably lifted from other sources, pirated from various cultural discourses, and then stitched back together to fashion Blaise Pascal's "incomprehensible monster" that I, but only with fear and trembling, call my "self" (*Pensées*, Bordas, 1991, p. 163).

Buffett hits explicitly upon this idea in his 1996 song "School Boy's Heart," one of the choruses of which goes:

> Cause I got a school boy heart, a novelist eye
> Stout sailor's legs and a license to fly
> I got a bartender's ear and beachcomber's style
> Piratical nerve and a Vaudevillian style.

It's tempting to read this song, and especially its chorus, as an attempt at self-definition, as a way of saying, "Here, *this* is what *I* am." But such a reading would be thoroughly misleading. This is because insofar as Buffett seems to be saying, "This is who I am," he is also pointing, if only obliquely, to the *impossibility* of ever saying, "This is who I am." And *this* is because the "I" of "I am Jimmy Buffett" is always already entangled in a web of antecedent models—of school boys and novelists, bartenders and beachcombers, sailors and vaudevilles. My "I" is not a stable, unified whole, Buffett seems to suggest, but rather a messy, imprecise, pirated mixture of different themes and ideas. And so if you want to understand me, you must first understand them, for *without* them "I" am nothing; without them, there is no "me."

The song's subsequent metaphors bear out this idea. At one point, for instance, Buffett describes himself as a "Swiss Army Knife" and a "Frankenstein." Both metaphors point to the "self" as an unnatural amalgamation of sources and parts that have no obvious unity and no single identity. Later he portrays the universe as a "cosmic shipwreck" and himself as the product of an "obscene and unscrupulous mind" which "pick[ed] up what he could find, / Added ice, shook me twice, and rolled the dice." Here the notion of a fragmented self gets linked up with the idea of a chaotic, meaningless world. If the Buffettian self is a haphazard jumble of different and contradictory elements, that's only because the universe itself is a kind of dizzying (indeed inebriating) array of shards and fragments that seem to have no coherence and no purpose, like bits of a wrecked ship strewn about on the ocean's surface.

From an intertextualist perspective, Buffett's vision is precisely what we should expect. For, according to that view, our world is indeed a kind of shipwreck, and we ourselves are indeed a bit like pirates who arrive on the scene too late and so must rummage through the debris and hope against hope that the drunken, dice-rolling universe looks favorably upon us. But (and here is the key point) for the intertextualist this goes not only for the self-described pirate—for a Buffett or a Calico Jack. Because, for the intertextualist, it is not only Buffett who is a pirate.

We all are.

But things are even more complicated than that. For Buffett, you will recall, says not only that he's a pirate (which should come as no surprise, since we all are), but also that he is somehow also "too late" to be a pirate. Now, if we follow my suggestion and understand piracy as a metaphor for intertextuality (or, if you like, intertextuality as a metaphor for piracy), then the notion of having arrived "too late" to be a pirate is a perplexing one indeed. This is because for Kristeva and Co., intertextuality is not something that you simply *decide* to do; it's not like consciously inserting a citation (although it includes that as well). Rather, intertextuality is a kind of *condition*, specifically, the condition of having to use a language that you didn't invent and whose meaning you cannot control. So being "post-piracy" (or "post-intertextuality") could only mean being outside of language all together. It could only mean being dead or being God.

Two Kinds of Piracy

To see how we might resolve this dilemma, I want to make a distinction between two kinds of people, whom I shall call "common-sense believers" and "ironic believers."[2] The common-sense believer and the ironic believer will agree about a wide range of things. Both will probably say, for instance, that genocide is bad, that we should be kind to one another, that peace is better than war, that democracy is better than fascism, that Mozart was a better composer than Salieri. Where they will differ, however, is in their attitudes toward these beliefs.

The common-sense believer, on the one hand, holds the beliefs I just mentioned unselfconsciously. She and most of the people around her take them as intuitively obvious, and so almost no one ever thinks to argue for them. Of course, these beliefs may sometimes be challenged. If they are, the common-sense believer may try to back them up with more general principles (such as "Democracy is better than fascism because human beings inherently desire freedom"). If that doesn't work she may seek recourse in something even more grandiose—something like the Word of God, or the deliverances of Reason, or the dictates of the Moral Law. But this usually won't be necessary. Things are "common sense" for a reason. They generally don't get questioned, and so there's generally no need to defend them.

The ironic believer, on the other hand, sees that what counts as common sense for one person may not count as such for another. "Democracy is best!" seems obvious to us inhabitants of rich, North Atlantic democracies, but it did not seem obvious to Caesar or Richard III or Mussolini. The ironic believer is impressed by this fact, just as she is impressed by the fact other people seem as deeply committed to their positions as she is to hers. This sense of astonishment leads her to have serious and ineradicable doubts about the adequacy of her own beliefs. She wonders a lot about whether the way she looks at things is the right way, and she may even begin to doubt whether there is anything like a Right Way of looking at things. And so although she is convinced, for instance, that "democracy is better than fascism" or that "killing people is wrong" she realizes that she has no reliable way of arguing for these positions, no neutral, unbiased language in which to frame her beliefs, no failsafe way of convincing a radical pro-lifer that he should stop murdering abortion doctors

---

[2] In elaborating this distinction I have borrowed from twentieth-century American philosopher Richard Rorty's *Contingency, Irony, and Solidarity* (Cambridge University Press, 1989), pp. 73ff.

or an Islamic fundamentalist that he should abjure jihad against the infidels.

Now to link this up with piracy: the intertextualist claim is that we are all in some sense pirates—that all we ever do is rearrange pre-existing elements into new, more-or-less interesting patterns. But just as there are common-sense believers and ironic believers, so, I want to suggest, there are also common-sense pirates and ironic pirates. On the one hand, the common-sense pirate, like the common-sense believer, goes about pirating (how could she do otherwise?) but is mostly oblivious to this fact. She lifts words, ideas, and beliefs from a variety of different sources (her parents, her church, the books she has read, the people she has met) and then assembles them into new patterns. But—and this is the key point—she, like the common-sense believer, takes her beliefs, thoughts, and ideas as obvious, as unproblematically natural. She sees them as her own, as something over which she has control. And, as a result, she *doesn't realize that she is a pirate.*

The ironic pirate, on the other hand, is obviously a pirate, but unlike the common-sense pirate, she is also aware of herself as a pirate; she *knows* that the only thing she ever does is take pre-existing words and thoughts and ideas and arrange them into new patterns. And so she has no illusions that through this reweaving of inherited (pirated) patterns she might somehow, someday hit upon the Right Pattern or the Right Meaning. She has taken to heart my suggestion that the construction of cultural (and personal) identity always involves an artificial, piratic amalgamation of different, pre-existing thoughts, ideas, and texts. What's more, she sees no way of getting back behind or down below these overlaid, superimposed texts to discover something like the Real Meaning of Life or the Right Way to Live. And so she accepts her lot. Unlike the common-sense pirate, she knows that she's only a pirate, and she knows there's nothing she can do about it.

I take Buffett's claim that he has arrived "too late" to be pirate as a confession of *ironic piracy.* I can perhaps make this point through a brief reading of the last few lines of "A Pirate Looks at Forty."

The first verse begins with an invocation of majestic "Mother Ocean," whose call the singer remembers from childhood. As the song moves along, however, the expansive, meaning-filled vision of the opening line quickly disintegrates into a series of discontinuous narrative fragments that run from smuggling and drug use to extended periods of drunkenness and cohabitation with younger women. The last stanza recapitulates the first, but, in light of the intervening narrative, the tone has changed. Most significantly, the distant echo of Mother Ocean's call has been replaced by Buffett's sober confession that forty years of living have taught him nothing about the Meaning of Life except that the Meaning of Life is nowhere to be found. "I feel like I'm drowned," he concludes, "Gonna head uptown."

Interestingly, the last line admits of a number of variations in live performance. Sometimes Buffett goes uptown to "check out Peachtree Street," sometimes to "get in trouble in old Boston Town," and sometimes just to get drunk. What this suggests, in the first place, is that if "heading uptown" is Buffett's ultimate solution to the problem of the disappearance of Mother Ocean as a source of meaning and purpose, then the question, "Head uptown to do *what?*" has as many potential answers as Buffett wants it to have. Another way of putting this point would be to say that the question, "Head uptown to do *what?*" has no *single* answer, no *correct* answer.

What Buffett seems to be intimating here is that after having given up on the prospect of figuring out *the* Meaning of Life, the appropriate response is not to substitute another Meaning, but rather lots of *different* meanings—lots of *different* possibilities, goals, and destinations. Since life has no single meaning (since the question, "Head uptown to do *what?*" has no single answer), our life opens up to the possibility of multiple meanings. In my view, however, to adopt this attitude is precisely to give oneself over to piracy—and specifically to ironic piracy. For the ironic pirate, like the ironic believer, realizes that there is no such thing as *the* meaning of life. At the same time, however, she knows that she has to go *somewhere*, that she has to do *something*, just as she knows that whatever she happens to do or believe can never be final and definitive.

The ironic believer, then, arrives "too late" to be a believer in the sense that she arrives too late to "just believe"—to hold her beliefs unselfconsciously and unreflectively. In the same way, the ironic pirate indeed arrives "too late" for piracy, not for any chronological reason, but rather because she is unable to engage in piracy unselfconsciously. She arrives too late to "just be" a pirate precisely because she must take a particular stance toward her piracy—a stance of awareness, a recognition that a pirate is all she will ever be. What this suggests, then, is that for Buffett, to have arrived "too late to be a pirate" does not mean to have arrived "too late to be a pirate"; rather, it means, paradoxically, to have arrived too late to be anything *except* a pirate.

How We Still Might Manage a Smile: Being Pirates and Making Meaning

The vision of Buffett's piracy I have presented so far is something of a depressing one. To be a pirate is to have arrived too late to grasp the Meaning of Life, and to be Buffett's kind of pirate (an ironic pirate) is to have abandoned the search for any such Meaning entirely.

But maybe it doesn't have to be so depressing after all. In a 1967 essay ("The Death of the Author," in *Image, Music, Text*, 1977) central to the development of intertextuality theory, Roland Barthes argued that the "death of the Author" must give way to the "birth of the reader" (p. 148). By invoking the "death of the Author" and the "birth of the reader," Barthes is making two points, one negative and one positive. The negative point is a variation of the (by now) familiar intertextualist claim that the author of a text has little or no control over the meaning of that text, over how her text will be construed by future generations of readers. The positive point is that, unchained from the shackles of the Author, we Readers are now free to construe the text any way we please. No longer haunted by the specter of Meaning, we may impose lots of other meanings.

We might enlarge upon this point by saying that, released from the constraints of Meaning or Purpose, we pirates may construe our lives in a variety of different ways. The pirate's life, then, is fundamentally a life of *freedom*: the freedom to make our own rules, to do exactly what we want. But the pirate's freedom is also a hard freedom. Just as it is the freedom to know that you can do anything you want, it is also the freedom to know that you can *never* know whether what you're doing is what you *should* be doing. And, perhaps most importantly, it is the freedom to recognize that, however we choose to live, it is we—and only we—who will be responsible for our choices.

It was just this sense of the unbearable weightiness of freedom that led French philosopher Albert Camus to declare, "There is only one truly serious philosophical problem, and that is suicide" (*The*

Myth of Sisyphus and Other Essays, Knopf, 1961, p. 3). In other words, if life *really* has no point, if there's really no reason we are here, then perhaps the best thing to do is to kill yourself. Of course, Camus eventually concluded that this was in fact *not* the best thing to do. But he, like the other existentialists, still took it as a genuine possibility.

I suspect that Buffett would not take it as a genuine possibility. In his travel diary-autobiography *A Pirate Looks at Fifty* (Random House, 1999), Buffett remarked that turning fifty "can be a ball of snakes that conjures up immediate thoughts of mortality and accountability. ('What have I done with my life?') Or, it can be a great excuse to reward yourself for just getting there. ('He who dies with the most toys wins.') I instinctively chose door number two" (p. 9).

Now, this is not exactly the vision of the Greek philosopher Socrates, who famously claimed that "the unexamined life is not worth living," and it probably strikes most of you as crudely hedonistic. But I think there is a more charitable way of taking it.

Instead of reading Buffett's "excuse to reward yourself for just getting there" as an expression of unreflective materialism, we might rather construe it as a recommendation to celebrate life as it is, to rejoice instinctively in the beauty of existence without worrying too much about whether we've "gotten things right," about whether our lives square up with the Meaning of the Universe.

This second interpretation chimes nicely with one of the points of German philosopher Friedrich Nietzsche's book *The Birth of Tragedy* (1872). There Nietzsche argued, among other things, that Socrates killed the joyous, affirmative spirit of Greek tragedy by convincing us that the point of being human was to reflect rationally on life rather than to *live* it. If we read Buffett as a kind of latter-day Nietzschean, then we can see him as saying that the meaning of life is life itself, and that there is no reason to look for anything else. We can see him as saying that if he *had* "pondered the question too long," he would have missed something much more important.

To take this line would be to say that whatever meaning life has is meaning we have put there. It would be to say that we have no access to anything bigger than us and that life is what we make of it. This sense that we don't have access to anything bigger than us also suggests that pirate living will be characterized by a certain degree of intellectual humility. In other words, if we can't point to a sacred text or to the dictates of Reason, then we must always be open to conversation with other people about what kinds of things are valuable, about what kind of life is worth living.

Now I, for one, think there is some grandeur in this vision. It is not, of course, the grandeur of the religious believer who thinks that if she can just discern the will of God everything else will fall into place. But it is perhaps the grandeur of the American poet Wallace Stevens, who wrote:

> It was when I said, "There is no such thing as truth,"
> That the grapes seemed fatter.
> The fox ran out of his hole. ("On the Road Home")

Stevens's point is that it is only when we declare, "There is no Truth!" that life appears in its most dramatic relief, acquires its deepest dimension of splendor. It is only *then* that the roses shine in all their majesty, that we taste the grapes in all their sweetness. I think this is Buffett's view. I think he would say that the question, "What is the meaning of life?" is as silly as the question, "What is the meaning of *Hamlet*?" And I think he would say that *even if* we agree that these questions are silly, we can still find joy in our *own* pirate lives, just as we can find joy in the lives of our children, our families, and our friends. And maybe, at the end of it all, we, like Buffett, "can still manage a smile"—a wry, ironic smile, but a smile nonetheless.

And yet! And yet I do not see how to escape Camus's worry. I do not see how to brush aside the possibility that, in the face of meaninglessness, the only option is to conclude that life really isn't worth living. And so the question, for me as well as for you, is this: which way to go? Does being a pirate mean wallowing in complete meaninglessness (or worse)? Or does it mean siding with joyous, affirmative Nietzsche and saying that the point of life is life itself, without subtraction, exception, or selection? (*The Will to Power*, Random House, 1967, p. 104)

Unfortunately, I do not see how to answer this question. I do not see how to answer because it seems to me that if we are too late even for piracy, then we are probably also too late to know with anything approaching certainty how properly to order our post-pirate lives. This is not to say, of course, that the question has no answer. Maybe it does. But how could we ever know? And who could ever tell us?

Buffett has made his choice. But should we follow him?

9

An Altar Boy Covers
His Ass

MATTHEW CALEB FLAMM and
JENNIFER A. REA

The rumors and the stories of my past I can't deny
I'm no Saint Ignatius but again I'm no barfly.
The wrong thing is the right thing until you lose control
I've got this bank of bad habits in a corner of my soul.

—"Bank of Bad Habits"

Remember in grade-school? That annoying friend who always exposed people's moral imperfections to the teacher and enjoyed it a little *too* much?

Up to a point, of course, he was right. While our tattling friend looked on in smug satisfaction, the teacher was forced to say we were probably not exercising the best judgment when we inserted flirtatious limericks in the new student's reader. We should have been listening to the lecture. The teacher explained that our disregard not only for class rules, but for the codes of conduct worthy of those considered to have moral character, was *unconscionable*. Still—whatever "unconscionable" meant—it *was* fun, and easily more interesting than the lecture.

"Sister Mary Mojo" was Jimmy Buffett's proverbial schoolteacher. He tells us in "That's My Story and I'm Stickin' to It" that he couldn't trick her, so when he gave his dog-eating-homework excuses he did so without apology, inviting her to accept him for the game-player he was. Caught in the act, he willingly tells tales to others, but they "love him anyway." (Or so he rationalizes.) While this may not be a model for morality it clues listeners in to the psychology that grounds Buffett's many observations concerning moral responsibility outside of the confines of *religious* moral law.

Although Buffett makes mostly mocking references to his youthful stint at St. Ignatius Catholic School, and later at the McGill Institute for Boys, the experiences at those places were obviously crucial for his later outlook and attitude. They may have given Buffett his first big musical break. "The Christian," a song opening his debut album *Down to Earth* (1970), caught the ear of Catholic convert Mike Shepherd, then manager of Barnaby Records. "It's a hell of a time to be thinking about heaven," Buffett croons in country twang, "you been acting like Jesus owes you a favor, but he's a little smart for you to fool." Chiding those spurred to belief only after they start feeling the pangs of mortality, "you pray a little more as you grow older, you get religion as your hair turns grey," this lyrical send-up of insincere Christians is a major preoccupation of Buffett's music and writings.

Why Moralists Hate Fruitcakes

Buffett agrees with Friedrich Nietzsche's memorable charge that "there was only one Christian, and he died on the cross" (*The Antichrist*, #39). Our Nietzsche in Bermuda shorts offers criticisms of Christianity that go deeper than simple disgust at the hypocrisies of moralists and preachers. To Buffett, as to Nietzsche, those many thousands of the allegedly religious who ignore the example of their own prophets are really only a symptom of a larger problem. Buffett understands this problem to be that of the inability of humans to accept themselves for who they are in their deepest, most basic inclinations and loyalties. Why are so many humans uncomfortable in their own skin?

To begin with, as Buffett suggests in 1994's "Fruitcakes," the cosmic bakers (whoever they are) seem to have taken humans out of the oven too early. The song explains with tongue only half lodged in cheek that the unfinished, half-baked nature of humans accounts for their mad behavior. The key to life is to embrace, rather than resist, this natural-born madness. The problem is that too many "bakers" (read: moralists) concoct recipes to cure humans of their undercooked madness, when what the world really needs is more fruitcakes. Buffett tells us that "we need more fruitcakes in this world and less bakers! We need people that care." For Buffett the people who care are "strutting naked towards eternity." This mad behavior is desirable, affirmative in its ability to offer individuals something more than a stale existence, cooling with gooey insides on a baking rack.

Fruitcakes: you know, the naked roller-skaters, raving prophets, artists, and freethinkers who dare, whether through constructive action or counter-cultural protest, to care about things. The unthinking, fear-driven bakers who deny or try to overcome their uncooked nature are the first to deride and censor fruitcakes. The best way to do so? Through moralism. Everyone knows that reputation is the better (for some the best) part of moral character. Our proverbial and clever baker-moralist wants to peg you and me with a bad reputation. "Give a dog a bad name and hang him," the centuries-old saying goes.

At the risk of being reckless in characterizing this Buffettian insight (that is, at the risk of following the example of our subject), we suggest that his critique of moralism is in a key sense, quintessentially Catholic. Catholic doctrine, to say nothing at all of Catholic practice, has long emphasized the need to distinguish *those who preach* morality from *those who are* moral; moralism, from this point of view, consists in the failure to make this distinction in some crucial respect. Such moralism is exposed in outward exhortations for behavioral change without indication of the means to effect such change. You've seen these moralistic phonies. The Robert Tiltons and Jim Bakkers, the ones Buffett affectionately calls the "crazy-ass people, television preachers with bad hair and dimples."

Mark P. Shea, senior editor for *Catholic Exchange* (www. Catholicexchange.com) and frequent columnist for InsideCatholic. com, articulates very nicely the Catholic perspective on moralism: "Some of history's greatest moralists have been monsters [Osama Bin Laden, Cromwell, Hitler] . . . it is . . . because they are in the business of shouting down their screaming consciences that deeply evil people can be profoundly moralistic." Monstrous moralists are thankfully rare, but their example aids one in understanding the character of all moralists, such as those inhabiting the much larger category of semi-monstrous or, like our televangelists, just-plain-irritating.

Shea goes on to explain that the zeal with which moralists endorse their views comes from the fact that they are aware of the immoral *means* by which they intend to achieve their targeted moral *ends*. So take a less than monstrous moralist, a tattling fellow student for example, and you will always be able to find a contradiction between the "good end" they seek (restoration of morality in the classroom), and the "bad means" by which they pursue that end (tattling).

To detect a Catholic "sense" for moralism in Buffett's music is one thing, to call the self-identified pagan a "Catholic," to say nothing of *religious*, is another. Buffett's songs expose the world's many misguided forms of madness that result from moralistic zeal, and so far, they share with Catholic and non-religious critics alike a concern for cultural arrogance, for the idea that *this* form of existence is the best there is or has been. But Buffett offers an explanation for the cause of this cultural delusion that parts with religious critique, Catholic or otherwise. As he psychoanalyzes in the speaking sections of "Fruitcakes," unthinking social conventions result from letting others think for us, pre-eminently others coming from governmental, religious, or personal positions of authority.

One Particular Baker

Eminent Catholic intellectuals from the early twentieth century like G.K. Chesterton (1874–1936) and Hilaire Belloc (1870–1953) also displayed a bombastic sense for the essential madness of modern life, and could easily spot phony milquetoast believers. Yet, unlike Buffett, their talents in this regard only reinforced their religiosity. In *Orthodoxy* (1908), Chesterton characterized his "revolt into orthodoxy" in terms that might well describe Buffett's own revolt into heterodoxy. Modern humans, Chesterton argued, need to commit themselves to a belief system that is a "practical romance, the combination of something that is strange with something that is secure." The religious orthodoxy Chesterton espoused importantly combines "an idea of wonder" with "an idea of welcome," (*Orthodoxy*, p. 2) suggesting the need for a world oscillating continually between the surprise and upset of settled belief (wonder) and confirmation (welcome) of the same.

The very same world-wise, practical romance is endorsed in Buffett's "One Particular Harbor." Reaching out in a time of inner turmoil, the song's protagonist gropes in imaginative contemplation towards a vision of things encompassing all that he has experienced, and known. That one *particular* harbor is metaphorically apt in its representing a kind of eternal return, a point of returning from all other places of returning. This cosmic harbor, "so far but yet so near" (both strange and secure), is where one sees the end, and it's okay. Everything's okay from the standpoint of the eternal harbor because one is humbled by one's cosmic littleness, and is able to place oneself in the scheme of a vast natural world. The Tahitian lines in the song's climax, delivered with gospel force by the all female "Chorale Epherona," translate loosely as: "Nature Lives (Life to Nature), Have pity for the Earth (Love the Earth)." A wonder of nature is combined here with solicitations of welcome and sympathy to that which is familiar and earthly, to that to which humans are fated even as they glimpse the cosmic beyond. Buffett's one particular harbor is the symbolic expression of that simultaneously wondrous and welcoming vision.

What convinced Chesterton of the necessity of religion inspired Buffett, with equal force, to naturalistic neo-paganism. How does it come about that the very same Catholic-rooted longing for cosmic romance produces such opposite commitments? Benedict Spinoza (1632–1677), a modern philosopher whose naturalistic perspective is amenable to Buffett's, invokes a phrase that helps explain the paradox. The phrase in Latin, "sub specie aeternitatis," translates to mean "under the aspect of eternity (timelessness)." Spinoza meant to convey the sense in which one sees things in their *necessary* rather than in their changing or *contingent* relation. While Spinoza saw this necessary relation of things as identical with the nature of God, his God was not at all the God of Abraham. Rather, Spinoza identified God with nature, earning himself the heretical label "pantheist." And here we find a real point of connection, because Spinoza, raised in an orthodox Dutch-Jewish community, was excommunicated in 1756 for his unorthodox opinions.

Both Chesterton and Buffett long for a vision of things from the Spinozistic standpoint, where all things are under the aspect of eternity, they simply differ in the nature of the object from which such timelessness flows. The God of Catholicism, Chesterton's preferred eternal object, is translated by Buffett, much as Spinoza translated the Judeo-Christian God, into naturalistic terms. And Buffett has more to say in support of the naturalistic point of view that anticipates its rejection by religious critics.

Let's return again to the bakers and fruitcakes. To whom does it occur as odd, unjust, or unthinking to restrict movie-snack choices to exorbitantly over-priced and sized items? To the fruitcakes of course. The rest fall back as cattle and trust to convention that such ways of arranging things are, after all, for the best. Our baker-moralist exploits those with cowed, passive responses, and his stock in trade is acceptable, conventional behavior. The result?

"I'll take the twelve pound Nestlé's Crunch for twenty-five dollars please."

Movie fare is of course a mundane example for Buffett to high-light, but one suggesting much food for thought, in particular with regard to religious behaviors and loyalties. And let's be frank, in the West the consumer world frequently sets the bar for moral behavior, a fact once lamented by religious authorities, but one more and more used by them to their great advantage to court followers. Buffett finds this situation absurd, and his frequent use of irony to express his ire is just the tonic needed to reach the mass of cattle he wants to sting into alertness. His keen sense for the intersections of morality and consumerism prepare the way for a deeper under-standing of the ironic complicity of religious authority and cultural convention. Examples in the consumer world abound that attest to the mad arrangement of human affairs and relations that is attributable, Buffett helps us realize, to the bakers: the moralists bent on keeping humans from accepting their incomplete natures.

So opposing the moralist is just an entry-point for Buffett, one that opens to the opposite danger of moralizing a new kind of *im*morality, something he is equally interested in avoiding. It's not bakers as such that Buffett opposes. After all, everyone's a baker to the extent that she wants the world to be better than it is. It's that one *particular* baker who makes the world *worse* than it is who deserves Buffett's boiling criticisms. And lord knows there're a lot of religious bakers, trained in diverse culinary settings.

The Dread Pirate Benedict de Buffett

There's more Spinoza in Buffett yet. Our singing Catholic rebel embodies, in both his life and music, Spinoza's spiritual quest as famously set out in his autobiographical opening to *Treatise on the Emendation of the Intellect* (in *A Spinoza Reader*, Princeton University Press, 1994, pp. 3–6). This was written sometime soon after his excommunication, when Spinoza had moved a few miles from Amsterdam and taken up the modest career of lens-grinder.

Spinoza explains the bold break from his orthodox beginnings. He begins to wonder, as we can imagine Buffett at the close of his Catholic school days doing, why all things in ordinary life appear empty and futile. More particularly he laments the shortcomings of living a life consisting only of the acquisition of three perceived "goods": wealth, honor, and pleasure. Spinoza vows to seek the greatest happiness, assuming it to be capable of attainment, and assuming it to be achievable only after the goods just listed cease to be sought for their own sake—cease to be falsely considered the "highest goods."

Without worrying about repercussions, Spinoza makes his greatest observation, one that is important to understanding how Buffett "broke out of the grip of Catholicism," and sailed down a naturalist rather than a religious path (*A Pirate Looks at Fifty*, p. 5). Spinoza comes to the realization that most humans are "so distracted" by the three illusory goods of wealth, honor, and pleasure, that they "cannot give the slightest thought to any other good" (p. 3). In Spinoza's estimation men are bogged down, mired in the narrow ponds of pursuit of wealth, honor and sensual pleasure. Spinoza's idea, and here's where Buffett's example is helpful, is to strike out beyond these obstacles, and to follow the small streams and tributaries of the mind into the open sea.

This is of course a paradoxical take. Buffett, a sage-like disavower of fleshly pleasures? Can we seriously find a parallel between the life of our rebel-pirate and the cloistered Spinoza? Actually, yes, on two fronts: first, there's the fact that many listeners of Buffett's music mistake the protagonists and characters as autobiography. Many of Buffett's songs are based on his own biography, but one must be cautious as to what parts of the songs are Buffett's own life experience and which parts are simply the artist trying to make sense of the world around him.

A good example of this is "A Pirate Looks at Forty," a song Buffett explains (on the *Feeding Frenzy* album and elsewhere) was written in sympathy for an "old friend" of his who, unable to find an "occupation" in the twentieth century, chose to live in a "fantasy world." Sympathy aside (pity is a more apt description given the melancholy nature of the song and its character), these characterizations are hardly celebratory or envious. In "Pirate" Buffett is neither celebrating a rebel life, nor romanticizing its loss, but rather calling into question, as Spinoza did, the lives of his orthodox contemporaries, the holding on to a wished-for ideal to the detriment of one's living vivacity and vitality.

Second, we can establish the Spinozism of Buffett's perspective if we reinforce the themes already discussed in the foregoing sections. Traditional religion, we have observed, tends to foster baker-moralists, bent on providing recipes for overcoming the undercooked nature of humans. They protest against human sins of course, the very behaviors Buffett lustily seems to celebrate, but they protest too much. Sinful objects and their choices, helpfully filed by Spinoza under general "goods," are not in themselves bad. For Spinoza, nature, we have said, is God, and further (here's where he *really* offended his religious community), that nature neither favors nor disfavors humans. What this means is that *nothing* in the created world was "meant to be." Least of all, humans!

Now this is really offensive stuff for any orthodox believer. Humans not special? Not favored? That's the very delusion that has so vexed Buffett and, two hundred years before him, vexed Spinoza (was he a pirate?). For Buffett and Spinoza orthodox religion embodies, and even encourages, confining one's intellect to false forms of happiness and the only sure way out of such confinement is a greater acknowledgement of one's natural situation.

Buffett's biography and discography are litanies of desire for wealth, honor, and most importantly, sensual pleasure (drugs, alcohol, and sex). But they are explorations in these "goods" for the sake of greater understanding. He, like Spinoza, and any red-blooded mammal for that matter, is swayed by these three categories of desire, not because he's a sinner but because he is human and a product of nature and a culture that fumblingly exploits its goods. Apparently humans have, at least since the seventeenth century, been pretty good at confusing supreme happiness with final acquisition of these general, natural goods. Buffett follows Spinoza in holding traditional religion accountable.

Yet, while Spinoza ground lenses (causing his untimely death at the age of forty-four) in sage-like, albeit productive retirement, Buffett has always returned to the open sea. Ah the sea: a great outlet for the cosmic longing so present in Buffett's music. The strict Catholic upbringing did nothing to settle the feeling that there was something better beyond these worldly pursuits. Buffett hauntingly sings in "A Salty Piece of Land" that he was "force fed my religion, But I somehow saved my smile, tapped into my instincts, as I headed towards exile," and he "took off for the ocean." Buffett reflects that the attraction of the "salty piece of land" is mysterious, yet he cannot stop himself from looking towards the sea, not "for salvation," but for a conduit towards something greater than the worldly (land) pursuits.

Once again, we're reminded here of our excommunicated philosopher-naturalist. Spinoza, too, "could not . . . put aside all greed, desire for sensual pleasure, and love of esteem, . . . however . . . so long as the mind was turned toward these thoughts, it was turned away from those things, and was thinking seriously about the new goal. That was a great comfort to me" (p. 5). The acquisition of wealth, honor and sensual pleasure "are only obstacles so long as they are sought for their own sakes, and not as a means to other things. But if they are sought as means, then they will have a limit, and will not be obstacles at all" (p. 5).

The end that Buffett seeks, then, is not the one that many cavorting Parrotheads think he desires. His wealth acquired from the concerts and sales of his records, his pride at being Jimmy Buffett, and his frequent lapses into sensual pleasure are simply a *means* for the man, not the end result and certainly not where his happiness lies.

On one level this persona is the antithesis of the conformity foisted upon him by his strict Catholic background, and yet it's also Buffett's way of seeking something beyond the three narrow pursuits of most humans, and of pursuing that which offers the greatest happiness. He's not simply a naughty schoolboy rebelling against the orthodoxy imposed by domineering nuns in Alabama. Buffett is on his own Spinoza-like quest for the greatest good and happiness. Whether or not he has found it is irrelevant. The important thing is the quest—the quest beyond the immediate satiation of wealth, honor, and sensual pleasure, to something deeper and more meaningful. Beyond *here* lies that one particular harbor.

Three-Finger Rule? Depends Which Is the Fourth

These thoughts bring to mind a moral rule one of the present author's parents used to recite. Know it? Some call it the "three-finger rule." By some genius arrangement of digits it occurs that when we point to others in moral judgment we humans can't help finding three fingers pointing back at ourselves. This is a rule that our annoying tattler in Bible-study would have done well to acknowledge.

We know how Jimmy Buffett approaches the three-finger rule. Like Falstaff in Shakespeare's plays, he chooses a different digit, and it's not the one used to make moral judgments (well, unless "Fuck you!" is a moral judgment). Wearing the ironic smile we enthusiasts must wear here, we might draw a further parallel between Shakespeare and Buffett. (Buffett would of course share the ironic smile.) Shakespeare, thought by a great many authorities to be one of the most irreligious of modern writers, was also peeved at phony moralists. A pre-eminent example of our baker-moralist can be found in *Twelfth Night*, with the character Malvolio, a fancy-socked, finger-wagging steward of a rich countess named Olivia. Malvolio plays foil to "Sir Toby Belch," the flatulent Falstaff-like rabble-rousing uncle of Olivia.

The Falstaffs and Tobys in Shakespeare's writings are of course the first and best examples in modern literature of the Jimmy Buffett ethic. As readers we sympathize with their misbehaving wit and whimsy, which always occur at the much-needed expense of moralists like Malvolio. In a brilliant scene in *Twelfth Night*, Malvolio has discovered Toby amidst his friends raising hell in the style of our Parrotheads, and warns: "If you can separate yourself and your misdemeanors, you are welcome to the house; if not, and it would please you to take leave of her, she is willing to bid you farewell." Olivia's stuffy steward's hair bristles at the caterwauling of Sir Toby and his friends. Malvolio despises all manner of fun and maintains a self-righteous belief that he is devoid of human sin.

Yet Shakespeare, via Toby, has the last laugh when a twist of plot creates in Malvolio a false belief that his boss Olivia has fallen in love with him. The Buffett-like Sir Toby instantly recognizes the Puritanical moralist in Malvolio and retorts "Art thou more than a steward? Dost thou think, because thou art virtuous, there shall be no cakes and ale?" Of course, this dig puts the moralist Malvolio in his well deserved place among those who believe that, simply because they abstain, they are virtuous. The blind eye they turn to human pleasures, to feasting and celebrating things of the flesh, is disingenuous. We see it as such in Toby's reprimand of Malvolio.

There is a further parallel involving this shared theme; that is, affirming one's natural madness in order to oppose moralism. It's no accident that Shakespeare and Buffett associate their critiques of moralism with the celebratory use of drugs and drink. The madness wrought by intoxicants is characterized by Nietzsche as "Dionysian," a kind of *blissful ecstasy welling up from the inner-most depths of man*. Dionysian ecstasy, Nietzsche suggested, is one side of a dynamic found in all human experience (the other is "Apollonian" reason), depicted in Ancient Greek tragedy and pre-eminently found in musical expression. The unstable, boundary-less, ecstatic, impulsive tendencies of humans are of course well accommodated by the use of chemical substances, and Buffett was fond of this Dionysian trait.

He associates such ecstatic celebration with religion in "God's Own Drunk," the hilarious tale of an intoxicated enthusiast transcendently inspired to stand up to a grizzly bear. The protagonist experiences in his intoxication a kind of universal love (one sign of what Nietzsche tells us is a mark of the Dionysian), and profound fearlessness; he achieves an inebriated plateau beyond the "knee crawlin'," "commode huggin'" drunk, and becomes: "God's own drunk." Of course he becomes God's own drunk just in time to encounter the bear, a big "Kodiak-lookin' fella" whom he verbally accosts, then placates by sharing the "honeydew vine water" responsible for his ecstasy.

Buffett's fondness for drunken wisdom, and for its use in putting moralists in their place reflects his insight that the virtue and vice symbolized in a Malvolio and a Sir Toby are two aspects of the same split personality existing within us all. This insight is most prominent in Buffett's many tributes to the "little" indulgences of life. Take a juicy burger with onion and tomato, Heinz fifty-seven and a pile of French fried potatoes and you have a mouthwatering description of virtue and vice on a sesame seed bun. With a cry of "Good God Almighty which way do I steer?" Buffett's catchy "Cheeseburger in Paradise" offers a small prayer to a higher power to show him the way to the ultimate sensual experience juicily combining virtue and vice. What more delicious way to capture the human condition?

"Cheeseburger" begins with a Christ-like sacrifice, and from the description this is as close to the ultimate sacrifice that Buffett can get: "tried to mend my carnivorous habits, Made it nearly seventy days, Losin' weight without speed, eatin'sunflower seeds, drinkin' lots of carrot juice and soaking up rays." After such brave abstentions the human carnival of desire enters Buffett's dreams and he begins to lust after "some kind of sensuous treat." Clearly, Buffett's paradise is not the Biblical Garden of Eden with righteous zucchini fettuccini and bulgar wheat, but one that also contains juicy hunks of pickle topped meat.

The virtue of healthy vegetables and green zucchini pasta is contrasted with the vice of humanly sinful quantities of decadent meat. Mmmmmmm! Buffett has given us Malvolio and Sir Toby on a sesame seed bun. What Buffett seeks is satisfaction of his carnal desire through the orgasmic relationship he has with the ultimate cheeseburger. He desires passion. For the Catholic schoolboy who has spent his adult life breaking the chains of his religious background, this cheeseburger is as powerful a middle finger for him as is Sir Toby's admonition to Malviolo.

An Altar Boy's Public Penance

So how does a former Catholic altar boy cover his ass? He spends his life doing penance. Jimmy Buffett's music is filled with Dionysian pleasures, with bawdy, raucous celebrations of debauchery. The sometimes flamboyant hedonism in many of his songs is nevertheless tempered by anthems of profound and melancholy love ("Come Monday," "Miss You So Badly"), and naturalistic affirmations of cosmic peace paralleling religious hymns ("I Have Found Me a Home," "One Particular Harbor"). Buffett pauses amidst his humorous indulgences to reflect on the grandeur and beauty of life, and it is most evident at such times that his audience has taken the place of his Priest. His message is ultimately confessional: he's asking his audience for absolution.

The Catholic Church's seven sacraments (baptism, confirmation, Eucharist, penance and reconciliation, anointing of the sick, holy orders, and matrimony) are seen as the necessary means of salvation for the faithful. Buffett's art takes on the role of the public confession in the act of penance, and while the formal act of openly confessing one's sins has become a private matter between priest and penitent, his music allows it a communal voice. The 1996 album *Banana Wind* contains one of Buffett's more confessional songs. He comes clean about his perception of himself as a "cultural infidel." The song craftily describes the characteristics of this manufactured persona: "I'm a cultural infidel, tryin' to draw a crowd, I'm a cultural infidel, singin' right out loud." The cultural infidel is a "free thinkin', hood-winkin', unblinkin' mon" who's a loose cannon among the preachers who monitor the behavior of the boys and girls on the dance floor.

Buffett's horror of people whose phony moral ideals straight-jacket their daily behavior is front and center here, and he fancies himself the true savior, because, of course "someone's got to talk about accountability, someone's got to raise some hell, it might as well be me." He places himself alongside "Al diablo Picasso, al diablo Manet, . . . al diablo Hemingway," the devils who "start trouble, burst-bubbles." The final lines of the song express Buffett's agnosticism: "Will I see you in Heaven? Will I see you in Hell? Will I see you tomorrow? Only time will tell."

Buffett visits the musical confessional. He clamors about his love of drinking, admits that he likes the odd pretty girl, sometimes just wants to "get drunk and screw," and unabashedly touts his desire for the life of the pirate: hardly the life of a saint. At the heart of his music is the penitent Buffett, confessing to the world sins for which he feels there is no need of cosmic apology, but for which he sometimes needs to perform an act of contrition. "Sins," Buffett once again helps us see, are really good old human quirks writ in moral code; behaviors that religions, especially Christianity, have marked in shame.

The question is, forgiveness from whom? Buffett is not asking absolution from a higher power via a Catholic priest, but if he needs any at all it is from the fallible humans who occupy space in his world. It is to his too-human Parrothead *audience* that Buffett is looking for some sort of absolution or solution. Buffett appeals to his audience, "and I don't know what I'm supposed to do, Maybe have me a boat drink or two . . . I've got some coastal confessions to make, How about you, how about you?" His desire to include his fan base in his confession is all a part of how Buffett reconciles himself to his Catholic background, and makes peace with the strict doctrinal chains that framed his youth through the public act of penance.

Buffett's music wears its heart on its sleeve. "Coastal Confessions" reflects a man trying to come clean with who he is: "so let's talk about the future, or the consequences of my past, I've got scars, I've got lines, I'm not hard to define, just an altar boy coverin' his ass." This altar boy eagerly confesses his sins to the world, and in the process leaves himself open. Open for what? Could be absolution. Could be eternity in Dante's second circle of hell where the lustful are tossed and turned as on the sea by a violent storm without hope of rest. One thing's for sure, the altar boy turned pirate has met many similar fates in his expansive life, travels, and art.

The Parrothead phenomenon has given to Buffett thousands of devoted fans. The members form clubs where they wear Hawaiian shirts and flip-flops and drink margaritas in homage to Buffett's confessional songs. His concerts have the feel of a Parrothead pilgrimage to see a holy man, and the holy man is nothing more than a mere penitent who confesses his sins through his music to create kinship with the other sinners of the world.

Buffett and his audience have a symbiotic relationship where each saves the other. And since we're all sinners, we have an affinity and understanding for this man in a Hawaiian shirt and Bermuda shorts.

Smart Women and Fruitcakes

10
A Feminist Looks at Jimmy Buffett

ERIN McKENNA

I am often asked how I, a feminist and a vegetarian, can like Jimmy Buffett. While there are questions about how I can like the song "Cheeseburger in Paradise" (which I love and sing loudly), the main concern for most people seems to be how a *feminist* can put up with him.

Isn't Buffett just about wild parties with lots of drunken sex? Aren't women portrayed as bait for men, problems for men to escape, and pieces of meat in bikinis? If my worried friends know Buffett's work at all (which they often don't) they point to songs they find problematic: "Fins" and "Why Don't We Get Drunk (and Screw)?" Given the huge number of songs Buffett has written and performed, I find it revealing that I'm regularly asked to respond to just these two. Nonetheless, these two are Parrothead anthems, and there are those who take them as permission to take a predatory and objectifying stance toward women.

This problem cannot be denied. In his songs and his books, there are plenty of references to women purely as objects of desire. Buffett himself says he got into music to meet girls (*A Pirate Looks at Fifty*, pp. 210–11). I believe, however, there is another message in much of his work. This message becomes clear when one approaches it from a pragmatist feminist angle. Unlike some other forms of feminism, pragmatist feminism starts with the fact that women and men are embodied minds. The senses and emotions, not just reason, play an important role in how we experience the world, and it is in experience that we start to find our place in the world. Denying experience, for the pragmatist, is like denying inquiry. Buffett's music and his books describe particular kinds of experiences—particular takes on the world. While some feminists may not like certain kinds of experience, they are real and must be taken into account. Further, when one listens and reads carefully, one finds that Buffett is actually undercutting the notion of women as playthings for men.

For instance, in the song "Smart Woman (in a Real Short Skirt)" Buffett is clear that he cares about the mind of the woman. He's looking for something more than the purely physical—"Bimbo limbo is wearing me thin." Do smart women have to deny their bodies, though? This is often the case in liberal feminism and a common critique of this kind of feminism is that it tries to make women into men. A pragmatist feminist seeks to embrace the full continuum of experience. This does not mean one cannot be critical of various portrayals and actions of people, but one has to be careful about being too dismissive.

In "Fins" we hear things like "fins to the left, fins to the right, and you're the only bait in town." But when Buffett talks about this song he says it's what he sees from his vantage point on stage (specifically inspired one night at a concert with beauty pageant contestants present). The men who are "circling" the bait are actually the object of critique. That the fin sign has become the greeting between Parrotheads (and even used by Buffett himself), shows us that the critique has not been as effective as it might be. But, when one adds Buffett's novels into the mix, I think the case for the critique of this kind of male behavior becomes stronger. The male characters in the novels who objectify women and spend their time in strip clubs, or just having sex and moving on, are the bad guys. They are also thieves, killers, or just generally unlikable. The male leads get in serious trouble when they become involved with "party girls" or when they begin to fall prey to the culture's stereotypes of "girls gone wild." In the end they end up with smart, serious women.

I'm not trying to make Buffett into a pragmatist or into a feminist, but rather to show that a pragmatist feminist reading allows for a different understanding of his work than what is commonly expressed by many of his devoted fans (Parrotheads) or those who find no value in his work at all—those who see it as mindless escapism and simple music. There's an important middle ground here that reveals a feminist message in an unexpected place—a place where many people live and party.

Smart Women (in Long Skirts)

Feminist philosophy is a huge field, with many differing theoretical perspectives. Technical definitions of feminism are even more abundant. However, I think we can use some common understandings of the word for our purposes here. On the cafepress.com.irregulargoods website we find the following bumper sticker definitions:

> Feminism is the radical idea that women are people.

> Fem . i . nism n. 1. Belief in the social, political and economic equality of the sexes. 2. The movement organized around this belief.

> "People call me a feminist whenever I express sentiments that differentiate me from a doormat or a prostitute."—Rebecca West.

> Feminism, the belief that women should have the same economic, social, and political rights as men, 1895.

> Feminist: a woman with self-respect.

These takes on feminism are not far off. Related ideas include:

> This princess saves herself.

> Justice is better than chivalry.

> I am not a well behaved woman.

> Sexism is a social disease.

> Uppity women unite.

> Well behaved women rarely make history.

These bumper stickers give voice to the concern that women have been held back from their full potential by social systems and rules of etiquette that require them to be polite, deferential, and dependent on men.

Women's independence, however, is a scary concept for some. This has given rise to terms like Femi-nazi. Feminists fight this perception with "Feminism is not a dirty word," and "fem . i. nism, coolest f-word ever." Women's equality and independence does require us all to rethink many of our social habits and change is usually a scary thing. It has almost always taken bloody conflict to put a country on the road of following the ideals of equality, fairness, and independence that are the basic notions behind the feminist 'movement'.

Philosophers add a layer of complexity to the concept of feminism by dividing it into various schools of thought. These schools of thought differ in some of their basic assumptions about sex, gender, and social systems. They also offer slightly different pictures of what an improved world would look like.

The most common type of feminism in the U.S. today is what's called liberal feminism. This school of thought takes the classical liberalism (social contract theory) of philosophers like Jean-Jacques Rousseau (1712–1778), Thomas Hobbes (1588–1679) and John Locke (1632–1704) as its starting place. Classical liberalism emerged during the Enlightenment and is usually seen as the basis for the American Revolution, the Constitution, and the Bill of Rights. The classical liberal view assumes that free, rational, and autonomous individuals must secure their freedom against the infringement of others. Leave these rational persons alone and through enlightened self-interest the best individual and social outcome will be achieved.

Right away there were women—and men—pointing out that the values of equality and liberty needed to be applied more widely. At first it was only landed white men, for instance (since they were the only ones considered fully rational), who could vote and so establish and protect their freedoms through government and by law. An extension of this view was made when in 1870 the vote was granted to black men. It was not until 1920 that women in the U.S. gained the vote. It's not that no one thought of it as a problem until then. Mary Wollstonecraft (1759–1797), a British woman writing around the time of the founding of the U.S., pointed out the logical problems with denying women equal education, equal employment opportunities, and an equal voice in politics. She was not a smart woman in a short skirt, but a smart woman in a long skirt who was called a hyena in petticoats for voicing her views.

When Jean-Jacques Rousseau wrote his books on social contract theory and the proper education of citizens who participate in their own governance, he made it clear that women should not participate in the public, political realm. Their role was as helpmates to free and autonomous men. While male citizens need to learn to be independent in their thinking, she was to take on her father's and then her husband's religion. She was to be pleasant in conversation, but not think deeply. Her will was to remain pliable so her husband could shape her as he pleased. The female leads in Buffett's novels are the opposite of Rousseau's ideal. Buffett's song "West Nashville Grand Ballroom Gown" is also about a woman who has rejected the restrictive expectations of her upbringing and struck out on her own. She doesn't have much money, she hasn't gone to church, and her message to her family is to fuck off.

Wollstonecraft (whose daughter Mary Shelley, author of *Frankenstein*, also took on the way in which liberal culture shapes life) was more than annoyed by the works of Rousseau. In 1792 she wrote *The Vindication of the Rights of Women*. This book, along with others, is a classic example of what liberal feminism is about.

Wollstonecraft argues that *if* women are less rational than men, less capable of performing certain tasks, or less moral, it's because they have not been provided with the same mental, physical, and moral education as men. She suggests that if women truly are not capable of being equal, there can be no harm in giving them the chance to try. Her argument is used to call for equal education, equal employment opportunities, and the vote. She doesn't challenge the Enlightenment ideals of reason, liberty, and equality, but simply asks that women be seen as full rational persons along with men. It's this kind of feminism that led to women gaining the vote in 1920 in the U.S. and to most of the educational and employment reforms many of us benefit from today. It's this kind of feminism that focuses on removing obstacles so that rational, free individuals have the opportunity to succeed.

While this kind of feminism has taken us a long way, it has shortcomings that inspired other schools of feminist thought including socialist feminists, Marxist feminists, radical cultural feminists, radical liberal feminists, ecofeminists, and pragmatist feminists. These later theories came to understand that it is not enough just to remove obstacles and provide the same education for women. Sexism is a deeply engrained social habit and there are social systems in place that perpetuate it, regardless of how particular individuals may think and act. This system is commonly referred to as patriarchy, and more recently as heteropatriarchy—as the sexist assumptions of compulsory heterosexuality became more visible. Different forms of feminism hope to dismantle patriarchy in different ways. (Another good bumper sticker says, "I'll be post-feminist in the post-patriarchy.")

Each kind of feminism argues that all people will be better off without patriarchal systems. While these systems oppress women, they also oppress racial and sexual minorities. And, as Wollstonecraft argued back in 1792, men suffer under patriarchal institutions, including white men with privileged economic status. For instance, they may find themselves as the sole economic support for emotionally and financially dependent women. This limits the options of men and creates the kind of situation that results in men viewing women as clingy and needy. This is how we get the view of women as something to be avoided—at least as partners. In fact, women can't be partners. Women will just hold you back from your dreams; it is best to stay footloose and fancy-free. Women are okay to have sex with, but more than that should be avoided. (This view of women is the stereotype of Buffett's message that I am trying to dispel.) Wollstonecraft argued that both men and women would be happier, and society would be better off, if women were more than mothers or sexual playthings. I think Buffett agrees.

While Wollstonecraft's critique and argument have taken us a long way in terms of women's access to education and jobs, she did not really push for a rethinking of our daily and domestic habits—habits very much informed by assumptions about sex and gender. Pragmatist feminism helps us do this kind of rethinking as it pushes us to examine our social habits very carefully. In so doing, it offers us an interesting take on the work of Jimmy Buffett. I will draw upon another smart woman in a long skirt (who worked to shorten them as part of her campaign for dress reform) as my main example—Charlotte Perkins Gilman.

Barnacle Brains and the Need to be Flexible

Classical American pragmatism emerged in the second half of the 1800s in the U.S. with the work of Charles Sanders Peirce (1839–1914), William James (1842–1910), and John Dewey (1859–1952). It was developed and put to work in the world by people like Jane Addams (1860–1935), who dealt with issues of immigration, poverty, and gender; Charlotte Perkins Gilman (1860–1935), who dealt with issues of gender and economics; and Alain Locke (1885–1954), who dealt with issues of race and violence.

Pragmatism is a philosophy that is naturalistic, pluralistic, developmental, and experimental.

- **Pragmatism is naturalistic in that it sees humans as part of the natural order of animals, subject to the same process of evolution. Humans are creatures who interact in various ways with other creatures and our environment. In these interactions we adapt to these various environments and adapt the environment to our needs (these adaptations are what we call habits).**

- **Pragmatism is pluralistic in that it notes that we each have only a partial take on the world and it seeks to incorporate as many viewpoints as possible.**

- **Pragmatism is developmental in that it sees the world and the creatures in it as being in process—not finished or static.**

- **Pragmatism is also experimental in that it does not seek final solutions, but better working hypotheses to help us cope with what we encounter in our lives. We must learn and develop—be flexible—if we are to survive and grow (even to grow older if not up).**

Pragmatism sees knowledge as helping us to organize experience in ways that are more or less satisfactory. It sees truths as beliefs backed by experience, but always open to revision. Pragmatism insists that our barnacle brains must bend!

What all this means is that pragmatism takes humans as creatures who grow and develop physically and psychologically throughout their lives. This happens through having various experiences, various transactions with one's physical and social environments. One can allow this to happen more or less as it will, or one can bring intelligence to bear on the process by paying attention to what experience teaches us (knowledge and truth) and continually testing and revising this knowledge and changing our habits of living. Some of the important insights for our purposes here are 1) that humans are fallible, that is we are always mistaken in one way or another; 2) given that we are mistaken and only have a partial take on the world, we need to embrace a pluralistic approach to life; 3) that through a pluralistic take on the world we can make the world better and arrive at more satisfactory relationships with others and the world—*better habits.*

These insights are important for feminism, and for our examination of Buffett, in that they suggest an open, pluralistic, and experimental approach to both identifying problems and approaching change. This means the insights of all forms of feminism are available for the pragmatist feminist to consider. It also calls on us to remain open to all forms of experience—this includes the *Girls Gone Wild* phenomenon, the *Sports Illustrated* swimsuit edition, and the fin salutes at a Buffett concert. This does not mean various forms of experience cannot be critiqued, however. In fact, we must offer critique and revision of various habits of experience if we are going to grow.

An example of this kind of critique can be found in the work of Charlotte Perkins Gilman (1860–1935). She was active in the movement for dress reform—shortening the skirts of women (as well as getting rid of their corsets) so they could participate in physical activity. Physically weakened by inactivity, and confined by their corsets and skirts, women were physically dependent on men. Gilman thought that while social interdependence was important to the growth of humanity, the dependence of one sex on the other hindered our growth and development.

Writing in 1914 (*The Man-made World*, Charlton) she says, "Humanity, thus considered, is not a thing made at once and unchangeable, but a stage of development; and is still . . . 'in the making'. Our humanness is seen to lie not so much in what we are individually, as in our relations to one another. It is in what we do and how we do it, rather than in what we are'" (pp. 16–17). Gilman goes on to observe that so far, though, we have lived in a "Man-made World." This has affected our habits, especially with regard to the relations of women and men. But habits and relations can change. Gilman spent her life writing and lecturing— helping to bring about change in our habits regarding men and women.

In general, Gilman is concerned about how the social and economic relationships of men and women have, through an evolutionary process, resulted in women being smaller and weaker than males. This results in a physical dependence that is furthered—especially for middle and upper class women—by an economic dependence resulting from a lack of education and career opportunities. Women are not only excluded from politics, but Gilman notes that women's domestic dependence and confinement harms the prospect of democracy for all, as men and boys learn to exercise power over women when they should be learning about equality and freedom.

As a pragmatist, Gilman realizes that before a problem can be addressed people must see it as a problem. Since most people accepted this division of the sexes, she had to demonstrate how it was a problem. That is, it had to be a problem for men—those who take pleasure in it and those with the power to change it. She did this by arguing that men and boys learned to be tyrants in the home, and so were not well prepared or interested in participating in a democracy. Further, as had Wollstonecraft, she argued that women would be more interesting sexual and life partners if they were more fully persons. Finally, for society to progress we need the best person for every job. Excluding half the human race right off the bat limits the chances of this happening. At least some women will be better than some men at some tasks. We need to find those women. In order to do this, though, we need to radically re-order the domestic sphere. If women are to get an education and have careers, we need different notions of home and family. Gilman proposes the professionalization of housework and childcare. These private and unpaid duties, should be public and paid. She rethinks the home—some without kitchens!—and the neighborhood. While the details of her proposals are very interesting, what concerns us here is her realization that the change in one habit requires a change in many habits—that's why feminism can seem so scary to some.

Following Gilman, a pragmatist feminist must first seek to understand the habits we have. What purposes do they serve? Are they still satisfactory for these purposes? Are there other, more satisfactory, approaches to life? So, what are the habits with regard to women that we find in the work of Jimmy Buffett? Do they need to change?

Fins, Bait, Drinking, and Sex

The work of Buffett is varied, and so are the portrayals of women. Buffett has written countless songs, several novels, and an autobiography. In all of these, we find a wide array of women. However, the common perception of women in Buffett's work seems to be that they are objects of desire, responsibility to be avoided, and the source of heartache. This heartache, of course, results in much drinking and running away to islands to get tattoos and get laid. But, this is not *really* the story one finds in Buffett.

"Margaritaville" is the one song that even non-Buffett people will have heard. In fact, they often think it's the sum total of his career. These same people don't listen to the song, though. They will tell me it's a song about drinking and sex. In fact, it's a song about heartache. Yes, there is drinking, but the point of the song is a man coming to admit that he fucked up. "Some people claim there's a woman to blame" becomes "I know it's my own damn fault." If the music that accompanies the lyrics wasn't upbeat, maybe more people would hear what is going on. One of the keys to Buffett is that his music is often upbeat, even when the lyrics aren't. While this may mask the point of the song, it does go with the pragmatists' "meliorism"—their concern with making things better. The music expresses the hope that things can get better; it points to the reality that life is precarious, uncertain, and can just suck, but we need to go on. And, in this song, we get the sense that a habit has been identified as not being satisfactory and there is at least the contemplation of change coming in the future—after another margarita.

Now, what about "Why Don't We Get Drunk (and Screw)"? Buffett tells us that this song was written as a satire of one of Conway Twitty's country songs ("Let's Go All the Way") and is based on an experience of watching a man try to pick up a hooker in an Atlanta diner. A feminist may not like the reality this line represents, but it is a particular reality. Prostitution has been part of the female experience for as long as we can remember. It has been both empowering and disempowering for women. It also says a lot about men and the sexual mores of a given society. Gilman would say it is the natural outcome of focusing women's attention on their physical and sexual attractiveness to men. If this is what women are for, might not a purely economic transaction make more sense than using marriage to hide the same money for sex exchange?

Most liberal feminists will argue that as long as it is a free choice, prostitution represents a woman doing as she chooses with her body. In fact, she's exploiting a weakness in men. This song can be seen as the ultimate kind of escape from the normal constraints of society—freeing for both participants. The "We" is an important part of the lyrics. However, with the increasing attention to date rape this song does represent a problematic attitude held by many men. There are men who intentionally get women drunk (or drugged) so they can do as they please. Again, this says a lot more about men than women. The fact that some men see this song as an anthem for this kind of behavior is disturbing. But it's not actually the point of the song.

And what about "Fins"? With the recent release of Margaritaville Brewing Company's Landshark Lager there is no denying that the image of a land shark is strongly identified with Buffett. Parrotheads greet each other with the fin sign and Buffett uses it as well. When men are proud of being land sharks, and when women are happy to be simply bait, we have a problem. However, once again, that does not seem to be the point of the song. He's warning the women about the circling men and I believe he's offering a critique of this kind of male behavior.

This interpretation of the song was recently supported in a conversation with a child of one of my friends. Alyssa is sixteen and loves Buffett (as do many of her friends). She first heard Buffett when out on a boat with one of her uncles. I asked her what her favorite song was and she said "Fins." I asked why, and she said the music was fun. (Again, I think the music in Buffett often distracts people from the point of the song.) When I pressed her about what the song is about she said it was about men who are hitting on women. She did not think that Buffett saw women as bait. Rather, the song draws attention to the behavior in a way that can serve as a warning about such men. It's the behavior, not the song, that's the problem. Men should change their outlook and behavior. (I asked her to text some of her friends and they gave similar interpretations of the song.)

Now this is not to say there's no problem here. One of the more graphic depictions of a land sharks comes in Buffett's novel *Where Is Joe Merchant?* (Harcourt Brace, 1992):

> Tuesday night was Land Shark Night. Curly and Shirley happily stripped down to their G-strings, and now they were part of a group of a dozen girls who swam provocatively in a see-through hot tub. . . . Rudy sported a large gray plastic fin strapped to his back. He had rented a mask, a snorkel, and an underwater camera, and he sat at the bar with the rest of the land sharks and waited for the cue from the emcee. "Feeding frenzy!" a fat man shrieked into a microphone, and Rudy dove into the pool. He landed in a pile with the rest of the spawners, splashing and snapping away at the naked mermaids in the waterfall. Curly and Shirley found him and made what they called a shark sandwich out of him. (p. 317)

Rudy is not a character in the book who is to be liked or admired. Buffett is relaying an experience of the world, not promoting it. However, the pride some men take in being land sharks is indicative of our culture. Women are sold as sex objects in our advertising and highly sexualized from a very young age in the entertainment industry. Young girls get plastic surgery and wear very suggestive clothing. They all want to dance like Madonna and Britney. Men come to expect this of women and many women internalize the norm themselves. There are many women who want to be bait. They crave male attention and seem to revel in the apparent power their sexual appeal provides. Charlotte Perkins Gilman, along with most other feminists, warns about relying on such power and playing into sexualized images of women. They are demeaning and temporary. If looking good in a bikini is how you get things out of life, at some point you will find you don't have the power you once had.

Further, if a woman relies on men for money and material goods, she makes herself vulnerable to abuse. If she is dependent she is not in a good position to leave should the man be abusive. In her book *Women and Economics* (Harper and Row, 1898) Gilman tells us that developing one's mind and body, and being capable of earning a living, are essential to being able to stand on one's own and so decrease the risk of being in such a position. As mentioned before, in Gilman's time there were women who worked outside the home, but careers were not open to women. Most middle- and upper-class women did not work. Further these same women were constrained by corsets and long skirts and their bodies were weakened by lack of physical activity. Gilman argued that female economic, physical, and mental dependence (humans being the only species in which the female can be found to be almost completely dependent on the male of the species for food, shelter, and protection) hinders the social development as a whole. Further, most men eventually find dependent women unattractive. This kind of relationship limits the possibilities of both men and women.

In Gilman's short stories, such as "The Cottagette," she tells stories of men who give up pursuing their dreams (like being a painter) because they must earn enough money to support their wife, daughters, sisters, and mother. In "What Diantha Did" we hear about a women who strikes out on her own to run a boarding house. The resulting economic independence from her father and her future husband have a liberating effect on her physical well-being and her mental powers. She eventually has a career as a writer and lecturer. We see the debilitating effects of female dependence in her most famous short story, "The Yellow Wallpaper." In this case, the lack of independence (the woman is shut in a room) and the inability to exercise her mind (she's forbidden to write) lead to a complete mental breakdown. Anything that encourages female dependence, then, should be a cause for concern.

In her novel *Herland*, Gilman provides a vision of what women could be like if there were no men around. In this society, the women are strong, well-educated, and have many interests. Not focused on getting attention from men, the women of Herland dress in a practical manner that allows free movement and don't worry about their hair and makeup. Women are, and should be seen as, more than objects of pleasure for men. Women and men should both be encouraged to be careful about images and behavior that reduce women to their bodies and to how they are seen by men. Given these concerns, the apparent pride in being a land shark is a problem. So is an internalized desire to be bait. Perhaps Buffett himself could set an example by not returning the fin salute (they could make the sign for the manatee instead).[1]

And what about Landshark lager? I recently found myself at a table with a bunch of philosophy graduate students. One of the women was drinking Landshark Lager. I had not yet tried the beer and I asked her how she liked it. She said she loved it; in fact it's the only beer she drinks. I then told her I was in the middle of co-editing this book on Jimmy Buffett. She stared at me blankly, though several of the male students began excitedly talking about Buffett and asking about the chapters in the book. Eventually I got back to the woman and asked her if she knew the song. She did not. Did she know Buffett's work at all? She did not. Did she know what a land shark was? She did not. She didn't seem to be the kind of woman who wants to be seen as bait, but here she was unwittingly participating in an image that does dehumanize women. The men at the table all knew what a land shark was, but it was too late

---

[1] Speaking of things a feminist might wish Jimmy Buffett didn't do, there's the song "Getting the Picture" and the accompanying video with the Sports Illustrated swimsuit models (2007). While there is clearly some irony or satire in this video, on the whole it serves to sexualize and objectify women. How does this connect to Buffett trying to raise two daughters to be smart and independent women?

to get their honest take on the song since they knew I work in feminist philosophy. As usual, they were surprised that I not only like Buffett, but that I was writing a feminist interpretation of Buffett for this book.

This experience demonstrates an awareness of the problems with the land shark image. Again, though, I think the song itself shows an awareness of the problems of this kind of male behavior. The behavior is real and predates the song. Buffett didn't create the problem. In fact, by pointing it out he puts us in a better position to identify and critique it. It provides an opening for men and women to talk about this kind of objectification and its consequences. Feminists shouldn't pretend men don't behave this way or deny that some women "want" to be treated this way. This is a strongly held habit we need to work to change. This is an ongoing project of consciousness-raising and I think Buffett's music and writing can play an important role. He has plenty of strong women characters in his songs and books. They are sexual, but not sexualized or objectified.

Desdemona, Trevor, Cleopatra, and Sophie

In Buffett's first novel, *Where Is Joe Merchant?* we encounter two strong women, Desdemona and Trevor. In his second novel, *A Salty Piece of Land* (2004), we meet Cleopatra and Sophie (and a strong girl in the character of Montana). Desdemona and Cleopatra are not really presented as sexual. They are older, smart, independent, and determined women who gain the loyalty, respect, and love of the male characters in the book. We hear about their past sexual lives; this aspect of their being is not denied or ignored. However, their lives have been about much more than their relationships with men. Trevor and Sophie are presented as sexual beings—they are the women the male leads want to be with. But they are smart, independent, and determined women as well. Their lives, like Cleopatra and Desdemona, are about more than their relationships with men. Trevor is an artist and Sophie is a photographer (both also turn out to be independently wealthy but we'll leave that aside for now). Both women have independent incomes, have their own "mental" pursuits, and are physically strong. The men have to "straighten" out their own lives and behavior in some way in order to be with them. The older women help the men see this. And, as Buffett says, it is not some fairy tale ending he is after, but "Happily ever after, now and then" (p. 286).

This is a clear and direct critique of the fairy tale endings that children internalize from an early age—girls looking for the prince to save them, and men, looking for a damsel in distress. That story is a recipe for disaster and Buffett is clear about this. Being with strong and independent women may mean the men aren't the center of the universe, but they aren't. One gets the sense that Buffett may have learned this lesson in his own life when he was separated from Jane—the woman he's now been married to for over thirty years. "Come Monday" and "Coast of Carolina" are songs that express such love. "Margaritaville," and "If the Phone Doesn't Ring It's Me" are songs that express some of the more difficult times one can encounter in a relationship. Let's look more closely at Buffett's account of non-fairy-tale relationships.

In *Where is Joe Merchant?* we meet Desdemona. Desdemona has had a career as a singer in a rock band and is a wonderful baker. She is psychically in tune with the universe and has set out on a mission to build a rocket ship. She sails her own boat and does her own thing. She is not afraid of anybody or anything. The song "Desdemona Is Building a Rocket Ship" picks up on the story (or the reverse as the case may be). It is Dedemona whom Trevor Kane is looking for because she thinks she can help her find her brother, Joe Merchant. She also gets advice on men. Desdemona says,

> "Men are a hell of a lot easier to understand than rocket ships. They'd rather stare at their watches than tell you they love you, but that doesn't make them bad. It makes them mysterious. We women are perceived as the mysterious gender, catlike, intangible. To me, men are the mysterious ones. They fight all their lives to figure out why the physical superiority they possess isn't the key they need to unlock the treasure chest called happiness. Once they find out, that's when they'll really be hard for us to deal with.
>
> "You're actually at the best stage of your relationship when you're past all that storybook-ending mumbo jumbo. Too many people waste too much time trying to make the reality of their lives conform to the unreality of the myth of romantic love. Happily ever after, now and then, is what you're looking for, and that takes work." (p. 286)

Desdemona is a sage and the time spent in her company transforms both Frank Bama and Trevor Kane.

Trevor Kane is more of a mess than the other women I will talk about, but she is still independent. She and Frank Bama (the male lead) have had a relationship before but broken up. She felt he loved his plane more than he loved her. She comes to him for help in finding her brother, but ultimately she finds herself (as does Frank) and they give things another try. An indication that he has grown comes when Trevor writes to Desdemona and says "Frank is talking and that makes me happy" (p. 378). We had an earlier indication that Frank was moving in a new direction—forming a new habit—when we read, "There weren't too many women around like Trevor Kane, and I wanted her back in my life. I was tired of trying to converse with twenty-year old college girls on vacation in Key West. I would rather cook myself dinner in the hangar and sit with Hoagy [his dog] in my lap, reading a good book" (p. 221). With a change in his habits, Frank has made a new life possible. They end up in Alaska, with Frank flying for a living and fishing on the side. Trevor works to preserve the wilderness (part of an environmental theme that runs throughout Buffett's work) and continues with her painting. In the end they are hoping for "happily ever after, now and then" (p. 286), following the advice from Desdemona! No princess or fairy tale ending here.

In *A Salty Piece of Land* we meet Cleopatra Highbourne. Cleopatra is nearing 102 years of age. Like Desdemona she captains her own ship and her own life. She too is wise. Tully Mars, the male lead, is rescued by her in more than one way. She keeps him safe from thugs, keeps him out of the grip of the law, and helps him find his way. We are told, "Cleopatra was the professor of living long and wise. The vast amount of knowledge she imparted was simply amazing" (p. 170). She had a love affair with a famous Cuban baseball player, but did not allow herself to be tied down. "Luis and I had a torrid affair. He asked me to marry him and come ashore countless times, . . . I never met anybody else who came close . . . so I just stopped looking and sailed on" (p. 175).

When we meet her she's trying to fulfill one last dream—the restoration of a lighthouse. She is not distracted from this project. She doesn't take shit from anybody. She lives, and dies, on her own terms. At her end she tell us, "We are all survivors . . . But the trouble with being a survivor is that you find yourself dancing alone a lot. It is a tricky seesaw on which the survivor has to sit. On the one side is your ability to be comfortable in a world inhabited only by yourself. On the other side is your desire to share your time with others. How do you balance? Being a survivor is not a bad thing, but you do run the risk of being the last one at the party . . . —like me" (p. 418). Her final advice for Tully is: "Have parties, find a woman, raise some children, and fish a lot." She's not complaining. She tells us she is married to the sea and to adventure. She briefly wonders what would have happened if she'd stayed home like her mother had wanted. The answer is clear. Her life, and the lives of the many she has sailed with, would have been a lot less interesting. As we know, for Buffett, a life well lived is an interesting life. Cleopatra is an exemplar of a life well lived.

We also meet Sophie Diament toward the end of *A Salty Piece of Land*. Her name alone, hints at the wisdom of women. She also sails her own ship and steers her own life. She turns out to be Cleopatra's niece. Her fiancé is dead, but she has their child (Montana). She is a nature photographer. Her arrival in the story is a turning point for Tully. "It is amazing how things unfold. I had come to Fortune Island to be alone with my thoughts, to fish in solitude, and then make the great leap into the new chapter in my life. The next thing I knew, I was being served breakfast on a picture-book ketch by an enchantress from Corsica who was going to the same place I was" (pp. 442–42). They settle into a life that honors both of their endeavors. Tully, the male lead, is designing boats. Sophie has published a best selling photography book. To make this relationship possible, Tully has had to change, and his change is largely due to the influence of Cleopatra. She helped Tully start to think with his head. Talking about his past mis-adventures Cleopatra says, "I am not sure it was stupidity. You men have that inherent problem when the little head thinks for the big one" (p. 328). Attracted to Sophie physically (she was diving off her boat naked when he first saw her), he sees much more than her physical beauty. He sees the strength of Cleopatra.

Gilman would like these women and the transformation of the men. We see in these characters women who are willing to challenge social habits. Desdemona and Cleopatra defy social conventions and lead their lives on their own terms. They have relationships with men, but they do not focus their energy on men. They focus their energy on their own dreams. Trevor and Sophie have also learned to follow their own dreams. The men who want in on these journeys have to learn to take care of themselves and be partners in relationships that promote mutual flourishing and growth. They have to grow beyond a focus on the physical and sexual and come to realize that the real attraction comes in finding a smart and independent partner. They have to realize they want a smart woman (in a short skirt).

"Happily Ever After, Now and Then"

So, what can we conclude from all of this? I think we can see that Buffett does indeed favor smart, independent women. However, he also gives voice to a real phenomenon of men who seek out young women in bikinis on spring break, and of young women who present themselves to the world in this way. Feminism cannot ignore the fact that our culture encourages this behavior in men and women, and should not condemn as anti-feminist all those who give voice to the experience. Reading and listening carefully we find that Buffett is a critic of this kind of habit of being and he encourages the formation of new habits. If we read Buffett with a pragmatist feminist eye, his work shows us that the men he depicts find that ways of being that were once thought to be satisfactory turn out not to be. These same men learn through experience and transform their habits. Those who do not learn and grow are not portrayed in a good light.

Women who lead independent lives come off well in Buffett. Independent does not mean man-hating, but it does mean these women do not arrange their lives around men and do not focus all their energy on achieving male attention. Land sharks are not attractive to such women. So how can a feminist be a Parrothead? Once we understand that Buffett's music and writing do not promote the objectification of women, it's not a problem. It does mean, however, that we have to take the opportunities to talk about Buffett's works and the message we find in it. We have to be willing to challenge simplistic understandings of his work and to argue with those who use it as a justification to treat women as meat. In other words, we must continue to engage and critique our world and the social habits we encounter. As Desdemona says, happily ever after, now and then, takes a lot of work.

11
Fruitcakes

JOHN KAAG

"Don't be such a fruitcake!" What exactly makes one a fruitcake? Why are fruitcakes such distasteful characters to the discerning, yet dull, tastes of mainstream America? How might fruitcakes function in the social and political sphere—as dissenters and participants?

To answer these questions, let's begin with Buffett's album, *Fruitcakes*. Buffett's music, in its typical levity and irony, takes on serious issues of existential alienation, social deviance, and political oppression. At the end of the title track, Buffett shouts that, "we need more fruitcakes in this world!" Fruitcake is an acquired taste, but a taste that might revive our palate, deadened by the effects of modern culture. This culture has attempted to co-opt Buffett's music, to draw it into its wake, and commercialize the Parrothead. "Fruitcakes," however, reasserts its independence from the mainstream by its elevation of the odd, the irregular, and the queer. This song hovers at the boundary of culture, and cannot be consumed as easily as some of his other songs, such as "Margaritaville" and "Cheeseburger." "Fruitcakes," despite its catchy refrain and cheery cadence, is harder to swallow. To Buffett's way of thinking, we need more, not fewer, of these interesting and deviant characters. "And (he is) mad as hell and (doesn't) want to take it anymore!"

The feminist philosopher Judith Butler has something to say that resonates closely with Buffett's remarks. Butler has observed that political, religious, and cultural institutions define what it means to be a "normal" and "natural" human subject. "The Man" cooks us just the way he wants us. More dramatically, these institutions construct the meaning of "human nature." This point is developed in detail in Butler's *Gender Trouble* and *Bodies that*

Matter. In later works, such as *Precarious Life*, her interest is in exposing the violence that is done in the process of forming human subjectivity and in highlighting the treatment of those individuals who fall outside the standard definitions of "normalcy." These are the "nobodies," the fruitcakes who are pushed to the margins of our culture.

At first glance, Butler and Buffet seem like a very poorly matched couple. One is a feminist, a queer theorist, and a Berkeley intellectual. The other has been described as a sexist, and a racist, and a shallow musician. The heterosexual currents in many of Buffett's songs restate norms and values that would undoubtedly strike many modern feminists as odd, if not obviously objectionable. When Buffett suggests that "we get drunk and screw," he could easily be accused of giving voice to the dreams of juvenile American males.

Such accusations, however, would mask an important point of convergence between the feminist and the musician. Buffett, in songs such as "The Death of an Unpopular Poet," speaks to the unappreciated genius of the individual who is born before his time. In "Cultural Infidel" and "Mental Floss" his lyrics border on the absurd as he states plainly that he is a cultural infidel who stands against the mainstream. This infidel advocates a counter cultural form of mental hygiene, clearing out the cultural and traditional rubbish that builds up between our ears.

Both Butler and Buffett suggest that something significant has been lost in the marginalization of the fruitcake, this counter-culture figure, and encourage us to reconsider the value of its uncanny existence. What has been lost is the particularity and singularity of individuals, and with it, our ability to value the unique and untapped possibilities of human existence. In a time when exceptional characteristics and powers are somehow leveled off and made manageable by bureaucracy and technology, the fruitcake remains as a rare embodiment of human particularity. Butler and Buffett allow us to take a second look at the individuals designated and branded as fruitcakes, and in this second look, we have the chance to re-spect these interesting figures. That is, after all, what it means to "look-again" at someone or something. Here, we also have the chance—and the *obligation* - to protest institutions of power that might do violence to these individuals, but also, and perhaps just as importantly, to recognize, in Buffett's words, "the little bit of fruitcake left in every one of us."

Baking Fruitcakes and the Performance
of Normalcy

"Fruitcakes" opens with an interesting sentiment, one that runs counter to our normal and seemingly seamless lives. He tells us that he has a friend Desdemona who runs the local "space station and bake shop" and that she says that, "human beings are flawed individuals, that the cosmic baker took us out of the oven a little too early. And that's the reason we're as crazy as we are." This insight—that we're all slightly half-baked, that our lives are not yet fully determined in the reasonableness of everyday life—is quickly lost in the mechanizing and institutionalizing of society. It is lost, or silenced by centers of power (governmental, economic, or cultural) that demand compliance and conformity from individuals in exchange for the chance to matter in social-political affairs.

From *Gender Trouble* (Routledge, 1999), to *Bodies that Matter* (Routledge, 1993), to *The Psychic Life of Power* (Stanford University Press, 1997), Butler has highlighted the way in which modernity has closed the question of matter, *of what and who matters,* before it was opened in a meaningful way. In these works, she asks a question that reflects what is often referred to as a constructivist position: How do bodies come to matter only in and through a social and cultural context? Tarrying with such open-ended questions has traditionally been considered both unwise and unnecessary for it shakes the bedrock of the "natural," a character that has been historically framed as necessary and enduring.

Before going forward, let's slow down and consider the constructivist position more carefully. The constructivist holds that the categories and classes by which we understand our worlds are constructed or made by the cultural and social forces that govern our lives. There is no natural or real basis of "race," or "gender," or "madness." Nature does not parse these categories for us to understand, rather *we* are responsible for these categories, their boundaries, and their exclusionary power.

Like Desdemona's comments, these points are drowned out before they have the chance to be explored. Too often we take for granted the organizing frameworks of Western society and, in so doing, neglect those "oddballs" who fall at the margins of so-called natural categories. Butler, in an act of defiance, however, consistently expresses and supports a belief that the "natural" is enduring only insofar as it is *always* constructed contingently through the social realm. The *mode* of this construction - its pervasiveness, its stability, its exclusionary force – seems to be Butler's abiding concern. Here, I hope to briefly explain Butler's analysis of exclusion as a means of subjectivity construction. This line of thinking is continuous with the rest of Buffett's *Fruitcakes*, but also echoes particular themes in Continental philosophy.

Butler understands "nature" and the notion of "matter" as emerging in the interpellation (the process by which something acquires a name) of cultural construction. In other words, the naming and designation of what is "natural" precedes and determines what is considered natural. Why do we call a woman a woman? According to Butler, it's because she acts like a 'normal' woman; she *performs* the part. Butler's feminist position echoes the account of many women who have claimed that cultural expectations, enacted by a group of individuals, get confused and internalized as the "natural state of womanhood." The natural state of womanhood would be considered a social construction, that is a practice that seems natural and obvious to those who accept it, but in fact, is a creation or outgrowth of a particular cultural norm.

Many post-modern theorists such as Butler aim to underscore the artificial nature of these constructions. Indeed, woman philosophers in previous eras have made a similar point. One of these women is Ella Lyman, whose journal entries from the nineteenth century give concrete expression to Butler's point. In describing her situation as a woman, Lyman writes that, "A girl's life is indefinitely harder than a man's in some ways. Girls are expected to keep a perpetual cruse of tenderness to oil their jarring tempers. And because she needs to be more alive to the feelings of others a girl is more quickly to be hurt, more sensitive. Is it strange that girls are naturally more subject to moods than men?"[1] For Lyman, "girls" are expected to act in a certain manner and, through this expectation, these manners become a girl's way of being in the world. A woman's "natural" sensitivity can be traced to the cultural norms and mores of a specific time and place.

Through a reiteration of norms, through the speaking and recognition of the cultural law, the revealed "nature" of bodies becomes sedimented, cemented, reified. It is only in this sedimentation that a human subject gets to matter. Butler notes that a

---

[1] Ella Lyman Cabot Papers. Schlesinger Library. Radcliffe Institute for Advanced Study. Accession number: A139-374.

"proper domain of 'sex'" is established through and in the power of the social realm, but solidified and demarcated at a certain expense. In *Bodies That Matter* Butler echoes the postmodern theorist, Michel Foucault, in asking: "How much does it cost the subject to be able to tell the truth about itself?" They answer in accord: the price is simply too high. Where natural boundaries and domains are formed, certain bodies and practices fall beyond the narrow scope of the "normal" and are quickly banished to a realm that simply does not matter: the true fruitcake.

In *Gender Trouble* Butler says that the law "produces both sanctioned heterosexuality and transgressive homosexuality" (p. 94). It is in this sense that gay and lesbian possibilities are abjected and excluded from the discourse of "natural" heterosexuality. They are banished for good reason. The fact that these possibilities *are* possibilities (despite any regulatory norm) exposes the contingent and performative aspect of "sex" itself. The social construction of "sex" marks the "boundaries of livable being." In the current debate on the "nature" and character of "sex" and gender, Butler hopes to show that, "the regulatory norms of 'sex' work in a performative fashion to constitute the materiality of bodies and, more specifically, to materialize the body's sex, to materialize sexual difference in the service of the consolidation of the heterosexual imperative" (p. 2).

This heterosexual imperative has co-opted science and technology in an effort to expedite this process of constructing the natural and, indeed, to mask the fact of its construction. As Butler notes, the sonogram, typical in its accuracy, repetition, and artificiality "shifts an infant from an 'it' to a 'she' or a 'he,' and through that naming [a] girl is 'girled,' brought into the domain of language and kinship through the interpellation of gender" (p. 7). The interpellation of gender refers to the typical practices that constitute male and female identities, practices that often determine the development of gendered children.

Girls are "girled" by way of a particular acculturation: They are taught to be caretakers, to tend to children, to attend to details, to be modest, to be submissive, to be "girls." This is the sort of ritualized, cultural performance that makes a body a *normal* human subject. Ironically, the rhetoric of these boundaries insists that no one and no*body*, falls outside these boundaries. Hence, it comes as no real surprise that gays, lesbians, trans-gendered, and inter-sexed individuals become the proverbial "nobodies" of the biological, political and social sphere. These are the individuals who defy definition, who refuse to be defined by cultural and scientific norms of their time.

The more rigorous and unequivocal the technology and ritualized performance becomes, the more necessary and "natural" categories, such as gender, seem. Modernity's emphatic understanding of "nature," through the rhetoric of science, culture, and politics has become the prevailing discourse that matters in the sense of having meaning and significance. Nature and human nature is understood in definitely concrete terms, leveled off to the common denominator of consumerism or scientific progress.

Buffett and Butler seem to laugh in the face of the serious attempts of modern, scientific Man to understand his world. Buffett laughs at the political figure who spends a "jillion dollars" in order to understand and categorize the cosmos, to "get a look at Mars." Just like the fruitcake, nature itself loves to defy the expectations of society and science. Nature is unruly and loves to hide from the investigator who would want to figure out its dynamics. According to Buffett, the complexity and singularity of the cosmos mocks the attempts of cone-head politicians and scientists; that is why Buffett tells us in "Fruitcakes" that, "I hear universal laughter ringing out among the stars." The universe is uniformly *irregular* and continually rejects any normal interpretations that seek to define and confine its workings.

Fruitcakes as Political Actors

But what happens when a nobody becomes somebody? What happens when a nobody speaks up, or speaks out, or is spoken about? What happens when a queer individual speaks out against oppression? This is what Buffett is up to in "Fruitcakes." Buffett believes that fruitcakes can do some very important social and political work. In Butler's description of the human subject and its creation through ritualized, cultural norms, she notes that the interesting peculiarity of a human being is silenced. The human subject is only given voice through the collective braying of societal norms.

In the second stanza of "Fruitcakes" Buffett recounts a trip to the movies in a description that makes us laugh—almost until we cry. The owners of the theater decide that people want "a twelve pound Nestlé Crunch for twenty-five dollars;" they decide what people want to watch; they decide that the people want eight extra ounces of watered down pop. In their insistence, these decisions, wants, and needs become equated with the will of the people. Indeed, most individuals *subject themselves* to this collective will and happily gorge themselves on generic food and generic cinema that—if they really thought about it for two minutes—they actually might detest. At least Buffett detests it and takes the time to say so. He says quite flatly that, "he does not want it," and explains that he "does not want other people thinking for" him. Buffett has his *own* desires—quirky, unique, singular—that depart from those of "the people." In speaking out against his culture, Buffett attempts to distance himself from the collective mass that the twentieth-century German philosopher, Martin Heidegger, called *"das Man"* (the They).

Having expressed the voice of the fruitcake, namely the refusal to have others think and speak for him, Buffett expands his critical project to address oppressive institutions that not only determine how one views a movie, but how an individual views herself and the world at large. In so doing, Buffett takes on his local church, or more accurately, takes on organized religion on the whole. He prepares us with a subtle refrain that could almost be confused with a sort of primitive beat. Indeed, in a certain respect, it is: "Mea culpa, mea culpa, mea maxima culpa / Mea culpa, mea culpa, mea maxima culpa."

This Latin phrase is translated: My fault, my fault, my most grievous fault; its expression is the lynchpin of the Roman Catholic prayer known as the *Confiteor* ("I confess"). In this prayer, one confesses her sins against the community and against the God who sanctions its normative laws. It goes, almost without saying, that that fruitcake is the one who ought to feel guilt and who is required to atone for the ways that he or she has transgressed against the Father and his Christian community. More generally, in *The Psychic Life of Power*, Butler notes that guilt and the identity of the modern subject is inextricably connected thanks to the power of Judeo-Christian institutions: "This readiness to accept guilt to gain purchase on identity is linked to the highly religious scenario of a (naming) call that comes from God and that constitutes the subject" (p. 109). Only through religious law and the corresponding guilt does one acquire an identity in the Christian West.

In concert, Butler and Buffett object to this rendering of religious practice. Butler's "The Value of Being Disturbed," underscores the value of questioning the sanctity of specific Christian symbols that tend to organize and "subject" religious practitioners. Many commentators have noted that Butler's works can be employed to denaturalize the gendered and sexed categories that are established in the Old and New Testament. God is not a man. Women do not, as the Bible has us believe, fall into only two categories: virgins and whores. The patriarchal and heterosexual norms of the Catholic church are oppressive to those unlucky individuals who fall outside, or fight against, their regulative power. The Catholic Church is not so catholic, in the literal sense of the word—it is no longer open to everyone.

Buffett's critique runs along these same lines and weds the earlier critique of commercialism and capitalism with a brief analysis of the exclusionary effects of religion and the death of true spiritualism: "Where's the church? Who took the steeple? Religion's in the hands of some crazy-ass people." He explains that religion has been hijacked by narrow evangelical interpretations and captured in sound-bites that "sell" in the blue-light market of ideas. He begs us to understand religion without these narrow definitions, saying that religion "is not that simple."

Instead of allowing doctrinal interpretations to ground religious sentiment, we ought to maintain a broader definition of 'the religious' in order to respect and maintain the individual spiritual preferences of others. Buffett sums this up succinctly in his suggestion that religious experience "Is the Buddhist in you; it's the pagan in me / It's the Muslim in him; She is Catholic ain't she / it is the born again look / it's the Wasp and the Jew." Following John Dewey, Buffett suggests that while specific religions may seem to run at cross purposes, there are similar religious experiences that might serve as a useful common ground between these traditions. When we look at this experience more closely, the definable characteristics of doctrine and creed fall away, leaving a process and sentiment that is difficult to define in "normal" terms. This experience is "had" by an individual. And while this experience is often had by an individual who is a member of a wider community, the experience cannot be generalized over this community. It remains peculiar to the individual, irreducible. In the end, Buffett asks about the nature of religious experience and seems to answer for all of us: "I ain't got a clue." Instead of allowing the customs and norms of a tradition to exhaustively define the individual experience of a practitioner, Buffett leaves the question of experience unanswered and open-ended.

The Fruitcake as Performative Exemplar

A Buffett concert is a fruitcake convention. Picture it: Four generations of men and women, wearing an array of technicolor shirts, coconut bras, and parrot hats, pack themselves in sweaty stadiums in order to pretend they have gone on a Caribbean vacation. They sway, and dance, and sing seemingly silly songs about cheeseburgers, and sharks, and library love affairs. They salute one another by placing their hands together over their heads. When the music comes to an end, onetime strangers hug and laugh as fast friends. Yes, this is not normal behavior. What fruitcakes!

What can philosophy tell us about these performances? What can we, as Buffett fans, tell philosophy? Butler notes that we spend most of our waking hours performing and reinforcing the identities of normal, everyday life. We dutifully perform our functions as men, and women, and realtors, and teachers, and janitors, and guidance counselors, and whatever else we do to "make our living." In the performance of normalcy, we eliminate and foreclose other possible identities that we might quietly like to perform, but that run against the grain of custom or law. Butler pays close attention to those rare and "freakish" performances that do deviate from the customary embodiment of identity, and more particularly, gender. Why? She believes that parody, such as the "acting out" involved in drag shows, destabilizes the categories of gender and exposes the contingent nature of "normal" identity formation. More simply, a drag show is a dramatic break from the humdrum of everyday life. In the "balls" of New York and San Francisco, the performance of drag takes on an interesting character. The "fruitcake" who occupies the borders of mainstream culture finds others who are also committed to nonconformity, who fail to "fit in." Together, these individuals constitute a unique borderland, an ironic community of dissent—just like a Buffett concert.

Going to a Buffett concert is not a form of escapism—or *only* a form of escapism. It's also a performance. Surprisingly, the performance does not take place on stage, but rather in the audience. In this case, Buffett's music serves as the occasion for the gathering of its fans who perform their freakish roles for a joyous four hours. During this time they dare to *act out* as fruitcakes. This is no drag show (even though many "men" like to wear coconut bras)—but it's as close as many nine-to-fivers and professionals get to acting out against the customs of their somewhat tedious lives.

It is a raucous good time, but it's also a quiet protest against the way that society pokes and prods us into mooing in unison. We do not want to moo! We want to squawk! We want to remain unique, singular, *peculiar* in the literal sense of the word. The word "peculiar" stems from *peculiaris,* meaning "of one's own property." We want to own, *and own up to,* the unique and uncanny aspects of ourselves. "Fruitcakes" articulates this sentiment by reminding a listener that, "there is a little bit of fruitcake left in everyone of us." We undoubtedly need this reminder. All too often, we leave the fruitcake convention and abandon our unique selves. Butler and Buffett both suspect that the abandonment of the fruitcake has ethical and political implications. A respect for the unique and the uncanny aspects of human life translates into a more sensitive, caring society. This is why Buffett cries out: "We need more fruitcakes in this world and less bakers! We need people that *care!*" Keep caring. Spread those crumbs around.

Margarita
Metaphysics

12

The American West as a Coral Reef

DUKE RICHEY

You're feeling great, with a fine attitude in hand. The pastels of the bluish-pink-orange Montana sky, which surrounds you for three hundred and sixty degrees on a circular horizon, remind you of the Caribbean; you say as much to the man sitting next to you. But this is Rocky Mountain wheat and cattle country, where the sun dies slow in summer; and you're driving on a black ribbon of highway, west of the snow-speckled Crazy Mountains.

You turn to the alpenglow on the Crazies and realize that the spectacular hue might also simply be the result of the rosy tint of your sunglasses helping nature shine in a sort of Vuarnet Technicolor. These thoughts about the colors on mountains—and any other thoughts, to be honest—are nothing more than cloudy suggestions under a wispy cloud-streaked twilight sky that is bigger than any sky you had ever imagined possible back in Tennessee when this journey started. You nudge your friend, Hooper, and pass him some attitude. He is curly-haired, and wiry, like any great young rock climber. He drinks his Rainier, then exhales his words in slow Southernese: "man, hit the rewind."

The two of you, and your brother, Kevin, are rattling along at fifty miles an hour in a 1979 Toyota Landcruiser. It is a "rig," as they call any truck-ish automobile in Montana, and it's not yet one decade old. Yet, it can barely make seventy, pedal to the metal and going downhill. Although the Cruiser came with an Eight Track Stereo, you have recently put in a used cassette deck, where *Living And Dying in $\frac{3}{4}$ Time* has been stuck (literally—it will not eject) for nearly three weeks. Needless to say, these are Jimmy Buffett songs that you know by heart.

Kevin is in a collapsible lawn chair that the three of you have crafted into a backseat. He is wedged between a sloshing cooler and duffel bags spilling over with dirty clothes, ropes, carabiners, hiking boots, flip flops, maps, tent poles, dry flies, the Bozeman newspaper, and a tattered copy of *Lonesome Dove* (a novel which, along with Buffett's entire Western repertoire, helped to inspire this trip in the first place). He is, against all odds, sleeping. Most importantly for this moment, the rig is littered with empty beer cans that the three of you—since escaping the historic fires in Yellowstone National Park days earlier—have planned to deposit into a mythical pile in a little town that is just this minute coming into view.

Miraculously, the rewind stops where you want it to stop and the strumming starts on "Ringling, Ringling," one of two songs to mention Montana on the Buffett record with one of the greatest pieces of cover art in the entire collection (our hero atop the half-sunken shrimper *Good Luck*). Then the pedal steel comes in, like the pleasant voice of someone you've missed badly who shows up with drinks at your favorite bar, and Jimmy Buffett describes yet again this latest stop on your Parrothead plot across Western America. You've had a beer in Leadville, Colorado, on the eleventh of June (the day John Wayne died). You've done a Saturday night in Livingston, Montana. You've made a point, several times, of hiking on a Tuesday. And you'll eventually have a very memorable stay at the Holiday Inn in Missoula.

But for now, the focus is Ringling, Montana: "Ringling, Ringling, slipping away, only forty people living there today." You sing now, Hooper and you, and Kevin, who is waking. You sing, loudly, with Buffett: "pile of beer cans been there twenty-seven years." Then you roll into Ringling . . . long-awaited, long-imagined Ringling, Ringling. You find no evidence of the pile of cans, no evidence of a sheriff (thankfully), no evidence of anything near forty people, but you do find a dog—a Blue Heeler that looks kind of like the dog you imagined in the song—lying in the middle of the street. You drive around him, looking for the church with broken windows, and the dog raises its head, briefly, cementing forever your image of what a dusty Montana cattle town ought to look like.

Lookin' Back at My Background

Now, years pass. You finish college, gain a little knowledge, then migrate from the mountains of Tennessee to South Florida, where you live in the old barroom of a defunct cypress-walled fishing lodge on the edge of the Everglades. You catch fish from a dock not ten feet from your door while listening to Burning Spear, Bob Marley, Dire Straits, and other musicians from the playlist of Radio Margaritaville, which at the time, in those last years before the internet explosion, does not yet exist. You read constantly and you never watch television. Almost daily for two winters, you put your hands over your head, as if imitating a hot air balloon in a game of charades, pleading with boaters to give it a brake for the manatee in the water near the canoes and kayaks of your students. On several occasions, you make the drive down to Key West and watch the sun set and rise again during the same pub crawl. And yes, you learn that buying chocolate milk at Fausto's can be a sublime experience. In short, you try to live your life like a song, many of which were inspired by Buffett, but re-written by you and your friends in what are now your own favorite places.

More years pass, as you meander again and again throughout Western America, before moving to Montana for graduate school. Eventually, you end up in Colorado, where you begin work on a history of Aspen. In addition to everything else, it's the town where Buffett married in the late seventies, where he wrote "Incommunicado," and where he still skis today. It's his western Key West, still occasionally lovely—even with too many people and all their stuff—but with the price tag to prove it when compared to much of the rest of America. While only tangentially connected to Jimmy Buffett, what interests you most about Aspen (the questions that bother you so, to be really cheesy) have to do with why people went there in the first place and how Aspen changed over time. Ultimately, your biggest questions, shaped over the years by your own travels and observations, are bigger than Aspen or any other one particular place. They are philosophical inquiries: what is community and why is it important? Also, how do individual and collective environmental ethics shape places? These are questions that Buffett has explored throughout his work, from his recording of "I Have Found Me a Home" in 1973 to his production of the film *Hoot* in 2006. Philosophers have asked these questions, too.

"Migration"

One of the best-known American philosophers to think about the importance of community and the importance of land use in shaping history was Josiah Royce, a professor at Harvard more than one hundred years ago. Royce spent his childhood in Grass Valley, California, one of the great boomtowns of the Gold Rush. His parents, who left Iowa and migrated across the Plains as Forty-niners, failed in their efforts to get rich at the diggings. By the time their son entered the world in 1855, the Royces scraped by in California, in part, on what Josiah's mother earned as a teacher and what little his father brought home as a traveling fruit salesman. Although young "Josie" moved to San Francisco at age eleven, and started college at the University of California five years later, "his western experience," one biographer noted of the years in Grass Valley, "composed a readily accessible part of his life, like an aquifer, a submerged but enduring sustenance" (Robert Hine, "The American West as Metaphysics: A Perspective on Josiah Royce," *The Pacific Historical Review*, August 1989, p. 270). Royce tapped into that aquifer to develop his "philosophy of community," which argued that individuals might only develop humane societies when they sacrifice selfish desires for the good of the whole. If this sounds simple, like something people say they learned in kindergarten, it's because it is a straightforward way of looking at things.

One great way to think about the goal of philosophy is to think about it as a way of looking at things. Much of Royce's philosophy has a kind of "golden rule" ring to it, reflecting his rearing in a mining community, where he saw how the plunder of an every-man-for-himself attitude could be destructive to landscapes and to individual lives. But his golden rule philosophy also reflects Royce's childhood in a devout Christian home. This is not to say that Royce was an overtly religious person in any traditional sense by the time he landed at Harvard after studying in Berkeley, in Germany, and elsewhere. Yet, Royce did *think* a lot about religion. He is the most well-known American practitioner of what philosophers call Absolute Idealism. This means, in part, that he believed in an Absolute, a.k.a. God In Some Form.

In his physical and intellectual migrations, Royce began with Western America but ended up explaining a major problem, as he saw it, for all of western civilization. While Royce felt, like the Progressives of his age (Jane Addams, Upton Sinclair, Teddy Roosevelt, to name some), that changes in society needed to be based on a personal moral code, he never shook it like a holy roller. A personal relationship to Jesus, for example, to quote a simple component of any modern evangelical's explanation of

Christianity, did not matter to Royce. It was this type of explanation—the divine incarnation experienced on an individual level—
that he actually saw as problematic when he wrote one of his most
well regarded books, *The Problem of Christianity* (New York:
Macmillan) in 1913. What mattered to Royce, what he saw as
important, was the gathering together in the Church itself of a *community* of people who shared a history of memories and a history
of hopes. "Those, I say, are right," Royce wrote, "who have held
that the Church, rather than the person of the founder, ought to be
viewed as the central idea of Christianity" (p. xxi).

The Church as a Roycean community in America would
arguably find its greatest success in the black community during the
Civil Rights movement, but ideal communities—with shared hopes
and memories—had existed in and outside of churches in America
throughout its history. From the time of the Pilgrims through the
Transcendentalists, Royce's adopted home of New England offered
prime examples of people seeking true community, what Royce
called the Beloved Community. On the contrary, in Royce's nineteenth-century Euro-American West, the boosters who did much of
the imagining did not root long in one community before moving
on to their next project.

Royce thought a great deal about the importance of community
and what he saw as the lack of it in much of California's history. In
addition to his work in philosophy, he wrote one of the first histories of his native state, *California: A Study of American Character*;
and he also penned his only novel, a western set in the hills east
of San Francisco, titled *The Feud of Oakfield Creek*. These two
books, published in 1886 and 1887, emphasized greed, violence,
conquest, and a lack of community as important themes in understanding California. Neither story won Royce many friends back
home, but he soldiered on. He felt strongly that people needed to
understand their histories, their pasts, especially the ugly parts, in
order to move upward as a society. Once people knew their histories, a "wise provincialism," whereby they could create healthy
communities, could make the West, other regions, and the entire
nation stronger. For Southerners—and Royce remembered the Civil
War well from his early childhood—a wise provincialism would
certainly require facing the legacies of slavery. For Westerners, wise
provincialism meant that the stereotypical wanderers (like Royce's
fruit-peddling father, but also the cowboys, miners, loggers, railroad men, and others) needed to come home and settle down into

stable communities. Twenty years after these first studies, Royce began to see evidence of strong communities in California—places where groups of people were able "to confront the standardizing, disorganizing, depersonalizing forces of modern industrial development" (Earl Pomeroy, "Josiah Royce, Historian in Quest of Community," *Pacific Historical Review*, February 1971, p. 8).

Although Royce's ideas tapped into the work of other philosophers—namely Georg Hegel, Charles Peirce, and Royce's close friend and colleague at Harvard, William James—his real aquifer was personal experience: knowing California as a native son and as a thinker. In his later works, he wrote about how climate and landscape in California—the environment—eventually shaped people and institutions. In what may be seen as an early twist on the idea that changes in latitudes can actually produce changes in attitudes, Royce wrote in 1908 that the Californian's "intimacy with nature," due to a mild climate, led to changes in how people there related to one another ("The Pacific Coast: A Psychological Study of the Relations of Climate and Civilization," in *Race Questions, Provincialism, and Other American Problems* (Macmillan, 1908), p. 202). He argued that knowing a place deeply, through nature, was important for transforming shaky places into real communities and bastions of democracy.

Take, for example, his conceptualizations of grace and salvation. These were not granted by God, but were, rather, ideals shaped by members of a community. He recalled that some early settlers in California built homes, and planted vineyards, thinking "not merely of gold nor yet of further wandering." They began, Royce wrote, "to regret their own former devastation of the landscape, and occasionally they would try to cover the wounds by gardens and by orchards." In this way, Royce's "wise provincialism" seems to approach a modern definition of "sustainable." In the "formation of a loyal local consciousness, in a wise provincialism," Royce argued, "lies the way towards social salvation" ("Provincialism: Based Upon a Study of Early Conditions in California," *Putnam's Magazine* (November 1909), pp. 235, 237). For Royce, nature shaped humans, and humans shaped nature in a never-ending process. When the latter happened responsibly, a true community—a Beloved Community—might begin to emerge.

Royce's philosophy of community would be repeated time and again by others throughout the twentieth century, some of them drawing on his work very deliberately. Frederick Jackson Turner, the most important historian of the American West, quoted Royce directly. Wallace Stegner, likely the region's finest writer, read Royce fervently, and wrote one of the better known summaries of the philosophy of community in the introduction to his collection of essays, *The Sound of Mountain Water*: "Angry as one may be at what careless people have done and still do to a noble habitat, it is hard to be pessimistic about the West. This is the native home of hope. When it finally learns that cooperation, not rugged individualism, is the pattern that most characterizes and preserves it, then it will have achieved itself and outlived its origins. Then it has a chance to create a society to match the scenery" (Doubleday, 1969, p. 38).

Westerners and Coral Reefs

You discover Stegner's writing in Montana. The discovery does not occur on the first trip, the one with visits to Livingston, Ringling, and with a memorable introduction to Missoula's finest after an early morning's splashy display of can openers and cannonballs into the indoor pool at the Holiday Inn. No, you discover Stegner on your second visit to Missoula, when you move there for graduate school after five years of bouncing between Florida, North Carolina, and Colorado. You're in the coffee shop-bookstore around the corner from your apartment, and it's one week before classes begin. You have heard others speak of Wallace Stegner, but you have never read him. You find *Angle of Repose* (Doubleday, 1971), his Pulitzer Prize winner from 1972, in a bin of used books. The price, two-fifty, is written in pencil on the inside cover. You love this novel from the start, when the narrator, who is in Grass Valley, California, living in the house where he stayed as a child with his grandmother, says, "My grandparents had to live their way out of one world and into another, or into several others, making new out of old the way corals live their reef upward. . . . We live in time and through it, we build our huts in its ruins . . ." (p. 18). Here's a metaphor that you can latch to as a Montana Parrothead: community in the American West as a coral reef. Years later, after you have read this five-hundred-plus-page tome a second time, you see in an interview where Stegner compares his grandmother character to Sarah Royce, Josiah's mother. But that first time through *Angle*, when you have never heard of Royce, you read the novel in a few days. At times, you're in the coffee shop, at other times,

your feet rest in an eddy pool of the Clark's Fork River. It's a fasci-
nating yet depressing story. As Stegner weaves a tale of a family
pulled through the ringer by too much movement across the West,
always in search of opportunity on the land in places like Leadville
(which is first described as "littered with wreckage, shacks, and
mine tailings . . . scalped of its timber"), you wish that Stegner's
characters would just find a place and stop (p. 236). Ultimately,
they do when they settle in Grass Valley, the actual hometown
Royce left as a child.

The next fortunate find in the used book bin is Ivan Doig's
memoir, *This House of Sky: Landscapes of a Western Mind*
(Harcourt Brace, 1978). You're drawn to this book not by the rev-
elatory title, but by the cover itself. It is not the artwork on the
cover that you notice, for the artwork on your edition is quite
bland—a sketch of cowboys—and says little of the rewards
inside. No, you are actually drawn originally to this astonishing
book because a previous owner (or browser in the coffee shop)
has stained it with the bottom of a coffee mug, forming a perfect
dark circle around the words "Western Mind." Like Stegner, Doig
grabs you early when he mentions his memory of "a Montana
community too tiny to be called a town." Later, when you read
the word "Ringling" at the beginning of a larger description of this
place, you literally get up out of your chair and stand up to read
the passage again. Doig published this memoir in 1978, four years
after Buffett wrote and sang his description of the town. After
reading and re-reading of

Doig's Ringling, where he lived during the 1940s and 1950s,
you put down the book and cue up *Living And Dying in 3/4 Time*
as you call your brother, then read him this passage: "Ringling lay
on the land, twenty miles to the south of White Sulphur Springs,
as the imprint of what had been a town, like the yellowed outline
on grass after a tent has been taken down." After explaining how
the town's original name, "Leader" (almost certainly the product
of a shameless booster), changed only when the circus promoter
John Ringling built a spur line to the railroad there from White
Sulphur, Doig wrote, "The adult population was about 50 persons, almost all of them undreamably old to me, and the liveli-
hoods were a saloon, a gas station, a post office, Mike Ryan's
store, the depot, and exactly through the middle of town, the railroad tracks which glinted and fled instantly in both directions" (p.
126). No mention of a pile of beer cans, but you're sure they were

there by the time Buffett throttled down the cruise control and rolled through town at the wheel of a rental car in the 1970s.

Besides the similarities in Buffett's descriptions of Ringling and in Doig's, what holds you and excites you in *This House of Sky* is Doig's idea of how a landscape, a place, imprints a philosophy, a way of seeing the world that suggests how we might live in it. For him, stories of people in particular places can connect landscapes of the mind with landscape histories. Histories are the roots for lives and also for the philosophies that drive people and their communities upward like grape vines or coral reefs, making new from old, and living in time and through it. You see this idea clearly when you eventually study Royce and his philosophy of community, then again when you discover Stegner's reflections on that same philosophy.

When asked specifically about Royce in the early 1980s—if westerners had ever had the type of community Royce imagined—Stegner answered in what must be one of the greatest short summaries of the region's Euro-American history: "The whole history of the West is a series of consecutive raids. The Beaver West gives way to the Gold West. Gives way to the Grass West, gives way to the Irrigation West. Everything has to be readjusted about once a generation. . . . It's difficult to establish a sense of community when everything changes so fast. . . . I expect the West will do it sooner or later, but I don't think it's done it very effectively yet" (Wallace Stegner and Richard Etulain, *Conver-sations with Wallace Stegner on Western History and Literature* (University of Utah Press, 1983), pp. 189–190). A wise provincialism, as Royce put it, built on Stegner's "cooperation, not rugged individualism," needed to develop. Once people in the West became rooted, real community—salvation, to use Royce's term—was possible.

But Stegner said all of this twenty-five years ago, nearly seventy years after Royce's death. Now, more than a century after Royce's last written thoughts on community in the West, land use debates rage in the region over gas and oil development, coal, declining fisheries, and urban sprawl from Winslow to Wasilla. The question remains: how might westerners shape a Beloved Community?

Whether Stegner realized it or not, his metaphorical nod toward coral reefs in *Angle of Repose* offers a useful lens for looking at Royce and answering this question again. As living organisms that protect themselves with a hard exoskeleton material, much like a fort, corals are akin to stereotypical westerners: seemingly tough on the outside, yet vulnerable. Coral reefs are ancient, built up incrementally by a few millimeters each year for centuries. They include some of the most endangered species on earth today. In other words, with coral, we see old, established communities that can still be changed relatively quickly. If you are coral, rootedness does you no good when a poisonous plume of waste from a cruise ship hits the reef. In a recent study, scientists pointed out that more than half of the world's reefs could be lost over the next twenty years. The three greatest dangers are pollution, over-fishing, and habitat destruction. The solution? "Reducing human impacts to coral reef ecosystems," the report stated, "often requires changing our collective behavior, beliefs, values, and decision making-criteria." The good news for coral reefs and for the American West, of course, is that when Royce wrote about communities, he referred to human ones. For coral, developing a philosophy for survival is not an option. Westerners, on the other hand, can think—and they can change "behavior, beliefs, values"—about how to develop humane societies where selfish desires are sacrificed for the good of the whole.

Wonder Why We Ever Go Home

Royce once wrote that "Americans spend far too much of our early strength and time in our newer communities upon injuring our landscapes, and far too little upon endeavoring to beautify our towns and cities" ("Provincialism," in *Race Questions, Provincialism, and Other American Problems*, Macmillan, 1908, p. 107). He also said, "All the threads are in our hands. We have only to weave them into a single knot" (*The Problem of Christianity*, p. 312). Royce made both statements in the context of spelling out his main point regarding a philosophy of community: that individuals are doomed without it. While the climber and the sailor need good knots to move safely over rocks or through wind over water, the writer needs to bring lines together to tie the reader to the point. So, here's my hitch: the philosophy of Jimmy Buffett is Roycean in that Buffett, too, finds salvation in communities where humans strive for sustainability. While acknowledging that Key West and Florida, broadly, have provided Buffett with the most inspiration (including the expression of a strong environmental ethic in *Hoot*) some of his most candid statements about man's need for a real sense of community, a home, have keyed in on the small towns and rural places in Western America.[1] This is not surprising, because the West, Stegner's "native home of hope," has played the role of the muse for countless American artists.

For Jimmy Buffett, the question of community in the West is explored most clearly in his original score for the neo-western *Rancho Deluxe*. This 1975 cult classic, written by Buffett's brother-in-law, Thomas McGuane (who studied under Stegner at Stanford), stars Jeff Bridges and Sam Waterston. The film, set in Livingston in the 1970s is about characters in the twentieth century who are seeking peace in their modern lives by drawing on parts of an idealized, or heavily mythologized Old West way of living off the land. The most important song to emerge from this soundtrack, "Wonder Why You Ever Go Home," revised and re-released as "Wonder Why We Ever Go Home" on 1977's *Changes in Latitudes, Changes in Attitudes*, asks the single most important question in the film and it offers one of the most important questions in the entire Buffett storehouse of tales about people and their escapes to particular places: What exactly are we looking for when we seek grace or salvation through community?

Put into the context of the film for which it was written originally, the song is about Bridges's character, Jack, who drives a muddy pickup truck with a gun rack, and with his partner, a "part Indian" named Cecil (played by Waterston), shoots and steals cows and barters away the meat in town. Jack loves Montana and his free-wheelin' way of life there, where as Cecil puts it, they live the lives of "the last of the plainsmen." Yet, the desire of the main character (Bridges's Jack) to wander outside the boundaries of communal decency as a cattle rustler is checked by his desire to make a real home for himself in Montana. This becomes clear when we find out that Jack is really from a wealthy suburban family that is not pleased with his life off in the Mountain West. The viewer and listener eventually realize why Jack's "Feelings for movin' grow stronger" when he goes back "home" to face his past: clueless, overly-consumptive parents (they drive a Rolls-Royce) and a nagging ex-lover; and we wonder, too, why someone in his situation might ever return to a place that seems so stifling. Juxtaposed to

---

[1] One of the main characters in *Hoot* is a boy who moves to Florida from Montana and helps lead a successful fight to protect a family of endangered owls threatened by a greedy businessman.

Jack's story is that of Cecil, who takes his father (this western's "wise" Native American) on a fishing trip in Montana. After asking Cecil if he has turned to crime in order to buy the fishing boat or his truck, the father defines what he calls The Pickup Truck Death: the Montanan's desire to sacrifice everything to buy a new rig.

In these two drastically different landscapes, we get the same Roycean message: selfish desires can hurt the broader community. In wondering why we ever go to places where people move quickly, humors in need of repair, with same occupations and same obligations, the key point to recall is that those ways of living are like driving around with no spare, having nothing to *share.* In the context of the film, at the heart of "Wonder Why We Ever Go Home," is a completely different question: how did we get into this predicament of every man for himself and how do we escape it? The answer is by striving to be part of a true community.

Restlessness is a character trait we see in many westerners and in the work of writers who deal with the West, including Royce, Stegner, Doig, McGuane, and Buffett. But while many restless western characters may be explained by a rugged individualism—a desire to succeed at all costs—these writers (or their characters) acknowledge the need for cooperation and they seek it out. Royce practically came up with the idea for a philosophy of community as it fit the American West, specifically, then the others built on the idea. It is clear by the end of *Rancho Deluxe* that the "last of the plainsmen," captured by the police and sanctioned by the community for their own greed in cattle rustling, have learned two things: that they can't trust the myths they had bought into about the ever abundant American West, and that the old Roycean idea—that individuals might only develop humane societies when they sacrifice selfish desires for the good of the whole—leads very directly for them to a society that matches the scenery in Montana. The irony for Jack and Cecil is that in going to "jail" for their own selfish desires, they actually become part of the truer community by working at the high country Rancho Deluxe as cowboys for the Montana Department of Corrections.

In closing, we return again to Ringling, the very image of a bygone, bypassed Montana town, shaped and then abandoned by boosters. For Buffett, like Royce, Stegner, Doig, and others, stories of people in particular places can connect landscapes of the mind directly with landscape histories. When we think about the philosophy of Jimmy Buffett, it's impossible to ignore Key West (the subject of "I Have Found Me a Home"). But we should also remember the key things about the other West in Buffett's life. When he writes of Tully Mars, the Wyoming cowboy who takes his horse to Florida and on to the Caribbean in *Tales From Margaritaville* and in *A Salty Piece of Land*, or when he laments the "dying little town" of Ringling, Buffett makes it clear that histories/stories are the roots for the lives we lead, but also for the philosophies that drive us and our good communities upward, slowly and sustainably, not unlike a healthy coral reef.

13
Fly-Fishing and the Ecology of Music

SCOTT L. PRATT

After a lecture I gave on the philosophy of music last year, an audience member asked: "What you have said is fine for Beethoven or Bach or Gounod [the composer of the opera I'd just finished talking about] but what about someone like Jimmy Buffett? Is 'Margaritaville' art in the same way? Or is it something else?"

The answer I gave clearly did not satisfy the questioner and, worse, it didn't satisfy me. There is, it appears, a world of difference between listening to Gounod's opera, *Faust*, and catchy tunes like "Fruitcakes" or "Come Monday." The question stuck with me and was part of the reason I became involved in this book. Is Jimmy Buffett's music art, or is it something else?

Before we explore Jimmy Buffett's view of this, let's take a quick look at the standard theories of art. These theories usually focus on the visual or the verbal, and treat music as an afterthought or an exception. Sometimes the effects of works of art are attributed to their overall form (things like the balance of colors, the texture of the object, shapes, spatial relations and so on) and sometimes to what the art object expresses (usually emotional experiences like anger, sadness, joy, adoration, or pain). Examples of visual art— paintings, sculptures, drawings and perhaps buildings—lend themselves to conceptions of art that emphasize the form and character of the work as it affects its audience. Examples of art constructed in language—poetry, stories, plays—can emphasize the formal and expressive aspects of art but also add the potential for understanding art as communicating particular content.

So a poem may have a certain form (a particular meter, a rhyme scheme) and may express a certain feeling (grief, joy, madness). A poem may also convey a particular content. For example, Simon Ortiz's poem, "Horizons and Rains" (www.hanksville.org/voyage/poems/I40_2.html), is a certain length (sixteen lines) with a pattern of repeated words (raining, losing, raining) and so on, and to most the poem expresses a kind of sadness and anger ("witness to the brown people / stumbling Sunday afternoons / northwards"). But it is also a poem that is about Native people in a particular place facing loss and poverty. The geography mentioned in the poem (Interstate 40 from Albuquerque to Gallup) also connects the poem to a particular place and a particular period of history. While a painting may lead to such specificity, the poem seems to present it more directly. In any case, art is often understood in terms of its formal structure, its expressiveness (or its ability to evoke a particular response in a viewer or listener), and its ability to be about something particular.

This last function has led some philosophers to claim that a key component of art is its ability to challenge social norms and provide a context for social change. In this case, all of the aspects of the art object come into play. An object can challenge expected forms, can express feelings of oppression, and, through the meaning of language, target the critique on aspects of society that the artist and audience believe need changing. While such theories have been readily applied to paintings and poetry, novels and sculpture, music has tended to be left out of the conversation.

A few philosophers have taken on questions of music as art. Historically, they include thinkers like Schopenhauer and Nietzsche, and more recently Suzanne Langer, Peter Kivy, Theodor Adorno, and a few others. The problem for coming up with a philosophical understanding of music, in part, has been that it's not clear what counts as the musical object, that is, the art itself. It's easy to point at a painting and refer someone to a poem, since these have a more or less unchanging presence. The Mona Lisa still hangs at the Louvre; Shakespeare's sonnets are available with or without modernized spellings and can be read by anyone, and Ortiz's poem is on the internet and accessible to all. There are differences, of course. A reproduction of the Mona Lisa seems to lack something that the original has, even though a reprinted edition of Shakespeare does not. Still, there is a sense of stability in most objects of visual art and most instances of poetry and prose.

Music has a different character. As an art object, music seems to come and go easily. Even if we refer to Beethoven's Fifth Symphony or Buffett's "King of Somewhere Hot," it's not clear what we're referring to. Since these musical objects do not hang on a wall, it's not obvious whether we refer to a particular instance of the symphony or some collection of instances (leaving out, perhaps, the ones where the violins are badly out of tune or the trumpets routinely miss their entries). We might imagine that the musical object is not any performance at all but an abstract idea, perhaps of the perfect performance. Or it might be something that is not related to an abstract idea, but rather to the music as recorded on paper, what Kivy calls in *Introduction to a Philosophy of Music* "score compliant" (Clarendon, 2002, pp. 224–234).

The problem with the conception of the musical object as an abstract idea is that it is not clear what an abstract idea sounds like. If music is finally something that is heard, how could something count as the real thing even though it can't be heard? Kivy tries to solve this problem by making the musical object something that "complies" with the score in performance. But in this case, compliance (the relation between the score and the sounds) becomes the art object and not the sounds in relation to the performer and the audience. Such a view may acknowledge music as a matter of form, but would have little to say about the expressiveness, content or transformative power of a given piece.

It might be that the musical object is simply a musical performance. Beethoven's Fifth Symphony has been performed thousands of times and taking into account changes in musicians, instruments, concert halls, and audience, among other things, every performance is different (some very different), enough so that when you and I talk about Beethoven's Fifth, we may be talking about two things that are only vaguely connected. It might be easier with "King of Somewhere Hot" if we talk about the recording that appears on *Hot Water*. But as we'll see later, Buffett himself recognizes very different performances of the song—different enough that one stands for him as *the* performance. Since that performance was not recorded and in this sense is lost, even starting a conversation about that song as art would seem to be a lost cause. It almost doesn't matter which notion of art we accept if the musical object is so easily lost that its best instances vanish even before the conversation gets started.

"Music for the Money"

Before we give up on Buffett's music (or music in general), it might be useful to think about whether these received notions of music are correct in the first place. Buffett himself may reject the debate from the start since at times he seems to reject the idea that his work should be taken as anything more than entertainment. His rejection of art, however, turns on what he takes the alternatives to be. If art is the kind of thing that the philosophers worry about—paintings by the masters, poetry by Shakespeare, novels by Austin or James—then he may be right. About the "Great Serious Writers" he says in *A Pirate Looks at Fifty*, "Well, I knew I wasn't one of those people. I was too warped by the court-jester-like behavior that's essential to being a good stage performer" (p. 12). If, on the other hand, art is roughly a kind of experience that has a particular character that sets it apart from ordinary experience, then Buffett's work may indeed be art.

Consider the song, "Makin' Music for the Money" on *A1A*. The song opens with Buffett exhausting himself by counting his money instead of sleeping. The experience is presented as a kind of revelation. He realizes that money is not the important thing. What really matters is "making music for me." If we set aside the irony of Buffett's vast financial success (and the fact that, like it or not, he is making music that, in turn, *makes* a lot of money), the point of the realization is that music is "in the making"—in the performance. The conclusion is important. In the chorus, Buffett declares that he doesn't care about money, so at first this appears to be a kind of insincere rejection of the music industry—insincere because he is clearly making money hand over fist. It isn't that Buffett doesn't care at all about money. It's rather that he doesn't care about it in the context of making music.

Suppose that we take for granted that music is a matter of performance, of making it, and we imagine that, as an activity, music is one that has a purpose or intent (as opposed to some unintentional body noise, for example). The declaration that he "won't make my music for money" is a declaration that the activity, the making, will have a purpose, but it will not be for the purpose of gaining money. This is significant for two reasons. First, it frames music or the musical object as a making or performance and second, that, as an intentional activity, it will have some purpose or end. This end, of course, is "me" or Buffett himself.

But what does it mean to have oneself as the purpose of an activity? At first, it might seem that this would mean that music is an activity of self-indulgence. After all, even if turning people on "is a good place to be," he doesn't aim to do that either. Music, if it is anything, appears to be a solo business for one's own satisfaction. The last verse of the song, however, undermines this conclusion. In the end, the singer finds a "place with much charm and much grace," untouched by the music industry, where "the people were havin' a good time / Makin' music all day long / And nobody cared if they ever got paid." The end of the song literally places music as a kind of performance in a community of musicians all participating in the process of music making. The purpose of the activity is transformed at the end of the song from something the singer does solely for himself, to something that he does for himself in the company of fellow musicians. Music is a particular kind of experience that involves the purposive engagement of a musician, a place, and others who share common purpose.

"A Permanent Reminder of a Temporary Feeling"

John Dewey's conception of art as experience provides a means for thinking about music as art that seems compatible with the notion of music in "Makin' Music for Money." For Dewey, what counts as art is not determined in advance by a definition that specifies its form, expressive character, content or even its compliance with a score or some other standard outside a given instance of art. Dewey argues that art is properly understood as an experience that has a particular character or quality. Where ordinary experience has a kind of routine or mundane quality, some other moments stand out. Moments when plans break down or old ways of doing things no longer produce results are instances of these more distinctive experiences.

Experiences of art, what can be called aesthetic experiences, are moments that are more than just a break in routine or an encounter with trouble. They are moments that are distinctive in that they are at once an experience in time with a beginning, a middle and an end, and at the same time are so unified as to stand out by themselves as somehow complete experiences. "A piece of work is finished in a way that is satisfactory," Dewey says in *Art as Experience*, "a problem receives its solution; a game is played through; a situation, whether that of eating a meal, playing a game of chess, carrying on a conversation, writing a book, or taking part in a political campaign, is so rounded out that its close is a consummation and not a cessation. Such an experience is a whole and carries with it its own individualizing quality and self-sufficiency. It is *an* experience" (Perigee, 1980, p. 36). A reviewer at EntertainmentAvenue.com, after a concert at Alpine Valley near Chicago, describes a Jimmy Buffett concert in this same way: "a Buffett show is an experience that must be lived" (www.entertainmentavenue.com/concert_hall/reviews/b/jimmy_buffett/jb060896.htm). Another reviewer, John Voket at LiveDaily.com, emphasizes the self-sufficient character of an "intimate" club show given by Buffett and his band in Connecticut. Despite Buffett's years of touring and hundreds of shows, Voket still concludes that the show was "a one-of-a-kind concert experience that most . . . fans only dream about" (www.livedaily.com/news/15201.html).

Experience of this sort, Dewey says, "we spontaneously refer to as being 'real experiences'; those things of which we say in recalling them, 'that *was* an experience'" (p. 36). Such an experience

> may have been something of tremendous importance—a quarrel with one who was once an intimate, a catastrophe finally averted by a hair's breadth. Or it may have been something that in comparison was slight. . . . There is that meal in a Paris restaurant of which one says 'that was an experience'. It stands out as an enduring memorial of what food may be. Then there is that storm one went through in crossing the Atlantic—the storm that seemed in its fury, as it was experienced, to sum up in itself all that a storm can be, complete in itself, standing out because marked out from what went before and what came after. (p. 36)

Such an experience may be *the* performance of a Beethoven symphony in terms of which all further ones are compared. Or it may be *the* performance of "Margaritaville," played in the midst of a concert on a particular evening in a particular arena. Like the music that Buffett finds in that place of "charm and grace," such experiences are somewhere, bound to a place and are in some sense both sufficient or complete and distinctive moments that serve to direct further experience.

But doesn't this make art simply what I like? When Buffett says that he wants to make music for himself, doesn't that mean that whether he is with other musicians or not, if what he plays is satisfying to him, it fits Dewey's definition of art—that is, it is sufficient or complete and distinctive, even if it is disparaged by every other listener? The sequence of verses in Buffett's song is instructive. After rejecting the idea that music can be made for money, he asserts that it can be made for himself. But he doesn't stop there. In the end, he finds (perhaps must find himself) a place where others are also engaged in the activity and there, in that community of artists, the music becomes part of a larger activity that is in some sense no longer just for Jimmy.

Art really comes in two phases. The first is the experience as one finds it: that performance of "King of Somewhere Hot" or that concert at the Waikiki Shell. If I declare that a particular performance has the characteristics of an aesthetic experience, it seems that there's little anyone else can say. It's my experience, after all, and though your experience is not an aesthetic one, that doesn't take away from mine. In fact, it's likely that while I'm singing along, I'm not even trying to decide if my own experience is aesthetic, let alone yours. But if I take the next step and claim that "King of Somewhere Hot" is art, then I'm making a broader claim: that the work when done again and for others, will continue to generate art experiences. My claim is open to debate and invites further performances. A central reason that certain classical works are "art" is that they have led to art experiences again and again across many audiences and across time.

The second phase of the experience is a reflective phase and an evaluative one. I think, "Now that was a great song!" And the woman next to me who has heard the same performance asks "Why do you say so?" and I start talking about the way the band played and Jimmy's changes in the lyrics from what I expected and that the song reminded me of some moment in the past when things were good, and so on. All of these reasons are inadequate to explaining fully what made the performance a complete experience, but all of them point back toward the now-lost sound and forward to the felt change that the performance has brought. My friend now adds her sense of the performance, agreeing that it was *an* experience, in Dewey's terms, and giving other reasons—the balance of voices, the enthusiasm of the crowd, the solos in the break and so on. In the first phase, the performance was *an* experience, but its character as a whole then becomes a kind of reflective standard that places the first phase in context and finds its meaning in the reasons we can give that it was a great performance.

"King of Somewhere Hot"

Buffett himself reinforces this conception of the aesthetic experience with his story, in *A Pirate Looks at Fifty*, about a performance of "King of Somewhere Hot" in Port of Spain. The performance was a rehearsal of the song in preparation for an upcoming concert in Miami. The sixty-piece steel drum band, WITCO Desperadoes, were a well known band in Trinidad and had agreed to open two benefit shows for Buffett in Key West and Miami. His co-writers on "King of Somewhere Hot," Ralph MacDonald and Bob Greenidge, went to Trinidad to rehearse the band and Buffett decided that he would join them when they were ready to rehearse the song (though Buffett makes a point of mentioning that he has a policy of not rehearsing very much).

Buffett finally arrived at the rehearsal site on top of a high hill in Port of Spain in a large open building surrounded by hundreds of people listening to the Desperadoes and dancing to the steel drum band. After a "wave of nervous fear" in front of this "musical force," Buffett picked up his guitar and began the rehearsal. "The song starts softly," he writes, "with just a guitar and one drum, but about twelve bars into it, when the Desperadoes came in, the goddamn thing exploded like a nuclear bomb. I was singing and listening and laughing inside, all at the same time. There is something about the sound of the steel drum that connects like a jumper cable to the musical fiber that I believe is in us all." Here, as both performer and audience, Buffett marks an extraordinary moment in which the experience comes "all at once." He continues: "There I was, this white boy on top of one of the toughest hills in Port of Spain, being picked up and flown by the power of the music and the place" (pp. 367–68).

The performance was quickly over, the unrecorded moment lost. The fact that the story appears years later in *A Pirate Looks at Fifty* suggests the experience nevertheless persisted, producing that second reflective and evaluative phase that makes sense of the original experience and transforms new ones. A week after the rehearsal, Buffett came on stage in Miami after the Desperadoes finished their opening songs and began "King of Somewhere Hot" again. "I would never have felt the same way about the song, or the performance, if I had just gone to the rehearsal hall and played through the songs with the band." Instead, on the floating stage at the Miami concert, "that night came" with "the whole experience of my trip up the hill" (p. 368). The earlier experience had not vanished but became part of the new experience, changing the character of the later performance so that "when the song ended, there was a split second of silence, like the vacuum that sucks out the air right before a lightning strike, and then they let loose. The crowd went nuts. The band went nuts. I went nuts and jumped into the bay" (pp. 368–69). The experience of the rehearsal carried forward to the performance in Miami, making it a new experience for Buffett, the band and the crowd who, Buffett concludes, "saw something special that night."

The musical experience, as an aesthetic experience, is not an isolated moment or an abstract idea or something lost at the moment it seems to end or even something necessarily confined within an individual. It is, from the philosophical perspective of Dewey's notion of experience and Buffett's own account, at once a complete experience and at the same time something without sharp boundaries that is connected to a wider context, a community of participants, a past and a future. It's both a "place of charm and grace" and an activity of makin' music.

It is possible that one could come to think of an art experience as a kind of singular event in which one is simply enveloped in a work and joins in the pervasive quality of the performance and its context as a single whole. Buffett suggests this possibility when, in his description of the Miami performance of "King of Somewhere Hot," he says that "I didn't play the song, I just climbed on board the groove that the Despos laid down and took a ride" (p. 368). From this angle, it seems that the performance really is a kind of singular experience with each participant potentially in their own "world" experiencing the music for themselves. The problem with this characterization is that it risks leaving out the relation between the creators of the experience: the musicians who perform, and the audience who listen.

This split is even implicit in Buffett's description of the experience where he leaves the performer role behind and becomes a kind of passive listener "riding the groove." Dewey seems to face a similar problem in his understanding of the aesthetic experience because it is at least not apparent where the relation between artist and audience figures in. It's true that for Dewey the artist is trying to establish the conditions necessary for an aesthetic experience of an audience (including the artist as audience). She will use her skills with the material of her art. Her knowledge of art, and her past experience about what works, shapes the materials at hand into something that will make an aesthetic experience of a certain type possible.

Musicians are no different and, of course, Buffett's own conception of himself as primarily a performer confirms that it is an ability to shape the experience of the audience that makes his performances successful as aesthetic experiences. In the end, is it enough of a relation that the performer prepared the way for an audience to be 'turned on'? Or is there more at work? The implausible place to look for a better model of the relation between artist and audience is not in Buffett's explicit take on music, but in his stories of fly-fishing.

"The Blue-Marlin Tango"

It's easy to overlook this passion since he has no songs about it. Still, in the voice of the hero of *A Salty Piece of Land*, Tully Mars, Buffett writes "the fishing pole bends heavier for some than others, and nobody has yet to figure out why—just as you never know, when you make a cast, if what attacks your fly is a finger-size baby snapper or a tiger shark that can turn you into bait. Still, we struggle with the rod just the same. Life to me is like a fish on the line. When it is there, you feel it. You fight it. You gain line. You lose line. But if that line suddenly snaps, or the pole breaks, or a thousand other problems occur that fishermen use as excuses when the tension is gone, you feel it even more" (p. 425). Fishing, especially fly-fishing, is no one-sided affair. There's no proverbial barrel that confines the fish for shooting; it is not target practice. It is also not leaving the activity to the fish while you sit and watch a bobber.

I have never really thought of fly-fishing as an art, though I suppose in its activity it is. Like other artistry, it is a complex activity whose greatest moments are short and intense, breaking from the routine and changing the feel of experience long after the moment has vanished. While the occasional novice fly-fisher can manage a lucky catch, it is more often a combination of luck and practice that brings the experience of a fish on the line. The fish on the line is also the result of a fly that has been made just right for the water and the light. The drift of the wind, the movement of the current, the clarity of the water, the presence of cover, the clouds in the sky, the angle of the sun all can be marked as critical elements of the experience of a fish on the line.

Buffett recounts his love of fishing, his occasional success and his frequent failure in *A Pirate Looks at Fifty*. There is, for example, his fly-fishing trip from Quepos, Costa Rica, in search of tarpons. The story reinforces the continuity of the experience. He finds a boat, the *Numero Uno*, and sets sail in search of fish. During a couple of days of fishing, the fish linger just out of range. When a blue marlin turns up in the wake of the boat, Buffett casts the fly close and the fish takes it. "All of a sudden the marlin hurls himself out of the water horizontally to the wake of the boat. Make way for the big enchilada. Here he comes: bill, fin, tail, and all. He crashes the fly and the line goes tight. My God, I have him on. I go to set the hook. A momentary tug and then nothing" (p. 259). The experience abruptly ends. The moment passes. The boat continues to churn slowly in search of another fish. The trip ends without a catch.

You might think that the failure to catch a fish marked an incomplete experience. On the return trip, however, he thinks again about the fish he had missed. "I looked down at my notebook," he writes, "quickly jotted down my final thoughts of the day, and realized that I had, in fact, landed the fish in the most perfect way. His brief appearance in our lives was now the best trophy I could want—a story" (p. 263). The two phases of experience emerge again. The first, the interaction with the marlin across the gunwale of the *Numero Uno*, marked the intersection of a vast number of environmental factors: the activity of the fish, the boat, the waves, the sun, Jimmy and so on. The second phase carried that intersection forward into a reflection that became a story that turns up again here, in the context of a discussion of the nature of music.

Buffett reinforces the interactive quality of his fly-fishing experience in an earlier story about the catch of his first striped sea bass on a fly rod in the rough waters of Long Island Sound not long after his near death experience in the crash of his seaplane off Nantucket. Buffett says "This little bass was more beautiful than he could have imagined." The key to that beauty was that he and the fish "were connected by more than the monofilament line that had brought him into my hands. I had used all my resources of modern materials and primeval stalking to fool him and catch him, and then I held him by the tail and moved him back and forth in the water so that the motion would fill his gills with water and replenish him . . ." (p. 67). The "more" in this case is the shared character of the experience. It is the hard connection between Buffett and the fish by fishing line *and* all the things that came to be focused in the monofilament connection. The experience was the interaction between the fisher and fish as embedded in a larger local environment.

The Ecology of Music

Without the attention of the fish, its characteristic behaviors, and its deviations from rigid habit, the experience would not be complete. Without the presence of the fisher and the environment that sustains them both, the experience could not be complete. While fishing is rarely listed among things ecological—at least not among those who are concerned with the survival and treatment of fish—fishing is in fact an ecological practice. 'Ecology' was first defined by the nineteenth-century German biologist, Ernst Haeckel. "By ecology," he said, "we mean the whole science of the relations of the organism to the environment including, in the broad sense, all the 'conditions of existence'. They are partly organic, partly inorganic in nature" (quoted in Carolyn Merchant, *The Columbia Guide to Environmental History*, Columbia University Press, 2005, p. 159).

From this perspective, the experience of fly-fishing is one that marks a particular range of interactions between organisms and environment. It is a multi-sided relation that under certain conditions becomes, for a moment, aesthetic in its unification of the environment and its organisms in the way that affects the ecosystem as it develops from that moment onward. After he released the little bass, Buffett was quiet. "The morning was complete, in a lot of ways. I had rediscovered my saline psyche" (p. 67). There is no report of how the fish recalled his morning.

In an important way, Buffett's story of the rehearsal performance in Port of Spain presents a comparable ecological conception, in this case of a musical experience. It is not simply the relation between the performers, or the performers and their audience; it is not Buffett himself, or even the place in some holistic sense, but rather the interaction between the organisms—performers and audience—and their environment. It was a warm Trinidad evening. Buffett sipped rum while he waited to go to the rehearsal. The building was like a pavilion, open to the surrounding hill, and was surrounded by an audience dancing to the music of the Desperadoes. The band was highly skilled and could play the complex rhythms and harmony of the song, the technology of steel drums and Fender guitars worked as expected.

Buffett left the performance a changed man, but there's no reason to assume that he was the only one taken up in the experience. During the later concert in Miami, Buffett mentions looking at his co-writers who had been present at the rehearsal and they "were laughing their heads off" (p. 368). Rather than being the experience of one alone, the nature of the musical experience is such that it is the interaction of agents and their environment.

Buffett recognizes the intimate connection between the participants and the environment of musical performance. Writing about his songs, he concludes that they are not his possessions. This fact becomes clear during concerts. He says, "When I forget a word or a phrase [, I] listen to the audience singing them to find my place. Songwriters write songs, but they really belong to the listener. I think of myself sometimes as a toymaker, who enjoys his work but who takes more pleasure from the fact that his toys live in a stranger's toy box, bringing that stranger constant joy" (p. 83). The task of a toymaker is not unlike that of a fisher who casts the line toward a disturbed patch of water. It is the connection between that leads to the experience. The toys (to shift the metaphor) live in a stranger's home, but this is just the monofilament stretched thin. When the box is opened and the tune is put into play again, the intimate bond is restored and the aesthetic possibilities return.

"Where Did All the Good Songs Go?"

In "Homemade Music," Buffett sets out a second conception of music to complement "Making' Music for Money." Here the music industry is still a target of ridicule. But what is "homemade music"? The question is explicitly ecological since 'eco' is derived from the Greek term *oikos* or home. 'Homemade music' is almost literally eco-music. Rather than mass produced music that leads to various modes of recording—"first there were records, cassettes and CD's"—homemade music is something live, or better, something alive. Unlike music produced and consumed through records that displace music from its ecosystem—its "home-system"—in order to make money, homemade music has a place even though it is also "on thin ice."

Buffett provides a sense of what he means by homemade music in his video "Party at the End of the World." He and his song-writing partners experiment with lyrics, stop the song, play phrases, laugh, and start again. But the video is also cut with clips from a live performance of the complete song and this connection is important. Homemade music is not just a performance for oneself or just with a few friends, but those performances *and* performances in other wider contexts: live concerts, recordings, and videos. It's the connection between these performances—their continuity—gained through the reflective and evaluative phase of experience that helps make the ecosystem in which the music lives and aesthetic experience is sustained.

I began this discussion thinking about the question of whether "Margaritaville" is art in a way comparable to works like Beethoven's Fifth Symphony and Gounod's *Faust*. Buffett himself seems to confirm the fundamental distinction between symphonies and his own tunes in "Six String Music": "Ain't no symphony / It's just six string music / So elementary." The difference is not one that defies comparison however. He admits that some people like Beethoven and some like Jimmy Reed, but we should "keep it simple" because "That's all we really need." While Buffett may be claiming that "simple" music is all we need, it's more likely that the music we need is simply the music that connects us: "a song from me to you."

Using Buffett's reflections on music and experience and the ideas of John Dewey and Ernst Haeckel, we have the resources to "keep it simple" and understand the aesthetic qualities of Buffett's music and Gounod's. "Margaritaville" and Gounod's *Faust* can be understood as elements of different ecosystems. Their comparison is at once pointless and at the same time helps to illustrate the larger importance of musical activity. *Faust* and "Margaritaville" are each part of complex relations that make them viable in one setting and not necessarily viable in others. A performance of *Faust* could only emerge in an environment that can sustain the complexities of opera performance with its space requirements, demands for musicians and singers trained in a particular style, and the money needed to make the performance a reality. The participants—performers and audience—will have been prepared with certain expectations so that the moment of Marguerita's damnation marks a turning point in the experience. If *Faust* is performed in some other setting, one where the musicians and singers are unfamiliar with the music and the style of performance and the audience expects some elitist and incomprehensible noise, the opera will be like a fish out of water.

"Margaritaville" is similarly bound to its own ecosystem of Parrotheads and pop culture, electronic music distribution and the practices of live concerts, giant performance halls and pitchers of margaritas, Jimmy's books and TV interviews and so on. The chance appearance of Jimmy at a bar in Key West to sing "Margaritaville" happens at the edges of this same ecosystem: the venue is small, the singer close to the audience, but the performance is still informed by years of listening to the song, of large concerts and Parrothead hats. And the performance at the bar will add to the system as a new story about the song and its performance. If the same song were played in some other venue, perhaps in a concert hall between a Schumann song cycle and a Mozart violin concerto, the performance would be radically out of place, another fish out of water.

The quality of "Margaritaville" and *Faust* as art is a matter of the experiences they are part of, not something inherent in their "music-ness" (whatever that would mean). Their viability as art is ecological. But the fact that they can both be understood in ecological terms also suggests some similarities. Both works, for example, lend themselves to repeated performances and new aesthetic experiences. "Margaritaville" is still played and sung decades after its peak in popularity while thousands of other songs are lost to time. Its ability to continue to be part of aesthetic experiences says something about its ability to thrive in its ecosystem. This probably involves its form (its melodic and harmonic lines), its ability to express something beyond a particular set of concerns (a lost shaker of salt) and its potential to raise larger issues (*somebody* is to blame after all).

The potential for *Faust* to persist for one hundred fifty years can similarly be understood. It thrives in its ecosystem as well and its formal characteristics continue to reach audiences like monofilament line. Its story is familiar and shared. It lends itself well to translation and it can be staged inexpensively or grandly depending upon the resources at hand.

The ecological conception of music that lies at the heart of Buffett's approach to music is one that can provide a valuable way to understand the activity of music and the nature of aesthetic experience. It's no wonder, then, that Buffett declares that homemade music—eco-music—performed and heard in its place is "part of his philosophy."

14

Dead Reckoning and Tacking in the Winds of Fortune and Fate

RANDALL E. AUXIER

Fortune favors the bold.

—Latin Proverb

When it comes to the basic questions of life and death, I have never considered myself a really deep thinker.

—JAMES WILLIAM BUFFETT, *A Pirate Looks at Fifty*

Others disagree with Jimmy's assessment of Jimmy. Our basic argument follows Jimmy's own logic. We can question whether all those allegedly "deep thinkers" are paying "way too much attention . . . to something that just can't be changed" (*A Pirate Looks at Fifty*, p. 35). To the list of things that just can't be changed, we can add taxes and bullshit, but whereas taxes and bullshit crop up all the time, it does seem like we're all going to get just one true shot at the bucket-kick, regardless of what may or may not come after it.

But speaking of life, rather than death, I guess this is where we find the questions that trouble us so. Here is where Jimmy has some thoughts for us, and I, for one, find them deep enough to ponder with appreciation. We can't take on every question, so I'm settling for one that I think every Parrothead has considered, and certainly Jimmy has. It's really one question, but philosophers use a number of different terms to describe the dilemma.

On one side we find the ideas of chance, luck, contingency, and freedom; on the other side we find destiny, fate, necessity and determinism. Our little brains get caught betwixt and between, which is one good reason to saturate those neurons with a good red wine from time to time. Administered in the right proportions, certain libations become catalysts for a cerebral emulsion. We find an elevated, or at least altered, form of *consciousness*, and the conflict between fortune and fate becomes pretty funny. So if you don't mind, or even if you do, I'm opening a bottle of my favorite stuff; I recommend that you do the same. If I start making sense to you along the way, you'll know you're gills are the right color of red (or at least the same color as mine).

A Dead White Dude and an Incarnation

Just about every philosopher who ever lived took the trouble to register an opinion about necessity and contingency—when something *cannot* be otherwise (which is necessity), and when something *can* be other than it is (which is contingency). The same is true of the issue of free will and determinism. Pretty much all the dead dudes talk about it. The discussions get tedious pretty fast, and nothing gets settled.

Jimmy has also weighed in on these subjects. On necessity and contingency, he chooses the hokey-pokey, on the suspicion that we are complicating the questions beyond what is advisable. Just put your head in, pull it out, shake it all about, and turn yourself around. On freedom and determinism Jimmy expresses his agreement with Forrest Gump: "he didn't know whether life was some kind of predestined plan or whether we were just floating around like a feather on the wind, but he thought it was probably both" (*A Pirate Looks at Fifty*, pp. 35–36). These may seem like contradictory answers, but as Jimmy confesses, "I can't help but be / Ruled by inconsistency" ("Distantly in Love"). This crap doesn't have to be worked out. We live the same way regardless of the answer.

On the other hand, relatively few philosophers, past or present, speak seriously about *fortune and fate*, but the list of those who do have something to say is intriguing: Aristotle (382–324 B.C.E.), Niccolò Machiavelli (1469–1527), and Giambattista Vico (1668–1744). The discussion of fortune and fate is not nearly so boring as those other topics. I think philosophers avoid these subjects because they have a vague feeling of superstition about them. Philosophers don't like to be seen as superstitious; they want to be Reason Incarnate, no matter how boring that makes them. And indeed, there is an important difference, however slight, between the ideas of "fortune" and "fate" and the other more "rational" ideas of necessity and contingency, freedom and determinism. Fortune and fate poke their conceptual fingers into the ribs of our primal ignorance. Sometimes that tickles, but Reason Incarnate isn't ticklish, and it isn't easily amused. Those other more "rational" ideas try to build our knowledge up from what we really *can* learn about ourselves, and our universe, by observation, experimentation, measurement, reasoning and the like. We may not come to any conclusions, but at least we feel like we *know* something when we're finished studying. But there aren't any "experiments" with fate and fortune, and even first hand experience with them isn't a reliable teacher.

There but for Fortune. . .

Aristotle had nothing to say about fate, but he spent some time wondering whether good and bad luck could actually determine a person's happiness in life. After a long discourse about it, he came to the conclusion that virtuous habits in both public and private life are the best defense against bad luck. Actually, he doesn't use the word "virtue," because he was Greek, and that isn't a Greek word. I'm saving the word "virtue" for something else in this heap of verbiage. Aristotle said that what you want to ward off bad luck is *aretē*, which sort of means "excellence," and in this case, not just an excellent fishing hole, but *moral* excellence. He pointed out that an "excellent" person could weather bad luck better than a person with all sorts of bad habits, vices, and moral failings. Even with tons of bad luck, a good person could still find ways to feel blessed and happy in life. On the other hand, a person of uneven character couldn't be contented with life even when all his luck was good, let alone when it was bad.

This sounds right to me, but I don't really want to do all the hard work required to be a genuinely excellent person, so Aristotle does *me* no good. And I'll bet I'm probably just like you (correct me if I'm wrong). I want to be *selectively* moral, and I also want the favor of good fortune to make up the difference between my vices and their natural consequences. In short, I don't want either justice or mercy—I don't deserve the latter and can't bear the former; I want to escape the natural order by just enough to enjoy my favorite toys, keep my vices, and die in my sleep. As Jimmy says, "a little escapism never hurt anybody. I should know, I've been selling it for years" (*A Pirate Looks at Fifty*, p. 58). Aristotle is right, but he's too austere for us. We want an easier way.

Machiavelli, on the other hand, might be just the ticket. He also has little to say about fate, but he says a lot about fortune. I know you've all heard of Machiavelli, since his name has become synonymous with ruthless politics and strategizing to take advantage of people. But there's a lot more to Machiavelli than that, and he deserved a better fate than to have his name become the ready-made epithet for all conniving assholes with limitless ambition and no scruples. I'm going to take a few tips from Machiavelli in what follows, because he may have the advice most needed by people like us—me, you, and Buffett (that is, people who don't want to sacrifice all of our vices just so that we can be serene in the face of all the bullshit that might or might not come down A1A).

An Over Forty Victim of Fate

Giambattista Vico also has a fair amount to say about fortune, cutting sort of a middle course between the ample wakes of Aristotle and Machiavelli, but what's more interesting and useful is what he has to say about fate. Vico carefully avoids saying there is "no such thing" as fate. I mean, how could we *know*? What he does say is that, "to be useful to the human race, philosophy must raise and direct weak and fallen man, not rend his nature or abandon him in his corruption." I don't wish to be rended or abandoned in my corruption, so Vico says I will have no use for those nasty old Stoics who are "chaining themselves to fate" or for Epicureans who are "abandoning themselves to chance" (*The New Science*, Cornell University Press, 1968, pp. 129–130).

The reason we need to look at this is because of what Jimmy has to say about fate. It doesn't show up too often in his songs, but it shows up famously: he was born two hundred years too late, and that was the work of fate. And Jimmy can't quite decide which way the wind blows on this—he has described the winds that fill life's sails as both fate (*A Pirate Looks at Fifty*, p. 15), and fortune (see "Mental Floss," his ode to the jellyfish). We need to find our way among the winds of life, to tack the craft toward one particular harbor.

Methinks There Is Madness in His Method

How to get at this? We need to get our bearings. Jimmy has always prided himself on having learned the art of dead reckoning, but even so, we have to have a fix on a position, a speed, and a distance. We can reckon our way through Buffett's philosophical moments if we can get a fix on them. I have noticed that Buffett songs follow sort of a pattern—it's not quite a "formula," but it's more than chance. Most of his songs contain the following: (1) a place, (2) a time, (3) a meeting, (4) a sentiment, and (5) a thought. Five things (I can still count the fingers on one hand, so no emulsion yet). Now there's plenty of variation in these five, so they aren't the fixed stars of the Buffett firmament, and I want to say something about the first four before we get to the last one, the *thought*, which is the part I'm really pondering. But first a story—or at least the beginning of one.

Meet Me in Memphis

A Place: Memphis. A Time: May 7–10, 1981. A Meeting: I was roped into working alongside that Parrothead. I won't name him, but the situation is worth recalling. If you're in the flower business, like this one particular Parrothead, Mother's Day is about the worst weekend of the year (Valentine's Day is the other main competitor). Every florist recruits friends, relations, acquaintances, and a few people off the streets to deliver flowers. I wasn't so much a friend of the Parrothead; I was more like a friend of an acquaintance of a cousin of a guy they pulled off the street. But every town has its own coconut telegraph, so I got a call to deliver flowers and pick up a little extra coin, which every thirsty student can use, for good ends or ill, or both. Final exams were, well, *almost* over. What followed was four straight days, Thursday through Sunday, in a ragged cargo van with a rabid Jimmy Buffett partisan, the first of that clan I'd encountered in all my twenty years. So while I knocked on doors with flowers for the resident matriarch, my new compadre charted a course for the next destination.

Like just about everyone, I had heard Buffett's hit songs. I liked them, even knew the words. But I didn't own a record and I'd never been to a concert, and I guess I would describe myself as "neutral" on matters pertaining to Buffett. That was about to change. The Parrothead had all and only Buffett recordings in the van, and it was *his* van. Our first conversation went something like this:

PARROTHEAD: You like Jimmy Buffett?
ME: Sure.
PARROTHEAD: He's the greatest songwriter who ever lived.
ME: Better than Bob Dylan?
PARROTHEAD: Way better.
ME: That's absurd.
PARROTHEAD: Listen to this . . .

He cued up "Why Don't We Get Drunk (And Screw)?" I had to admit that I'd never heard a Dylan song quite like that one, unless it was "Lay Lady Lay," where the message was a little more between the lines, the bed was brass, and Dylan was interested in a "lady." Jimmy wasn't talking to a "lady" in any but the loosest sense. Then my new friend played "God's Own Drunk." That was different. Then "Fins." I began to feel like remora. Then "Livingston Saturday Night." I was forming a notion that Jimmy Buffett was fond of a party, and who isn't? I found little in the next four days to disconfirm the hypothesis. But here was something weird, and I'll bet you've had the same experience. I actually didn't like this Parrothead guy very much, and I'm pretty sure he didn't care for me either. He would have to educate me, which was a bother, but I would do in a pinch, and this was something like a four-day pinch.

All of the Places

Back to the method. The *places* in Buffett's songs are just places that have been special to Jimmy—Paris, the Islands, Alabama, Florida, you know them. Once in a while he sings about places he doesn't like, such as the list of places he doesn't want to land when the volcano blows, but mainly he sings about places that have meant something good to him. It's a long list. Somehow though, there are places that are Buffettish and places that just aren't, and it's not easy to explain how we know which is which. It isn't just the weather. For example, Montana is cold, but it's Buffettish, while Vermont is cold too, but it isn't. It's the same with cities. New Orleans is extremely Buffettish. Houston isn't. And with countries, France is, Spain is, Germany isn't. It's not easy to say what makes a place suitable, but here is a litmus test: try to imagine whether Frank and Lola could get together again there, and if so, it's probably a Buffett place. This test explains why, for instance, San Diego won't work, but Paris will. But it isn't failsafe. You also have to study up to find out where Jimmy crossed paths with some ass-holes, since assholes are nearly everywhere, even Key West. When you know his stories, you'll see why some places make the grade and others don't. But any place that people are in too much of a hurry for Frank and Lola to rekindle their marriage, or too caught up in the future or the past, that place isn't worth your time.

Makes Me Want to Go Back Again

The *times* in Buffett songs are everything from times of day, to days of the week, to seasons, to whole swaths of years. These might be in the present or the past, but Jimmy will tell you when it is or was, just like he'll tell you where he is, was, or would rather be. He has a pretty consistent set of attitudes about these things. He likes the night time, but not the morning after; he likes summer, but not win-ter; and he likes the past, but not as much as the present. And most importantly, Jimmy is deeply ambivalent about the future. He tries to avoid hoping, wishing, predicting, or trying to control the way things turn out. This will be good to remember when we get around to discussing the "thoughts" about fortune and fate, if we can still remember our own names by then. But the "past" for Buffett isn't really history (in spite of his degree in it); it's not songs about the French Revolution or even the Civil War, it's the past as *remembered*, in personal experiences or in the way others have told him their own stories. Past times in his songs and books are times ripe for a moment of reflection, a memory, a realization. But we can't look backward too long. You may miss what's in front of you in the present.

The good "present" times are of three kinds: solitude (that's mainly fishing, flying, or sailing alone), a conversation, or a party. That's about it for the present, and so if you're wondering whether a given time, day, or season belongs to Buffett temporality, just ask whether it would be good for a conversation or a party, since time disappears in solitude—which can be a very good thing. That's your acid test, conversation or party. So "morning" is fine for a con-versation, even very, very early, when the fish aren't biting, but *not* the morning after. Summer is always good for a party, but fall, after the tourists are gone, is better for a conversation. Winter isn't good for very much. Spring just doesn't seem to show up at all in Buffett's songs or books, maybe because spring is all about the future. The only time always to be avoided is the future. If you start worrying about the future, bullshit is sure to overtake you. I admit that there are a couple of songs about the future—near future in "Come Monday," and distant future in "Little Miss Magic," but these are the exceptions that prove the rule. The point is not to fret about the future when it comes up, and it's wiser to avoid the subject as much as possible.

All of the Faces

The "meeting" is a constant in the Buffett song catalogue. It's in just about every song. Often the meeting is remembered, like his African friend, or the bear in "God's Own Drunk," or Jimmy's partner in crime in the peanut butter conspiracy (do you think they ever paid the Mini-mart back? I'm thinking not.). Sometimes it's a present meeting, and occasionally the meeting is missed, like when the phone doesn't ring. But whether it's a gathering of friends or a romantic encounter, what we get from these meetings is a cast of characters filling Jimmy's life with the weird, the wonderful, and even the worrisome meeting that may cost him two good years.

Before we get to sentiments and thoughts, let's take a drink and do a little experiment. Think of your favorite Jimmy Buffett character. I have to admit, mine is the bear . . . buddy bear in "God's Own Drunk." Now choose another one. I also have a soft spot for the old man in "He Went to Paris." You choose your own favorite characters. Now let's have a little fun. Choose a Buffett-place and a Buffett-time, and have them meet. What, maybe a bar in Bimini, long after dark. The bear bellies up, orders a plate of raw fish, the old man says "I can't recall your face, but you smell like a Scotsman I used to know . . ." You take the story from there. I think it ends with the bear selling the old man a homemade still. This much— the place, time, and meeting—might get you a story, and maybe you could make it rhyme with the heroic couplets Buffett is so fond of. But I think you'll see that it won't quite make for a song. There are two things missing, and those two things are the beating heart and the thinking brain of any Buffett song—the sentiment and the thought. And when we've taken a look at those, and how they fit together, we're getting pretty close to tacking the winds of fortune and fate.

"It's Five o'Clock Somewhere"

Suburban streets of Memphis. May 7, 1981, 11:00 A.M., or there-abouts. You might not be surprised to learn that, among the many uses of Buffett music, it makes a good accompaniment to delivering flowers for fourteen hours a day, four days in a row. By now I've heard the whole of *A1A*, and *White Sports Coat*, and I'm wanting to go to Key West. "Nautical Wheelers" has imprinted itself as my new favorite song. I still don't like this Parrothead, but I'm beginning to feel something like gratitude (and that's my sentiment for this story). There was something carefree, something ineffably fun about the feel of the music; just turns drudgery and repetition into a party. I mean, why *shouldn't* there be a party? But I wasn't altogether comfortable when *mon ami du jour* began to drink beer (while driving) before lunch, which is part of the reason I am not naming him. I am not certain it was even illegal to do that back then, but it wasn't wise in any case, and I certainly shouldn't have joined him. My main memories of the weekend are all from before noon. I think it went by pretty fast, but I can't say for sure.

Even four albums in, I wasn't prepared to allow that Jimmy Buffett was either the greatest songwriter ever, or better than Bob Dylan, and I'm still not, but I no longer think the idea is absurd. It sort of depends on what you're looking for in your music, and here is what I think I can say: nobody does what Buffett does better than Buffett, and that is partly because Buffett *invented* what Buffett does to suit what Buffett can do better than anybody else. It's actually kind of pathetic when anyone else even *tries* to do a Buffett-kinda-thing. I mean, for example, I'm sure Alan Jackson is a great guy, but the only, and I mean the *only* thing that makes "It's Five o'Clock Somewhere" an interesting song is when Jackson wisely defers to the much more interesting perspective of Jimmy Buffett. Jackson may have been to Margaritaville a time or two, but he didn't build it from his own imagination.

Alan Jackson, for all his ample integrity, and his admirable defense of traditional country music, is still one of a thousand Nashville frozen concoctions playing the part of the redneck with an attitude, or I should really say "the good ol' boy with a chip." The only difference between a "redneck with an attitude" and a "good ol' boy with a chip" is a two-year string of bad luck. I don't think Alan Jackson ever had such a string, but I'm willing to be corrected. And I think Alan is probably the real thing too—he actually *is* a good ol' boy from Georgia, writing and singing about what he knows, and doing it very well, and there's nothing in the world wrong with that. But that is what Nashville thrives on, new incarnations of the same persona. It's a tired persona if you ask me (and I realize you didn't).

Now, by comparison, how many Jimmy Buffetts are there? Nothing could be more obvious when Jackson steps on the stage with Buffett in that video—Jackson is the real thing, by Nashville standards, but any of a hundred Nashville stars could have filled his place in that song—Big and Rich, George Strait, Toby Keith, Brooks and Dunn, even Steve Earle. You choose and rewrite the video. You'll see that it works. But whoever you choose to play Alan Jackson, there is only *one* Buffett, and only *he* can finish the video. One of them created the whole genre of music he plays, and the other one simply stepped into a pre-fabricated role, adding his slight variations. That's my "thought" for this story, even if the story isn't over, and even if that silly song was twenty-two years away from making sense back in 1981, when that Parrothead changed my point of view. So, long before Jackson had emerged from the woods of north Georgia, the Parrothead was trying to help me "get it." He wasn't an articulate fellow—plenty smart, but not a word guy—and in the end mostly what he had to say was "listen to this" . . . and he'd fast forward to another tune.

Permanent Reminder of a Temporary Feeling

What sorts of sentiments does Buffett convey? Of course, it's *almost* the whole human complement, but we get no hate, wrath, anger, or rage. Rather than those, we get a bit of disdain, annoyance, and their close kin, but from Jimmy we get no blaming of other people, and precious little blaming of himself. We get considerable lust and nostalgia, but no remorse and only a bit of regret. He wouldn't do anything *differently* (except the great filling station hold-up), but he also doesn't want to do it *over*. There's only an occasional hint of light-hearted envy or revenge (I'm thinking of "Gypsies in the Palace" here). But what overall quality can we name that helps us recognize which sentiments do and don't belong in Margaritaville? I think I've figured it out, but let me get at it indirectly. Maybe the key to this treasure chest is hidden in Jimmy's way with words.

Shared sentiment is probably more important than *like-minded-ness* in binding Buffett to his fans. Poets thrive on shared sentiment, but I don't think Jimmy Buffett is first and foremost a poet. He has a fine turn of phrase, and rumor has it that he's a pretty smooth talker, but when I consider the William Blakes and Dylan Thomases of our mother tongue, I think Jimmy is up to something else. Even among singer-songwriters, there are the "pure poets," Dylan, Springsteen, and the like, who seem to think of words in the way Van Gogh must have thought of hues and tints. For Jimmy, words are nice, but they are a means not an end.

The *poet* type wants artistic intensity in his relation to his audience, he wants to share his *art* more than his feelings, so his feelings get all arted up. It's hard to know whether to trust the genuineness of those feelings. I don't think Dylan *has* any feelings of his own, but if he does, he wouldn't share them with *us*. We aren't *worthy*. Poets are too much trouble to mess with. Jimmy wants a party. There's an art to that too, but it's not exactly art for art's sake. A really big difference between a Parrothead and, say, a Springsteen fan is that when we hear Jimmy talking about how he feels or felt, we say "yeah, I been there too," whereas Springsteen fans are more likely to hear the words and believe that Bruce somehow, magically, just *knows* how *they* feel. That's fine, but it isn't exactly the truth about life. Springsteen is an honest guy. He would never *really* claim to know how someone else feels, but he makes them *feel* like he *does* know, and that is the magic of poetry. Of course, a concert, whether Springsteen or Buffett, *can* be a party either way, but the two have a different overall atmosphere, I think you'll agree. If his songs and books are any guide, Jimmy isn't always even sure how *he* feels, let alone how we feel. So Parrotheads see Jimmy as an ideal drinking buddy and a potential partner in crime, not as a prophet or a pure artist. If Jimmy became too intense, too dramatic, too Springsteen-esque, it would spoil his mystique and the persona he has worked so hard to create. The key to his feelings does not lie in the poetry.

What about the stories? Some would say, and Jimmy has said this himself, that he's really a *storyteller* (*A Pirate Looks at Fifty*, pp. 12, 444). If that's true, then his words are toggles for telling stories—and you have to choose the right words if you want to tell a *good* story. There's surely some truth to saying Jimmy is a storyteller, but what kind? He isn't like Pete Seeger, old school, morality tales filled with mythic images and symbols. And he doesn't even tell very many tall tales, those fantastical yarns like his hero Mark Twain used to invent. There are only a few of those, and while Jimmy is not one to let the truth spoil a good story, he stays closer to fact than Mark Twain. Jimmy is really more of a journalist than a traditional storyteller—he has more in common with Hunter S. Thompson than with Seeger or Twain. He tells his own story, and does so in ways that entertain us, and that we can relate to.

So the feelings are, I think, of the sort you get when you read or hear a good story, first person, like a travel journal—and maybe that's why Jimmy liked Mark Twain's travel books, like *Following the Equator*, better than the more celebrated "tall tales" about jumping frogs and prince-paupers and Connecticut Yankees. So, thinking of Jimmy as a sort of travel journalist, what kind? He's not ebullient like Rick Steves or irritable like Bill Bryson. But he is a little like Tom Bodett or Garrison Keillor, if not quite so folksy. Yet, there's something common about the sentiments here. I have a name for it: "wistful." And that is like Bodett and Keillor, without the Yankee pathos. Any feeling that can be felt *wistfully* fits in a Jimmy Buffett song, and things that can't be felt with wist don't belong. That's not to say that Jimmy's always wistful, only that the sentiments and feelings that show up in the stuff he writes would be ones that *could* be tacked to a wistful wind. So, go down the list of feelings that show up, add a little wist and you'll see what I mean. It may be that wistful habits of feeling give a person just enough detachment to laugh at the cruelties of fate—folly chasing death, as Jimmy described it (*A Pirate Looks at Fifty*, pp. 39, 449). If we couldn't laugh, we'd all go insane. The key to the treasure chest is cut wistfully, and damned if it doesn't fit the lock. It's better to be lucky than good, sometimes.

A Prince of a Guy

Adding up what we've got so far: places where Frank and Lola can get together again, times that are good for a conversation or a party, memorable meetings that make for good stories, and sentiments in a wistful key. We're ready for a lesson from Machiavelli, because these are the very *tools* of fortune. He has an interesting take on fortune. We usually think of 'fortune' as something good, but we also use phrases like 'a trick of fortune' and other sorts of verbal tics that show we don't always see fortune as favorable. The Latin goddess of chance is Fortuna. This is the same as "Lady Luck," upon whom Jimmy occasionally calls (*A Pirate Looks at Fifty*, p, 8).

Following the sense of his times, Machiavelli sees Fortuna more as a playful trickster who throws up obstacles before any and all of us, and our success or failure in any endeavor depends upon how we meet those obstacles. Sooner or later, Fortuna defeats most people, but Machiavelli says that there are some things you can do to evade her wiles. But first, well, you have to *marry* her, he says, and *then* you'll need a big stick.

I don't like violence, and neither does Jimmy, but if anybody ever decided to marry Fortuna, Jimmy did. So let's hear Machiavelli out because, after all, fortune isn't actually a woman, and the stick you need to hit her with doesn't grow on a tree. It's just a metaphor. So what stick is this? It's "virtue," says Machiavelli. Now that word also doesn't mean what you might think. It's the Latin "virtutem," which means moral strength, but also manliness, potency. The word "virile" comes from the same root, "vir," which means both a man and a hero. The sort of person who can marry Fortuna and then make her a co-operative partner is a kind of *hero*, a *man's* man—and by his own accounting, Jimmy has read dozens of books about heroes and crooks, and learned much from both of their styles. I wouldn't be surprised if Machiavelli is on Jimmy's book list, since the man wrote the ultimate travel guide for heroes and crooks. The point is that, since no one can avoid the tricks and wiles of Fortuna, it's wise to keep her close at hand, cultivate your strength and your boldness, and above all learn to read the winds—choose the right places, times, friends, and feelings, and when you think you have them, move decisively. Look before you leap, but he who hesitates is lost.

For example, you might decide to tell everyone in Nashville to just kiss your ass and go to the beach with Jerry Jeff. That seems pretty decisive to me. If you made the right move, you might even live to see Nashville come to *your* doorstep with a song praising your choice. You win Jimmy, you're a prince of a guy.[1] I wondered

---

[1] But everyone knows that Nashville plays the game by Machiavelli's book, which is why we don't want to land there when the volcano blows. Fortune favors the bold, the Latin proverb says, but Machiavelli adds that Fortune also favors the *young*. Jimmy was young when he made his big move, and I'm not recommending this sort of huge step for most of you, and certainly not for myself. I'm only pointing out how it describes a certain brash and successful songwriter we all know. But here's a *kind* of virtue that can make full use of your own *vices* (and those of others). That's good work if you can get it. We could all do with some of *this* kind of virtue (indeed, I could do with more than I have).

about the song "It's Five o'Clock Somewhere," and since one of its co-writers, Don Rollins, is a friend of a friend, I asked how much these guys plotted what they were doing, since it looked like the work of Parrotheads. It turns out that Rollins was not the plotter, but Jim "Moose" Brown was. As Rollins explained, he really didn't know how extensive Jimmy's fan base was, but since Moose Brown is friends with Michael Utley and Mac McAnally, he thinks that maybe Moose was more aware of how the scenario would play out. My suspicion is that Moose Brown knew *exactly* what would happen.

I Really Do Appreciate the Fact You're Sittin' Here

Later in May, 1981; Memphis Comics and Used Records, towards the end of the "B" bin. You never know what effects a weekend may have. I know that you and I aren't intimate enough for 'my story' to be of much interest to you, and I promise this is not a prelude to a suggestion about a waterbed. But I'm almost finished with what I have now decided will be just my *first* bottle of Pinot Noir today, and if you took my advice earlier, we are drinking buddies by now. In any case, you're not looking so clear to me at this point, so if you'll hold me steady, I'm pulling in the anchor. We have a lot in common, you and me. We like most of the same times, places, meetings, and sentiments. We like Buffett. Maybe you'll put up with the rest of the story, even if I'm not quite your favorite drinking buddy, and this isn't really a pinch you're in.

The final exams went rather poorly—five F's that semester and I was on my way to dropping out of college. The flower deliveries went somewhat better, as far as I can recall, and I got hired part-time into the business with that Parrothead. That would put food on the table for the next couple of years while I foolishly tried to become a rock star. Fortune may favor the young, but it generally shits upon the talent-less. It's hard to say whether it's fortune or fate, but either way, I exercised my Machiavellian virtues, such as they were, and went semi-heroically to the best used record store in town. I bought every Jimmy Buffett album then available. Jimmy didn't get any royalties from me then, since I bought them used, but I was poor, and he has been spending my money foolishly ever since. I'm proud that I probably spent enough in later years to finance the port-a-potties for the workers building the first Margaritaville Café (or at least this was my thought, when I ate there). Anyway, I bought the records and, like many of you reading this, I started learning Buffett songs on the guitar—songs I still know by heart. It amazes me how many people learned to play the guitar for the sake of singing those songs, and fortunately, most are easy. But I meet other Parrotheads on a regular basis who did that. I've run across a couple of these who never even learned anything else.

The Fickle Finger

To make it in the brutal music business you need some luck, but you also have to be *good* (better than I was). There's no sense at all in saying that it was fate that sent Jimmy to the beach, although fortune may have had a good bit to do with it, as he readily admits. When Jimmy contemplates fate, he reserves it for matters that seem beyond control—like when his wonderful little hotel on St. Barts burned to the ground. He suspected malice at first, but "as fate would have it, the fire started in the deejay booth of the disco" (*A Pirate Looks at Fifty*, p. 450). I'll leave the interesting symbolism of that for you to ponder. Like Vico, Jimmy is careful not to say there's no such thing as fate, but if it really exists, maybe the thing to do is to twist fate by tricking fortune.

That's sort of the way Vico tells the story. He says that if you want to know why things happen as they do, you have to consider three main things: the "natural causes," the "moral causes" and "the occasions of fortune." *Natural* causes are things like, if you don't see the wake in time, your flying boat will go out of control—because that's how the wake affects flying boats, and no amount of Machiavellian virtue can help that. *Moral* causes are things like being prepared for the plane crash by some U.S. Navy water survival training. The "occasions of fortune" are like this (and look closely here at what Jimmy says): the crash "would have killed me if it hadn't been for the intervention of God, Buddha, St. Christopher, my guardian angel, my fishing buddies, luck, and the United States Navy water-survival training" (p. 42). You can see that Fortune is called by her other name here, Mrs. Luck (remembering that Jimmy married her), and that the *moral* cause is named too (Be Prepared), but the *rest*—God, Buddha, St. Christopher, and the guardian angel, all rolled together—has a different name. Vico calls it "Providence."

I'm not going to go religious on you here, I promise. "Providence," apart from being an un-Buffetish place in Rhode Island, is more like a way of seeing the cosmic balance between fortune and fate. It comes from the same word as "provide," and it has to do with the resources in life that are *provided* for us—including the order of nature (natural causes), the order of virtue (the opportunities we have for developing our own character), and the ways in which fortune can be seen as a series of obstacles that we can meet. And here's Vico's point: you're not utterly at the mercy of either fortune or fate, if you make use of what is *provided*, but you also can't foresee all the consequences of your actions. And here's the chorus to that song: no matter what happens, it *can* be turned to good ends, to the end of providing *for others*, even if not for ourselves.

So let's discuss a nightmare. What if Jimmy *had* died in the plane crash? (After all, John Denver did.) What would we have said? That isn't a hard question. We would have said: "He died the way he lived, doing something he loved, and by the way, thank you Jimmy for the music and the books and for your life. We love you, and your music and life provide us with the means for confronting our own lives, with wist and wisdom." That is what we would say. And if Jimmy could answer us from beyond, I know he would say this: "Some of it's magic and some of it's tragic, but I had a good life all the way." *That* is "providence." We provide for each other, at the very least, the means with which to confront the obstacles that Fortune sends on the wind. You could think of Machiavelli's "big stick" as a main mast and Vico's providence as the mainsail. Vico says that whatever courses of action we set out upon, no matter how wicked or wise, these actions can serve the greater purposes of providence. Tack it right, and any wind can get you to harbor.

We are weak beings, "fallen man," as Vico says, but we don't want to be chained to fate or abandoned to the winds of chance. We want something to hope for and to be grateful about, and when you focus on that, with enough detachment to laugh about it, you'll see that the wistful sentiments are the right ones. That's the gift, the "intervention" of God, Buddha, St. Christopher or your guardian angel. They don't bring you safety, they bring you a sense of perspective about things, at least if you'll think about providence as being greater than fortune and fate. That seems like good advice to me, especially since it lets me hold on to my selected vices, with a clear understanding that they may do more to deter *others* from taking the same course than they do for *me*. I may have to be contented as a good bad example for others not to follow, but I might also get off scot-free. And that word "contented" is the emotional complement that rounds out the feeling of gratitude. Think about it. I'll bring that up again at the end, which is very near.

Providence

July 12th, 1986, Clinton, Kentucky. A meeting of the dearly beloved. Indulge me one last time, so that I can finish the story. Luckily, within a few years, I was actually able to marry a Parrothead, which is the next best thing to marrying Fortuna. (I'm no hero.) I'm not saying I married her *because* she was a Parrothead, but that may have been the only reason she married *me*. Providence. I didn't have much else to offer at the time, so I gave her flowers that I got for free (from among the stock too old to sell at the Parrothead's shop), and I serenaded her with Jimmy Buffett songs on my dad's old Gibson. She already knew the harmonies. Between the two of us, she was the one who had a real job, so she bought me a Martin guitar (this is God's own truth). We are all looking for the right sort of stick to tame fortune. In this case, the stick had six strings and was fashioned with care in Pennsylvania. These days I don't believe in mixed marriages (one Parrothead, and one who doesn't get it). That union is doomed. No stick is big enough. This may be more important than religion or politics, because it bears on the following five things: (1) the right places; (2) the right times; (3) the right meetings; (4) the right sentiments; and (5) the right thoughts. The five-fold path to providence. Now you're beginning to understand the full wistful weight of my gratitude to that Parrothead, wherever he is.

I think most of you have a story like mine, because we Parrotheads don't become the way we are by the ordinary channels. You don't come to this passion by watching VH1 or listening to hit songs on the radio. There *is* some dumb luck involved, but it isn't just fate. This kind of providential understanding of life spreads by subtler means, first-hand experiences, and by recognizing a providential moment when it shines. Maybe somebody who "gets it" comes to suspect that *you* might have the makings of a good Parrothead and takes the trouble to educate you until you can squawk on your own. I don't know if it's more like Amway or Catholicism, but whatever it is that spreads the good news, you can't bottle it. Alan Jackson likes us, I think, but he is *not* one of *us*. Don Rollins and Moose Brown, who wrote that song, mischievously plotted Jimmy's final revenge on Nashville, but if the best revenge is living well, then the perfect revenge is to live better than the people you told to kiss your ass when you finally learned that life is too short to put up with their bullshit. Thanks to Rollins and Brown for making us all smile, and to Alan Jackson for playing along. He got in his own kind of jab with the song, no doubt. I certainly am grateful to those guys for holding Nashville down while Jimmy got to tickle it into submission. And being grateful, I find myself *contented*.

"Livin' and Dyin' in Three-Quarter Time"

Maybe the secret to it all is as simple as being contented to live and die in three-quarter time. This is not defeat or fatalism by any stretch. The two key ideas are "contentment" and "three quarter time," and the second idea is the basis of the first one. If you want contentment, then it's a good idea to take the gift of time and make it into a tempo, organize it into a rhythm that works for you. If you're a Nautical Wheeler (that was a square dance group in Key West, apparently), then three-quarter time may be the way you want to go about that. But we all need rhythms, and I think people who can't find contentment are of two sorts: there are the ones who can't decide on the right rhythm, and there are those who don't notice and appreciate the rhythm they've found.

That weekend in 1981, I think I heard the call of Providence, because the line I could not leave alone, in my thinking, was "everyone here is just more than contented to be livin' and dyin' in three-quarter time." It went round and round my brain. It still does, and that is still my favorite Jimmy Buffett song, and on the weight of that one line: words to live and die by, if contentment with your Fortune is what you seek, and gratitude is what you offer in exchange, to appease Fate. As Jimmy says, "You know I can't help but be / Part of my own philosophy."

Songs Referred to in This Book

All songs are the property and copyright of their owners. They are quoted, cited, or listed in *Jimmy Buffett and Philosophy* for educational purposes only.

"American Dream." Rodney Crowell.
"A Pirate Looks at Forty." Jimmy Buffett.
"A Salty Piece of Land." Jimmy Buffett.
"Ballad of Skip Wiley." Jimmy Buffett, Russ Kunkel, Jay Oliver, Roger Guth, Peter Mayer.
"Banana Republics." Steve Goodman, Jim Rothermel, Steve Burgh.
"Bank of Bad Habits." Jimmy Buffett, Russ Kunkel, Jay Oliver, Roger Guth, Peter Mayer.
"Barometer Soup." Jimmy Buffett, Russ Kunkel, Jay Oliver, Roger Guth, Peter Mayer.
"Bend a Little." Jimmy Buffett.
"Boat Drinks." Jimmy Buffett.
"Changes in Latitudes, Changes in Attitudes." Jimmy Buffett.
"Cheeseburger in Paradise." Jimmy Buffett.
"Coast of Carolina." Jimmy Buffett and Mac McAnally.
"Coastal Confessions." Jimmy Buffett.
"Come Monday." Jimmy Buffett.
"Cultural Infidel." Jimmy Buffett, Russ Kunkel, Roger Guth, P. Mayer, J. Mayer.
"Desdemona's Building a Rocket Ship." Jimmy Buffett, Russ Kunkel, Roger Guth, P. Mayer, J. Mayer.
"Distantly in Love." Jimmy Buffett.

"Everybody's on the Phone." Jimmy Buffett, Roger Guth, Will
    Kimbrough, Peter Meyer.
"Fins." Jimmy Buffett, Deborah McColl, Barry Chance, Tom
    Corcoran.
"Five o'Clock Somewhere." Jim Brown and Don Rollins.
"Fool Button." Jimmy Buffett.
"Frank and Lola." Jimmy Buffett and Steve Goodman.
"Fruitcakes." Jimmy Buffett.
"God's Own Drunk." Lord Buckley.
"Grapefruit-Juicy Fruit." Jimmy Buffett.
"Gravity Storm." Jimmy Buffett and Jay Oliver.
"Growing Older but Not Up." Jimmy Buffett.
"Gypsies in the Palace." Jimmy Buffett.
"Happily Ever After (Now and Then)." Jimmy Buffet and Dave
    Loggins.
"He Went to Paris." Jimmy Buffett.
"Holiday." Jimmy Buffett, Ralph MacDonald, Bill Eaton, William
    Salter.
"Homemade Music." Jimmy Buffett, Michael Utley, Russell Kunkel.
"Hula Girl at Heart." Jimmy Buffett, Roger Guth, Will Kimbrough,
    Peter Mayer.
"I Can't Be Your Hero." Jimmy Buffett.
"I Don't Know and I Don't Care." Jim Mayer and Jimmy Buffett.
"If the Phone Doesn't Ring It's Me." Jimmy Buffett, Will Jennings,
    Michael Utley.
"I Have Found Me a Home." Jimmy Buffett.
"Incommunicado." Jimmy Buffett, Deborah McColl, M.L. Benoit.
"It's My Job." Mac McAnally.
"King of Somewhere Hot." Jimmy Buffett, Ralph MacDonald,
    William Salter, Robert Greenidge.
"Last Man Standing." Jimmy Buffett, Mac McAnally, Russ Titelman.
"License to Chill." Jimmy Buffett, Mac McAnally, Al Anderson.
"Little Miss Magic." Jimmy Buffett.
"Livingston Saturday Night." Jimmy Buffett.
"Makin' Music for the Money." Alex Harvey.
"Margaritaville." Jimmy Buffett.
"Mental Floss." Jimmy Buffet, Russell Kunkel, Roger Guth,
    P. Mayer, J. Mayer.
"Migration." Jimmy Buffett.
"Miss You So Badly." Jimmy Buffett and Greg Taylor.
"Nautical Wheelers." Jimmy Buffett.

"Off to See the Lizard." Jimmy Buffet and Jay Oliver.

"One Particular Harbor." Jimmy Buffett and Bobby Holcomb.

"Pascagoula Run." Jimmy Buffett and Jay Oliver.

"Peanut Butter Conspiracy." Jimmy Buffett.

"Pencil Thin Mustache." Jimmy Buffett.

"Permanent Reminder of a Temporary Feeling." Jimmy Buffett.

"Ringling, Ringling." Jimmy Buffett.

"School Boy Heart." Jimmy Buffett and Matt Betton.

"Semi-True Stories." Mac McAnally.

"Smart Woman (in a Real Short Skirt)." Jimmy Buffett and Marshall Chapman.

"Son of a Son of a Sailor." Jimmy Buffett.

"Strange Bird." Jimmy Buffett and Jay Oliver.

"Take Another Road." Jimmy Buffett, Roger Guth, Jay Oliver.

"That's My Story and I'm Stickin' to It." Jimmy Buffett and Jay Oliver.

"That's What Living Is to Me." Jimmy Buffett.

"The Christian." M. Brown and Jimmy Buffett.

"The Missionary." Jimmy Buffett.

"The Stories We Could Tell." John B Sabastian.

"The Tiki Bar Is Open." J. Hiatt.

"The Weather Is Here, Wish You Were Beautiful." Jimmy Buffett.

"The Wino and I Know." Jimmy Buffett.

"Tin Cup Chalice." Jimmy Buffett.

"Tonight I Just Need My Guitar." Jimmy Buffett and Mac McAnally.

"Trip Around the Sun." Al Anderson, Steve Bruton, Sharon Vaughn.

"Trouble on the Horizon." Jimmy Buffett.

"Truckstop Salvation." Jimmy Buffett.

"Trying to Reason with Hurricane Season." Jimmy Buffett.

"Weather with You." Neil Fin and Time Finn.

"When the Coast Is Clear." Jimmy Buffett.

"Why Don't We Get Drunk (and Screw)." Marvin Gardens (aka Jimmy Buffett).

"Wonder Why I Ever Go Home." Jimmy Buffett.

"Wonder Why We Ever Go Home." Jimmy Buffett.

Pirates in Paradise

Doug Anderson's infatuation with Buffett's music was foreshadowed when his grandmother's introduced him to the musics of the Caribbean. Growing up with a Gibson guitar in hand, and country music in the air, he first heard Buffett as the sound of calypso-country. This Buffettesque sound has remained at the center of his musical interest from then till now. When not playing music he can be found teaching philosophy to young folks at Southern Illinois University.

Randy Auxier strums a six-string on his front porch swing in southern Illinois, not far from Southern Illinois University, Carbondale, where he is a Professor of Philosophy. He has had the good fortune of having Parrotheads for neighbors during four years in Atlanta and almost nine years in his current locale. As he types his silly little bio, his neighbor is plugging in the electric palm trees in the backyard, and, if his eyes don't deceive him, she's mixing up some sort of frozen concoction. And it's only half past twelve, but hey, it's spring break.

Celia T. Bardwell-Jones is an Assistant Professor teaching at Towson University jointly in the Philosophy and Women's Studies Departments. Her research interests include Feminist Philosophy, American pragmatism, philosophy of travel and philosophy of the sea. She is currently working on a grant to teach Philosophy and the Sea in which she will take students sailing on the Chesapeake Bay. Desperate to change her latitudes to more warmer climes, she seeks to change the attitudes of her students instead. She still wonders, what is a pop top?

Drew Dalton currently teaches philosophy at Saint Anselm College in Manchester, New Hampshire, where he has assumed the self-appointed title of Supreme Mugwamp of the Parrothead Collation of

Southern New Hampshire Liberal Arts Colleges. When not extolling the benefits of a life lived on the sea and yearning for Key West, Dalton can be found penning articles on the idea of longing and has a book forthcoming entitled *Human and Divine Longing: Levinas in Dialogue*. When not in the classroom or on campus, Dalton can be found wandering the parking lots of Jimmy Buffett concert with tin-cup for a chalice and shark fin for a crown. His therapist has recently recommended him for an extended asylum stay.

ADAM GLOVER is a graduate student in Hispanic Literature at the University of Kentucky. He likes mystical poetry and twentieth-century French philosophy. He is also trying to grow a pencil-thin mustache."

AMANDA FELLER is a professor at Pacific Lutheran University located in tropical Tacoma. She earned her Ph.D. from the California Institute of Integral Studies located in the more-tropical city of San Francisco. Her teaching, research, and consultations center on the integral relationship of communication and transformation. This gives her an excuse (opportunity) to use and observe a range of practices, for instance artistic expression, mind-body-spirit forms like yoga and hiking, travel, and more. Amanda strongly suspects that the best practice is a change of latitude and is currently planning her next adventure. She's hoping to match her parent's lifetime tour of seventy countries (and counting) and is frequently heard saying, could you beam me somewhere, Mr. Scott?

MATTHEW CALEB FLAMM doesn't go to church, but he will wear his underwear and cut his hair at least until a couple of years from now when, pending good behavior, he is awarded tenure at Rockford College, in Rockford, Illinois. Meanwhile he enjoys teaching philosophy, re-reading and writing on George Santayana (a laughing naturalist-philosopher after Jimmy Buffett's own heart), and living his life like a song.

CHRISTOPHER HOYT is assistant professor of philosophy at Western Carolina University, in the Smoky Mountains. His scholarly research is focused on the philosophy of Ludwig Wittgenstein, religion, and contemporary culture. His essays include "Wittgenstein and Religious Dogma," "The Worldview of Personalism," and "Lotze's Failed Psychology." His interest in Jimmy Buffett dates back to his high school days in Miami, when the Man from Margaritaville provided the soundtrack to many happy days of fishing and secret pilgrimages to Key West with his friends (sorry, Mom and Dad).

JOHN KAAG is an assistant professor of philosophy at the University of Massachusetts, Lowell. He's working on two books that explore the American philosophical tradition. He is a youngish Buffett fan, but would like to thank Bill Pors who is a veteran Parrothead and helped John work through the finer points of Buffett.

ERIN MCKENNA is Professor of Philosophy at Pacific Lutheran University in Tacoma. When the rain is too much, listening to Buffett helps her "hang on." She prefers mojitos to margaritas and time at the beach is always in order. She is the author of works on pragmatism, feminism, vegetarianism, and animal and environmental issues. She likes informing non-Buffett fans about his work on behalf of the manatees and homeless dogs, and hopes to highlight some of this work in a book on animals that is in process.

PHIL OLIVER's academic specialty is American Philosophy, in particular the thought of William James and John Dewey. His book William James's *Springs of Delight* explores "personal enthusiasms and habitual 'delights' and their power to make our days meaningful, delightful, spiritual, and even transcendent"—in other words, to make life a kind of Buffett like experience! His other research interests include the philosophy of childhood and education, biotechnology, ethics, the environment, and philosophical ideas in contemporary literature. He was born near St. Louis, Missouri—which possibly explains his unreasoning love of baseball (about which he has also published), and his partisan preference for the Cardinals. He lives with his family in Nashville.

AARON L. PRATT is a third-year Senior at Pacific University in Forest Grove, Oregon, majoring in English Literature. His love of the sea and scuba diving fostered his appreciation for the music of Jimmy Buffett. Despite the fact that the weather is far from tropical on the Oregon Coast, and the ocean temperature hangs around a bone-chilling fifty degrees, Aaron and his father have been avidly diving together there for more than five years, incorporating Buffett's album *License to Chill* into almost every excursion. Aaron and his wife Holly are looking forward to his graduation from Pacific in May 2009 and a future in graduate-level studies in Philosophy and Theology.

SCOTT L. PRATT teaches philosophy at the University of Oregon. He is the author of articles on pluralism, American philosophy, philosophy of music, and logic, and of the book, *Native Pragmatism: Rethinking the Roots of American Philosophy*. In the moments when he is not teaching or writing, he fly fishes in the Cascade Mountains, scuba dives at the Oregon coast, or sips a prize-winning home-brewed beer while listening to *License to Chill*.

JENNIFER A. REA believes that if she couldn't laugh she would just go insane in Rockford, Illinois, where her version of a cheeseburger in paradise is a Guinness in Ireland. Her changes in latitudes and attitudes have led to teaching rhetoric at Rockford College and working in Irish Studies, all the while longing for that one particular harbor. Jimmy Buffett's epicurean appeal is always a delight to her, and she loves the idea that there is a little bit of fruitcake in every one of us.

DUKE RICHEY teaches in the Department of History at the University of North Texas, where he specializes in the American West and U.S. environmental history. He is currently at work on his first book, tentatively titled "The Apenization of Aspen: Ski Bums and the Creation of Exurbia in the American West." To ensure that no one ever confuses him with a glittery rock and roll star, Richey wears Hush Puppies, without socks, on a regular basis.

Index